W9-BNA-500

The Children of Noah

The Children of Noah

JEWISH SEAFARING IN
ANCIENT TIMES

Raphael Patai

With Contributions by
James Hornell and
John M. Lundquist

PRINCETON UNIVERSITY PRESS

PRINCETON, NEW JERSEY

Library of Congress Cataloging-in-Publication Data

Patai, Raphael, 1910–
The children of Noah : Jewish seafaring in ancient times / Raphael
Patai ; with contributions by James Hornell and John M. Lundquist.
p.   cm.
Includes bibliographical references and index.
1. Navigation—Palestine—History.   I. Hornell, James,
1865–1949.   II. Lundquist, John M.   III. Title.
VK113.P3P32   1998   387.5′0933—dc21   97-40059

ISBN 0-691-01580-5 (cl. : alk. paper)

This book has been composed in Galliard

An earlier version of the foreword by Howard M. Sachar
was first published in *Fields of Offerings: Studies in
Honor of Raphael Patai,* copyright © 1983 by
Fairleigh Dickinson University Press, East Rutherford,
New Jersey.

http://pup.princeton.edu

Printed in the United States of America

3   5   7   9   10   8   6   4   2

CONTENTS

LIST OF ILLUSTRATIONS

FIGURES

MAPS

FOREWORD

ON JULY 20, 1996, Raphael Patai died, a mercifully short time after being diagnosed with cancer. Thereby ended one of the most extraordinary careers in twentieth-century scholarship. Periodically, if rarely, there appear on the cultural horizon those monumental figures whose intellectual achievements serve as benchmarks for entire generations of colleagues and students. Such a man, surely, was Raphael Patai. For over half a century his career was a standing inspiration to those who toiled in the vineyards of anthropology, sociology, and history, and a tacit reproach to those, lacking his genius, who were unprepared to accept his own heroic standards of disciplined, self-sacrificing research.

One need only measure the stunning prodigality of the man. The hundreds of articles and the thirty-odd books that flowed from his pen would have challenged the absorptive powers of all but a handful of scholars— essentially those willing to devote their most vigorous years simply to a critical evaluation of Raphael Patai's own life and work. Consider, as well, the erudition, the plain and simple cultural and linguistic virtuosity resonating in this accumulated Pataiana. The *embarras de richesses* extends from studies of Shabbatai Zvi (in Hungarian), of the history of the Jews in Hungary (in German and English), of Josephus (in French), of Moroccan Jewry (in Hebrew), to an explosion of books and articles in Hebrew and English covering every facet of ancient and modern folk mores, from *Man and Temple in Ancient Jewish Myth and Ritual* and *The Jewish Alchemists*, to Patai's more popular but equally acclaimed volumes on *The Arab Mind* and *The Jewish Mind*.

Indeed, for academic "purists," fixated by disciplinary categorization, there is a lesson to be learned in the awesome breadth of Raphael Patai's terrain. Not for him artificial margins between the social sciences and the humanities, between Middle Eastern and Western cultures. He erased, devoured those barriers by force of will, stamina, and sheer intellectual muscularity. Whether applying his talents to subjects as diverse as "Hebrew Installation Rites," "The Jewish Indians in Mexico," *On Culture Contact and Its Working in Modern Palestine*, to *Women in the Modern World*, *The Republic of Syria*, *The Republic of Lebanon*, or *The Kingdom of Jordan*, he infused his works with an identical thoroughness and exactitude of documentation, with a magisterial command of historical and regional setting, and with an intuitive balance, perspective, and tolerance that, one suspects, reflected Raphael Patai's character no less than his learning.

It is instructive, moreover, to recall that this overpowering monographic superstructure was erected on a career enjoying few of the luxuries normally provided by Western academe. To be sure, Raphael Patai's own academic training and teaching experience were as densely upholstered as those of any of his professional colleagues. Born in Hungary, the son of the distinguished Zionist author and activist Joseph Patai, he earned doctorates at both the University of Budapest and the Hebrew University of Jerusalem (indeed, Patai's was the first Ph.D. to be awarded by the latter institution), as well as ordination at the Rabbinical Seminary of Budapest. Thereafter, he taught and acquired devoted protégés at the Hebrew University, at Columbia, Princeton, New York University, the New School for Social Research, the University of Pennsylvania, Ohio State University, and Fairleigh Dickinson University.

Yet, by contrast with those legions of academicians who ceaselessly bemoan the lack of fellowships and paid leaves of absence without which, they insist, there can be no "free time" for research and publication, Raphael Patai managed simultaneously to pursue his scholarship and to shoulder numerous challenging administrative responsibilities. Over the course of six decades, he served variously as research director of the Palestine Institute of Folklore and Ethnology; as director of the Syrian-Jordan-Lebanon Research Project; as administrative secretary of the Palestine and later Israel Institute of Technology (the Technion); and, most significantly, as research director of the Herzl Institute, in this latter capacity building the largest Zionist research center in the United States.

It was perhaps the confluence of these executive achievements, no less than a vivid, unifying strand in his publications, that revealed the élan behind Raphael Patai's intellect. There is, after all, a certain particularity within the ambit of every cultural galaxy, and Raphael Patai was no exception to this rule. Notwithstanding his devotion to scholarship in its broadest, most universalist dimensions, his transcending love affair unquestionably remained with Jewish civilization. At once intricate and austere, tradition-freighted and dynamically adaptive, intellectually cosmopolitan and ethnically defiant, that civilization is the coruscating penumbra of one of history's most vibrant and protean peoples.

Those who venture to interpret this complex and multifaceted phenomenon ideally should embody at least some of its characteristics. As it happened, Raphael Patai incarnated virtually all of them. In the most authentic sense of the word, he was a protean human being. His death, like his life, matters. "The wind blows through the stubble," wrote Theodor Herzl in 1901, aware that his time was running out. It is the wind that now has cut down Raphael Patai, ideological heir of the great Zionist father, whose majestic intellectual legacy signifies a comparable devotion to the fate and fortune of his people. For two generations of his students and admirers, the void left by his departure will not soon or easily be made good.

Howard M. Sachar

PREFACE
HOW THIS BOOK WAS WRITTEN

THE WRITING of this book spans a period of more than sixty years, many times longer than it took me to write any other of the thirty or so books I have authored in my lifetime. The next longest after this was my *The Jewish Alchemists*, on which I worked, on and off, for about ten years, and which was published in 1994 by Princeton University Press. None of my other books took longer than a period of one to two years to produce.

The history of the present book goes back to 1933, when I arrived in Jerusalem from Budapest, became a graduate student at the Hebrew University, and started to work on my doctoral dissertation, which dealt with water in ancient Palestinian folklore. While gathering source material for that book—I spent about two years doing little else beside reading the Bible and the Rabbinic sources and taking notes—I also jotted down what I found in those historical records on seafaring. I completed my dissertation by the end of 1935 (it turned out to be close to a three-hundred-page book, which was published in 1936 by the Dvir Publishing House of Tel Aviv), and earned the Ph.D. degree from the Hebrew University in June of that year—incidentally, the first Ph.D. to be awarded by that school. Right away I returned to my notes on seafaring, basing on them my Hebrew book *Jewish Seafaring in Ancient Times*, published in Jerusalem in 1938 by the Jewish Palestine Exploration Society. A brief English summary of it was published in 1941 in the *Jewish Quarterly Review*.

This done, my interest turned from the sea to the land, and more and more from historical to contemporary issues, resulting in a number of Hebrew books, published in small editions.

In 1944 I became a fellow of the Royal Anthropological Institute, and as such began to receive its journal, *Man*. In its March/April 1945 issue I found an article written by James Hornell on "Palm Leaves on Boats' Prows of Gerzian Age," the illustrations in which reminded me of a sketch in the Jewish burial caves at Beth Sh'arim near Haifa, which had been excavated shortly before. I sent in to *Man* a note on the subject, which was published in its March/April 1946 issue under the title "Palm Leaves on Boats' Prows in Palestine." In my note I pointed out the surprising similarity between the palm leaves on the Gerzian boats discussed by Hornell and those on the Beth Sh'arim ship, dating from the second or third century CE.

A few weeks later, to my great surprise, I got a letter from Mr. Hornell (it was forwarded by the editorial office of *Man*), in which he expressed his interest in the Beth Sh'arim find, and inquired whether I had more material pertaining to Jewish seafaring in ancient times. Delighted in the interest shown by a man who I knew was a foremost authority on ancient seafaring and the author of many important studies on the subject, I sent him a copy of my Hebrew book, and asked him whether he thought the book could be published in an English translation or adaptation. His answer was so positive that I felt encouraged to ask him whether he would be willing to read the English version I would prepare, and consider adding his own comments to it, or possibly even augment it with data from other ancient cultures that would throw light on what the Jewish sources have to say about seafaring. His answer again was positive, and I went to work on translating my book into English, a language in which by that time I was sufficiently at home, and in which I had even published several scholarly papers.

In the fall of 1947 a fellowship from the Viking Fund (subsequently renamed Wenner-Gren Foundation for Anthropological Research) brought me to America, but before I left Jerusalem I sent off the completed manuscript of my English translation to Mr. Hornell. Several months later I received the manuscript back from him in New York, in a revised, retyped, and occasionally expanded form. However, at the time I was totally involved in writing my book *Israel between East and West: A Study in Human Relations* (which was to be published in 1953 by the Jewish Publication Society), and was unable to tear myself away from problems of the present and to return to issues of the remote past. Hence, although I duly acknowledged to Mr. Hornell the receipt of the typescript, I also informed him that it would take some time before I could go over it and give him my reaction to the changes and additions he introduced. Here things stood when, in 1949, the news reached me that Mr. Hornell had passed away. He was eighty-four years old.

With Mr. Hornell's death the incentive to work on the seafaring book disappeared, and I put the typescript at the back of my filing cabinet, thinking that I would return to it once my current research engagements eased up and I would be left with some time on my hands. However, I got more and more involved in studies relating to the modern Middle East, other contemporary Jewish communities, the Arab mind, and the Jewish mind, so that the seafaring typescript remained untouched year after year—in fact, decade after decade.

Then, in the late 1980s, I was asked by my friend Dr. John M. Lundquist, head of the Oriental Division of the New York Public Library, to contribute a paper to the Festschrift he, together with Dr. Stephen D. Ricks of Brigham Young University, planned to publish in honor of the eightieth birthday of Hugh W. Nibley. Thinking about what would be most suitable for a collection of essays in honor of an outstanding Mormon scholar, and knowing that according to the traditions of the Mormons their ancestors sailed to America from the Land of Israel about the time of the destruction of Jerusalem by the Babylonians, I felt that a paper discussing some aspect of Jewish seafaring in ancient times would be most appropriate. So I went back to the seafaring typescript, and reworked the chapter that dealt with Rabbinic legal provisions related to seafaring. It was published in volume one of the Nibley Festschrift in 1990, and is reprinted here in a slightly changed form as Chapter 10.

This broke the "writer's block" I had with reference to the seafaring book. Working on that chapter, I saw that in order to produce a publishable English manuscript, the typescript that Mr. Hornell had sent me, in which he adhered very closely to my translation of my original Hebrew text, would have to be not only thoroughly restyled but also largely reorganized. In other words, I would have to produce a new manuscript, for which the old text would serve as nothing more than a collection of source material.

An additional factor that motivated me to go back to the seafaring book was that in 1993, after a hiatus of some thirty-five years, I was again under contract with Princeton University Press for a book. In 1958 they had published my book entitled *The Kingdom of Jordan*, and now they undertook to publish my *The Jewish Alchemists: A History and Source Book*. It was actually published in 1994. I happened to know that Princeton was interested in ancient seafaring. In 1951 they published George F. Hourani's *Arab Seafaring* (expanded edition 1995), and in 1991 they issued the second edition of Lionel Casson's *The Ancient Mariners*. Hence I felt that my book on Jewish seafaring in ancient times would also be of interest to them, and resolved that as soon as I finished seeing my alchemy book through the press I would go back to seafaring, rewrite it, and submit it to Princeton. My editor, Brigitta van Rheinberg, to whom I spoke about it, liked the idea and encouraged me to go ahead with it. I did, and the present book is the result. So, sixty-three years after I started dealing with the subject, *The Children of Noah: Jewish Seafaring in Ancient Times* is ready to embark on the hazardous voyage of facing the public and the critics.

A word has to be said about the share of James Hornell in the book in its present final shape. His contribution to the English manuscript I sent him in 1947 was twofold: first, he added brief comments to various passages, explaining technical details of shipbuilding, the parts of ships, and the operation of ships. Most of these comments I took over from his typescript into the present text. Regrettably, in my move from Jerusalem to New York, my copy of the manuscript I had sent was lost (as was my entire correspondence with him), and thus I was unable to be sure what precisely were Mr. Hornell's additions of this nature. Occasionally he put his comments in square brackets and signed them with his initials: these brackets and signatures have been retained in the present text.

His other contribution consisted of sending me offprints of two of his published papers, and suggesting that I include them as chapters in the book. One was a highly original article on "The Role of Birds in Early Navigation," published in the British journal *Antiquity*, vol. 20 (September 1946), pp. 142–49. After careful consideration I came to the conclusion, back in the late 1940s, not to include it in the book, because it had only tangential reference to Jewish seafaring in ancient times. The other article, entitled "Naval Activity in the Days of Solomon and Rameses III," was published in *Antiquity*, vol. 21 (June 1947), pp. 66–73. It dealt mainly with the naval encounters between Rameses III and the Sea Peoples, and contained speculations about the Ophir expeditions of Solomon and the location of Ophir. Again, after careful consideration, I came to the conclusion not to include this paper either, first because, like the earlier one, it had been published in a prestigious British journal and thus was known to those interested in the subject and, second and mainly, because it touched only upon what was the best known and most frequently commented upon incident in ancient Jewish seafaring—Solomon's Ophir venture. Now (in 1995), when I was working on the present version of my book, I reconsidered those two chapters again, but saw no reason to change my 1948 decision. What I did, however, was to incorporate the essential findings of Mr. Hornell about birds as winged scouts for ancient mariners on the high seas into my chapter on the ark of Noah, where they belong.

Thus the contribution of Mr. Hornell to the book turned out to be rather less substantial than both he and I originally thought it would be; however, his elucidations of shipbuilding details and of seafaring practices, which are scattered all through the text of several chapters, are of great value, and do—I like to hope—lend this book the same reliability that characterizes Mr. Hornell's many writings on the history of seafaring. Today, fifty years after he made these contributions, I remain as indebted to him as I was then, and want to express my sincere thanks to his shade.

Raphael Patai
Forest Hills, N.Y., 1995

INTRODUCTION

LET ME BEGIN by setting out briefly why I feel it is interesting—and, more than that, important—to write about ancient Jewish seafaring, what subjects fall under that general theme, how the book is organized, and whom I intend to address in it.

Seafaring, as will become evident as chapter after chapter unfolds, was an integral part of the economic, social, and emotional world of the Hebrews in biblical times and of their heirs, the Jews, in the days of the Second Jewish Commonwealth, of the Hellenistic period, and of the Talmudic era (until about 500 CE). At the time I started working on my Hebrew book on this subject (in the mid-1930s) the significance of seafaring in the life of the ancient Jews had been unrecognized or unconsidered by Jewish historical scholarship, and practically no studies about it were available. Even in the course of the more than half a century that has passed since the appearance of my Hebrew book (1938), which I never considered as more than a first attempt, no additional book on the subject has been published. Consequently, the picture presented by historical studies of that long early period in the life of the Jewish people remained incomplete: it showed the Jews as a landlocked people, whose world—with the exception of one or two episodes—ended where the sea began. As against this, a study of Jewish seafaring clearly demonstrates that after an initial period during which the Philistines and other peoples barred the Children of Israel from the sea, they learned to use the sea as a path to other lands in a manner no different from that of the other circum-Mediterranean cultures. This insight in itself has important bearing on the question of the early relationship between the cultures of the Aegean peoples and that of the biblical Hebrews.

As for the subjects that go into a study of ancient Jewish seafaring, they comprise an impressive variety of themes, ranging from such technical minutiae as the names of the many component parts of ships to descriptions of sea voyages and fantastic accounts of seamen's encounters with monsters of the sea. In ancient Hebrew, Jewish, and Aramaic sources, sea lore is in many ways intertwined with the references to concrete aspects of seafaring, and complement the latter by providing an insight into the emotional aspects of the relationship of the ancient Hebrews and Jews to the sea. Hence, it has been my feeling throughout that in order to give a rounded picture of "the Jews and the sea" hard data and fantastic stories have to be given equal attention in the book. In between are themes such as commercial and legal aspects of seafaring, naval warfare, life on board ships, the dangers of shipwreck, sailors' attitudes and experiences in the harbor, and a description of the many ports of ancient Palestine in which life was colored and enriched by the intermittent presence of seafarers.

The manner in which the book is organized is simple. I start by following the example of the Bible, in which all information about ships begins with the fascinating legendary account of the ark of Noah, and have placed a chapter on that subject at the head of the book. It presents all the data I could find on that great first navigational venture recorded in biblical and Rabbinical literature, and I believe that it serves as a good introduction to the later, historical details contained in the Bible about the first actual experiences the Hebrews had with the sea. Next follow the technical details found in biblical and especially in post-biblical Jewish literature about the building of ships, the parts that went into the ships, and the types of ships that were used and known to the Jews in ancient Palestine and Babylonia (Chapters 3 and 4). Once we are acquainted with the vessels, we are ready to have a closer look at the crews that manned the ships (Chapter 5), and at the maritime trade that gave the Jews (as well as other peoples) the basic impetus "to go down to the sea in ships" (Chapter 6). Next follows the information available on life in the harbor and aboard the ship on high seas. Especially rich in lively detail are the descriptions of the efforts made by the crew and the passengers to save the ship and themselves in case of a storm, when desperate measures had to be resorted to (Chapters 7 and 8).

The ancient Jews did not differ from the other peoples of the Mediterranean in using ships in naval warfare (Chapter 9). They also developed, again like other peoples, a corpus of laws governing property relations, chartering, buying and selling ships, and including, in the Jewish case, a body of religious laws that prescribed what *mitzvoth* (religious commandments) must be observed aboard, on high seas, in the harbor, while loading and unloading ships, and so on (Chapter 10). The next two chapters (11 and 12) introduce us to sea lore, and provide an insight into the place the sea, its awesome power, and its miraculous denizens occupied in Jewish imagination. Finally, the last two chapters (13 and 14) present the gist of the available historical information on the ports that existed in ancient Palestine along its long Mediterranean coastline, on the Red Sea, and around the Sea of Galilee. The usual notes and index complete the book.

In writing this book I have assumed that not only historians but also the proverbial "intelligent reader" will take an interest in it, and hence, "in order to enable the reader to run in it" (as the old Hebrew phrase puts it), I have kept all scholarly apparatus out of the text as far as this was possible, relegating it to notes at the end of the book.

It is an oft-stated fact that the sea has played a role of vital importance in human development. As the noted German natural philosopher Raoul Heinrich Francé (Vienna, 1874–Budapest, 1943) wrote in his 1924 book *Das Buch des Lebens*, the sea is "the greatest educator humanity has had. It showed man the way to culture. It gave and continues to give him food freely, and even today nourishes with its animal life one-fourth of the inhabitants of Europe. The sea taught man how to conquer distance, and opened before him a road around the globe."[1]

The sea began to function as the teacher of mankind at the very dawn of history. By the early third millennium BCE, peoples living on the Levant coast of the Mediterranean and its southeast corner, where the great river Nile flows into it, had developed regular commercial traffic across the sea, which played a crucial role in their economies. The historian of ancient seafaring, Lionel Casson, tells of a fleet of "forty ships filled with cedar logs" that set out from a Phoenician harbor and sailed down along the coast of Palestine to Egypt to supply Lebanese timber for the building plans of Pharaoh Snefru, about 2600 BCE.[2] For centuries thereafter shipments of cedars, copper, and other merchandise were loaded on ships at Byblos, not far north of modern Beirut, and sent south to Egypt's Mediterranean ports. In even earlier times, jars, flasks, and pitchers made in Palestine and Syria found their way to Egypt, and objects of Egyptian make were used along the Levant coast. The sea traffic between Byblos and Egypt was of such primary importance that seagoing merchantmen, whether or not they actually sailed to or from Byblos, were called "Byblos ships," just as many centuries later in biblical seamen's parlance overseas vessels were called "Tarshish ships," even if they sailed on the Red Sea and waters to the southeast of it, a direction opposite to Tarshish, which probably was located on the coast of the Iberian peninsula.

After Pharaoh Snefru's time, Egyptian overseas trade fell into abeyance for several centuries, but it was revived under Thutmose III (ca. fifteenth century BCE), who established Egyptian dominion over Palestine, Phoenicia, and Syria, and initiated a period of some three hundred years of intensive commercial interchange between these countries and Egypt. Egypt imported livestock and a large variety of luxury items, including chariots, delicacies, fine textiles, copper, timber, and so on, from the countries and islands of the eastern Mediterranean, as well as perfumes, incense, ivory, spices, sandalwood, pearls, and peacocks from countries it could reach from its Red Sea ports.

This import was counterbalanced by the export of merchandise produced in Egypt—canvas, embroideries, inlaid furniture, weapons, pottery, glass, and alabaster ornaments—for which a ready market was found in those overseas lands. One of the most important overseas trading partners of the Egyptians was Crete: the Minoans of Crete exported their wares not only to Egypt but also to other countries they could reach by sea, including Phoenicia, and in return imported the products of those countries. All this is well attested by archaeological finds, which of course can bring to light only nonperishable objects, and hence provide nothing more than a limited one-sided picture of the great variety of merchandise shipped in those days back and forth across the Mediterranean and the Red Sea.

Almost coeval with the initiation of sea trade was the inception of the utilization of ships as instruments of war. In the middle of the twenty-fifth century BCE, Pharaoh Sahure is reported to have used a fleet to transport his army to the Levant Coast, and about a millennium later Egyptian documentation shows that Thutmose III likewise used the fleet to send his soldiers on repeated expeditions against that region. This involved the conquest of existing ports, or the building and securing of new ones, which also served as places for the construction and repair of ships on the very spot where the requisite timber was available.

In the late thirteenth and early twelfth centuries BCE bands of Sea Peoples from the northern parts of the Mediterranean launched repeated naval attacks against Egypt, until, in 1174 BCE, Ramses III, unable to stop their advances, settled them as mercenaries in Egyptian strongholds along the coast of Palestine. Thus the Sikils became established in the Dor region of northern Palestine, the Sherdani settled in the Acre (Akko) plain north of Haifa, and the Philistines gained control over the southern coast of Palestine, gave the country their name, and came to play an important role in the history of the Hebrews in the age of the Judges (twelfth to eleventh centuries BCE). It seems that the Philistines dominated much of Palestine until the days of David, and they kept their national identity and political autonomy until the Babylonian Exile of 586 BCE.[3]

It was in the seventh century BCE that Israel's neighbors along the western and southeastern shores of the Mediterranean struck out at greater and greater distances across the sea. Large and dangerous as the Mediterranean was for ancient seafarers, they nevertheless, willy-nilly, ventured beyond it into the unknown waters of the faraway Atlantic Ocean. According to Herodotus, in about 650 BCE the ship of Colaeus, a captain from the island of Samos off the west coast of Asia Minor, was blown by gale winds all along the Mediterranean and through the Straits of Gibraltar to Tartessus on the Atlantic coast of Spain (possibly identical with the Tarshish of the Bible). About fifty years after him mariners from Phocaea, a city on the west coast of Asia Minor, were rumored to have ventured even farther out into the Atlantic in both northerly and southerly directions.[4]

Another few years later, again according to Herodotus, the Phoenicians, in the service of Pharaoh Necho (610–595 BCE), reached the Atlantic by setting out from an Egyptian Red Sea port and sailing around Africa, and then, sailing eastward on the Mediterranean, returned to Egypt.[5] About a century after this great feat of circumnavigating the African continent, Hanno, king of Carthage, recorded on a bronze plaque he placed in a temple in Carthage that he "set sail with sixty vessels of fifty oars" past the Pillars of Hercules (that is, the Straits of Gibraltar), and down the west coast of Africa to places whose identification is still not agreed upon by scholars.[6]

These few data suffice to indicate the role seafaring played in the lives of the peoples who lived in the vicinity of biblical Israel to its north and southwest. As soon as Israel was strong enough to gain access to the seas that surrounded it and to establish diplomatic and commercial relations with its neighbors, it began to derive benefits from their sea trade, and then to mount overseas expeditions of its own. How this came about, and to what developments it led, will form a central subject of this book.

The Children of Noah

Chapter 1

THE ARK OF NOAH

THE BIBLE, that unique literary masterpiece, opens with an account of the mythical beginnings of the history of the world, of mankind, and of the people of Israel, proceeds with an admixture of myth and history in which the former gradually diminishes as the latter gains ground, and then continues with a theocentric historical account of developments in the united, and subsequently divided, Hebrew monarchy, and of what happened to the Jews after their return from the Babylonian exile. In telling the story of Jewish seafaring in ancient times we shall try to follow this great example, at least to the extent of beginning our account with myth, then surveying the actual beginnings of Jewish shipbuilding and seafaring activity as these can be culled from the rather meager biblical references, before proceeding to the much richer data on ships, sailing, and fishing practiced by the Jews of Palestine and Babylonia that are contained in the post-biblical ancient Jewish and non-Jewish sources.

The Bible, in conformity with the mythical traditions of many ancient peoples, presents the story of a primeval great flood that wiped out mankind except for a few persons, who survived in some sort of water craft. In that connection, old traditions also give some details about how that craft was built, and make it clear that in antiquity shipbuilding was regarded as an art not invented by man himself but bestowed upon him by a benevolent deity. From the Sumerian myth of the deluge, preserved only in a very fragmentary form, we learn that the gods, or a god, instruct Ziusudra, a pious, god-fearing king, to build "a giant boat," and thus save himself from destruction by the deluge that the assembly of the gods has decided to let loose on mankind.[1] Likewise in the Akkadian Epic of Gilgamesh, Utnapishtim, the Babylonian Noah, recounts to Gilgamesh that "when the heart of the great gods led them to produce a flood," the god Ea instructed him (Utnapishtim) to build a ship, whose dimensions are described as follows: "Ten dozen cubits the height of each of its walls, ten dozen cubits each edge of the square deck."[2] That is to say, the ship is imagined as having been an exact cube, which of course is an impossible shape for a water craft. Clearly, what the tradition envisaged was not a ship at all but a cubic structure, a house with exaggerated dimensions. Since a cubit can be taken as having equaled a foot and a half, 120 cubits would correspond to 180 feet: this was the size of Utnapishtim's "giant boat." In the sequel it is stated that it had "six decks, dividing her into seven parts," and that "her floor plan [was] divided into nine parts."

In another Akkadian text, known as the Atrahasis Epic, when the god Ea commands Atrahasis to build a ship, Atrahasis says to him, "I have never built a ship; draw a design of it on the ground, that, seeing the design, I may build the ship."[3] The rest of the tablet is destroyed, but it evidently told how the god Ea fulfilled Atrahasis's request and drew for him a plan of the ship.

The Greeks believed that the gods were the first builders of ships, and Homer tells us that shipbuilding enjoyed the protection of Pallas Athene.[4] As a consequence of this traditionally assumed divine origin of shipbuilding, it has long been a common practice among seamen to place their ships under the protection of a particular god or, more frequently, goddess. Lucian tells us of an Egyptian ship called the *Goddess Isis*,[5] which designation clearly indicates that Isis was considered the protector of that ship. The passage of millennia changed little in this custom: to the present day, owners of ships and fishing boats all around the Mediterranean often dedicate their vessels to the Madonna, either explicitly or under some allusive name such as "Star of the Sea." In Italy, Spain, and Portugal fishing boats are commonly dedicated to some saint of local repute in order that this patron may ensure safety while they ride the waves.[6]

The ancient Hebrews constituted no exception in attributing the construction of the first water craft to a builder who followed divine instruction. According to the Book of Genesis, it was God himself who gave instructions to Noah, the first and only shipbuilder mentioned in the Bible, concerning the measurements and other constructional details of the ark (*tēvāh*) which he was to build—the earliest vessel mentioned in Hebrew literature. The divine instructions were:

> Make thee an ark of gopher wood; with rooms shalt thou make the ark, and shalt pitch it within and without with pitch. And this is how thou shalt make it: the length of the ark three hundred cubits, the breadth of it fifty cubits, and the height of it thirty cubits. A light shalt thou make to the ark, and to a cubit shalt thou finish it upward; and the door of the ark shalt thou set in the side thereof; with lower, second, and third stories shalt thou make it. (Gen. 6:14–16)

What, if anything, can we learn from this biblical description of the construction of Noah's ark, not forgetting that we are discussing an old mythical tradition? The first thing we notice is that Noah's vessel, although called "ark" (*tēvāh*) and not "ship" (*oniyāh*), was much more shipshape than Utnapishtim's "great ship," which is described as a huge cube. The relations between the length, width, and height of Noah's ark (30:5:3) are such as might be observed in ancient times at any seaport in which war galleys might be seen—a type of vessel characterized by a comparatively narrow beam combined with considerable relative length of hull and shallowness of draught.

As to the absolute measurements, there is undoubtedly a fanciful exaggeration in the account of Noah's ark, such as appeared necessary when telling about a ship that played a crucial role in the ancient mythical history of the world, built not only to save Noah and his family but to provide space for seven pairs of every species of clean animals, and for two pairs of every unclean animal found on earth (Gen. 7:2–3). Taking a cubit as approximately equal to a foot and a half, the ark as described would be about 450 feet long, 75 feet in width, and 45 feet in height. These dimensions are impossibly great for vessels of the date when the biblical story was put into writing, or for antiquity in general.

No seagoing ships even approaching such large dimensions were built by either the Greeks or the Romans even at the most advanced stage of their technical development of shipbuilding, when magnificent triremes were being constructed in Attic shipyards. The usual length of an Attic trireme was 37 meters (122 feet) with a beam of 5 meters (16 feet).[7]

As we shall see in the chapter dealing with the types of craft that were in use by, or known to, the Jews in Talmudic times (cf. Chapter 4), the largest ships are usually described as having had a capacity of 10,000 talents or amphorae, which is equal in burden to about 250 tons. It would therefore appear as probable that the author of the passage about the ark of Noah, after observing the proportions of the ships available to his inspection, solved rather simply the difficulty of having to describe a vessel that could carry a great multitude of animals: he multiplied the measurements of the ships he saw by a round number, such as seven or ten; then, ignoring the units under ten, he arrived at the arbitrary sizes of 300, 50, and 30 cubits for the length, breadth, and height of Noah's ark. From the fact that the ratio of beam to length is one to six we can infer that the basis of the calculation was the dimensions of a slender galley propelled by oars, rather than the average measurements of tubby merchantmen such as the grain ships that ran from Alexandria to Rome during the period when Rome held Egypt in her grip.

The biblical exaggeration of the size of Noah's ark appears as modest in relation to the measurements given by Berosus, the third-century BCE Babylonian historian, to the vessel that survived the deluge. According to him the length of that ship was five stadia or furlongs—about 1,000 yards—and its breadth was two stadia—about 400 yards.[8] Nor are these the maximum dimensions attributed to the ship of the Babylonian Noah. In the Armenian version of Eusebius's *Chronicles* based on Berosus (whose original has not survived), the length of the ship is given as fifteen furlongs, that is, nearly two miles.[9]

Legendary dimensions apart, the Talmudic sages looked upon the ark of Noah as having possessed the ideal dimensions of a seagoing vessel. A Midrash observed: "The Torah taught you a practical measure: If a man build a ship which has to be able to stand in the harbor, let him make its beam one sixth, and its height one tenth, of its length."[10] The expression "to stand in the harbor" is the usual one employed in Rabbinic literature to designate the way a ship floats upright in the water, with part of its hull below the water level and part of it rising above the water. Thus Rabbi Pinḥas said in the name of Rabbi Levi: "The ark of Noah was sunk into the water like a ship that stands in the harbor." As to the depth to which the ark of Noah was immersed in the water, it is stated in a Midrash that it was eleven cubits (that is, 16.5 feet).[11]

To return to the biblical account: as we saw, in addition to the dimensions of the ark, it contains some details about the materials that, according to tradition, Noah used in building his ark: they were gopher wood and pitch. It can be assumed that these materials were those actually used in shipbuilding in the place and at the time the biblical deluge and ark story originated. Gopher wood seems to refer to the Lebanese cedar (*cedrus libani*), once plentiful on the slopes of the Lebanon mountains, a fragrant and durable wood of light red color that was in great demand in Egypt for shipbuilding, coffin making, and cabinetry. The story of the troubles of Wen-Amon, sent about 1100 BCE by one of the Pharaohs to Phoenicia to buy a supply of "woodwork" for the building of "a great and august barque of Amon-Re, king of the gods," well illustrates the need which the Egyptians had for this wood and, incidentally, shows that the Egyptian treasury sometimes had difficulty in providing the funds required by the prince of Byblos as payment for the timber desired. In that story the ship itself is called a "cedar ship," and the text tells that the same kind of purchase was made several times during the lifetimes of the father and grandfather of the prince.[12]

As for the pitch (Hebrew: *kopher*) that Noah was instructed by God to apply to his vessel "within and without" (Gen. 6:14), it seems to be identical with the material that Gilgamesh used for making his ship watertight, and that, in E. A. Speiser's translation, is rendered "bitumen" and "asphalt."[13]

The use of bitumen to make hulls of ships watertight was a common practice in Egypt, particularly in the case of those vessels compacted of bundles of reeds and papyrus stems. Models of such vessels have been found in tombs and furnish evidence that they had received a waterproofing coat to prevent them from becoming sodden and waterlogged through prolonged immersion in water. Biblical evidence of this treatment is afforded by the story of the infant Moses in the ark made of bulrushes.

According to the story as preserved in the Book of Exodus, the mother of Moses, in order to save her child's life from Pharaoh's decree that all male children born to Hebrew parents should be killed, made for him an "ark of bulrushes, and daubed it with slime (*ḥēmar*) and with pitch (*zepheth*) (Ex. 2:3). The use of the two nouns (which, incidentally, correspond to the bitumen and asphalt mentioned in the Gilgamesh epic) caught the attention of the Talmudic sages, who commented on the difference between the double coating of pitch with which the ark of Noah was covered, and the "slime and pitch" used for Moses's ark of bulrushes. The waters of the Nile, they say, were weak, and so a single coating on the inside was enough to keep them out of the cradle-like ark of bulrushes; the coating of pitch was applied only to keep away from the child the unpleasant smell of the stagnant water.[14]

This explanation is rather fanciful. If we assume that the story is based on an actual incident, the bathing place of an Egyptian princess would certainly not have been located amidst stagnant, evil-smelling waters. It would rather seem probable that the *ḥēmar* was clay, applied to the inside of the child's ark, whereas *zepheth* was bitumen or asphalt, applied on its outside to prevent it from becoming waterlogged. If so, the interior coating with clay was done in order to afford a smooth surface that would not irk even the sensitive skin of a newborn infant, who, because of the heat, could not be wrapped into much protective clothing.

Pliny also bears witness to the Egyptian custom of making small boats of plaited papyrus watertight by an application of bitumen. An advantage of the use of a clay layer on the inside of reed canoes, rather than another coating of bitumen, is that bitumen may become sticky in the heat and adhere to the passengers' bodies, whereas clay is not affected by heat and remains hard as long as it is dry.

To return again to the ark of Noah: in addition to its dimensions and the materials used in its construction, it is described as a three-storied ship, with each story divided into rooms (Hebrew *qinnim*). It is also stated that it had a window ("light," Hebrew *tzohar*) and a door set in its side, and was "finished in a cubit above" (Gen. 6:14, 16). These details, too, elicited Talmudic comment. The word *qinnim* is explained as "compartments and rooms," with the word for "compartments" (*qelin*) borrowed from the Greek *kella, kellion*, that is, "cell." According to Rabbi Yehuda, "there were in it 330 cells, with each cell measuring ten by ten cubits, and two corridors of four cubits each [in width], with cells on both sides, and two cubits on the outside."[15] The word used by R. Yehuda for alleyway, *platya*, is again borrowed from the Greek *plateia*, meaning aisle. This rather laconic statement by R. Yehuda is explained by medieval commentators as follows: the lowest and middle deck of the ark each had four rows of cells. Each row consisted of thirty cells, so that the two lower decks had 120 cells each. The two inner rows were placed back to back, and were separated from the two outer rows by two corridors four cubits in width. In addition, there was a gangway of one cubit in width running along the outer sides of the two outer rows and separating the cells from the bulwark. Thus the total width of these sections was $1 + 10 + 4 + 10 + 10 + 4 + 10 + 1 = 50$ cubits. On the top deck of the ark the arrangement was similar, except that there were only three rows of thirty cells each, or a total of ninety cells, since the shape of the ark narrowed upward, so that on that deck there was room for only three rows of cells. Thus the total number of cells according to R. Yehuda was $120 + 120 + 90 = 330$.[16]

The calculation is ingenious and accounts for the biblical length (300 cubits) and width (50 cubits) of the ark, except for three flaws: it does not take into account the thickness of the dividing walls of the cells; it assumes that the ark had an oblong boxlike shape, so that the total measurement of the cells (30 times 10 cubits) equaled precisely the total length of the ark (300 cubits), which does not allow for the additional several dozens of cubits required to account for the narrowing of the beam fore and aft so as to give the whole structure a shiplike shape; and it leaves no space for stairs between the decks.

The same criticism must be leveled against the alternative view of R. Nehemiah, according to which there were 900 cells in the ark, each measuring six by six cubits.[17] Nehemiah also explains the biblical expression "in a cubit shalt thou finish it above" (Gen. 6:16) by saying that over the top of the third (uppermost) deck there was a roofing like that of the tilt of a wagon (the expression he uses is borrowed from the Greek *kamaroton*), and that it was curved so that the summit was only a single cubit in width.[18]

An entirely different arrangement for the compartments in the ark is suggested in a late Midrash in the name of R. Shema'yah: "The Holy One, blessed be He, showed Noah with his finger, saying: 'This is how you should make the ark. A hundred and fifty compartments should be along its right-side length, [a hundred] and fifty along its left side, and thirty-three compartments along its width on the prow, and thirty-three along its width on the stern, with ten in the middle to serve as store rooms for the food. Five meeting places [*apantiyot*, from the Greek *apanté*; or perhaps *aftaniyot*, store rooms] along the right side of the ark and five others along the left side. . . . And thus in the lower story, and thus in the middle story, and thus in the upper story.'"[19]

As to the *tzohar* which, according to the Genesis story, God commanded Noah to make for the ark, and which modern biblical scholarship takes to mean a light or an opening to let in light, the Talmudic rabbis were baffled by the word and gave it varied explanations: some considered it to mean window, others explained it as sails, and still others as a pearl. This last alternative is in accordance with a legend first recorded in the second century CE:

> R. Pinḥas in the name of R. Levi said: "During all the twelve months that Noah spent in the ark he did not need the light of the sun by day, nor the light of the moon by night, for he had a pearl which served this purpose when it was hung up. When he saw that the pearl was dull, he knew that it was daytime; and when the pearl was seen to shine [brightly], he knew that it was nighttime."[20]

In a later version of the same legend it is related in the name of R. Meir: "A pearl hung in the ark and shone for all the creatures that were in it like a candle that shines in the house, and like the sun shining at noontide."[21]

Rabbinic authors also devoted attention to the question of how the inmates of the ark were allocated among its three decks. According to one opinion, the lowest deck served for the disposal of the offal, the second for the accommodation of Noah and his family and the clean animals, and the upper deck for the unclean animals. A variant version has it that the lowest deck served for the unclean animals, the second deck for Noah, his family and the clean animals, and the third one for the offal. Yet another opinion considered that the lowest deck was for the cattle and the wild animals, the middle deck for all the fowl, and the top deck for "the creeping things and reptiles" and the human beings. There was also a trap-door ("*kataraklin*," from the Greek *katarraktos*) in the ark, through which Noah could shovel the sweepings of the compartments sideways into the water.[22]

Of course, all the statements presented above are but typical examples of the Rabbinic Aggada, legendary embellishments of the biblical text, or speculations on words and phrases in the biblical narrative that seemed obscure to the sages and triggered their ingenuity in appending their explanations. The very divergences, for instance, in the suggested numbers and arrangements of the cells in the ark are sufficient to show that the plans described are nothing more than ingenious attempts of the learned to explain how a vessel could have been subdivided for the purpose envisaged. The interest the sages evidently had in the size, construction, and structure of Noah's ark, although it led into the realm of fantasy, may have been nourished by the importance ships and seaborne traffic had for the life of the Jews in the Talmudic age in Palestine along the Mediterranean coast and in Babylonia, sustained by its great twin rivers.

To move now from the size and shape of Noah's ark to the navigational aspect of his staying afloat for the 150 days of the duration of the deluge, and his landfall (Gen. 7:24; 8:3–4)—on all this the biblical story supplies only laconic references. All we are told is that "the ark went upon the face of the waters" (Gen. 7:18), that it "rested in the seventh month, on the seventeenth day of the month, upon the mountain of Ararat" (Gen. 8:4), and that thereafter the "waters decreased continually," until, almost two and a half months later, "in the tenth month, on the first day of the month, the tops of the mountains were seen" (Gen. 8:4–5).

"At the end of forty days," counted from an unspecified starting point, Noah began to send out birds in order "to see if the waters were abated from off the face of the ground" (Gen. 8:8). First he sent out a raven several times, then he sent out a dove at seven-day intervals: the first time the dove returned empty-handed, or rather empty-billed; the second time she brought in her mouth an olive leaf, and the third time she no longer returned, from which Noah concluded that she had found a resting place in the dried-up land.

A very similar sequence of sending out birds to find dry land as the waters of the deluge subsided is given in the Akkadian Gilgamesh Epic, in which Utnapishtim says:

> When the seventh day arrived,
> I sent forth and set free a dove.
> The dove went forth, but came back;
> Since no resting place for it was visible, she turned round.
> Then I sent forth and set free a swallow.
> The swallow went forth but came back;
> Since no resting place for it was visible, she turned round.
> Then I sent forth and set free a raven.
> The raven went forth, and seeing that the waters had diminished,
> He eats, circles, caws, and turns not round.
> Then I let out (all) to the four winds,
> And offered a sacrifice.[23]

The sending out of birds to find out whether dry land is within reach forms part of the flood stories of other peoples as well.[24] It has been made the point of departure of a remarkable study by James Hornell entitled "The Role of Birds in Early Navigation,"[25] whose gravamen is to show that several ancient peoples used birds for the purpose of finding out whether there was land within a navigable distance, and in what direction. Hornell adduces references to the practice of carrying aboard several "shore-sighting birds" among the ancient Hindu merchants when sailing on overseas voyages contained in the Hindu *Sutta Pitaka* (fifth century BCE), according to which these birds were "used to locate the nearest land when the ship's position became doubtful." The same practice is mentioned in the Buddhist *Kevaddha Sutta* of Digha, written about the same period. Five centuries later Pliny mentions the same custom as practiced by the seamen of Ceylon when making sea voyages, as they were unable to steer by the stars.[26] Again, according to Cosmas Indicopleustes, the same practice was still followed by Ceylonese seamen in the sixth century CE. Hornell refers to data concerning the use of such "shore-sighting birds" from several cultures all around the globe, and his study makes it likely that the traces of some such practice were preserved in the Akkadian and the biblical legends about the birds sent out by Utna-pishtim and Noah to espy dry land.

Chapter 2

SHIPS AND SEAFARING
IN THE BIBLE

APART FROM the legendary description of the ark of Noah in the Book of
Genesis, the only biblical passage in which shipbuilding is mentioned is
found in 1 Kings 9:26–27. There it is stated with tantalizing brevity that
"King Solomon made a navy of ships in Ezion-Gebher which is beside
Eloth [Elath] on the shore of the Red Sea in the Land of Edom. And
Hiram sent in the navy his servants, shipmen that had knowledge of sea,
with the servants of Solomon."

The word translated as "navy of ships" reads *oni* in the Hebrew text of
the Bible. *Oni* is an abbreviated form of the more common *oniyah*,
meaning ship, and thus can mean either "ship" or "fleet." The translations take it to mean the latter, but in the very next chapter of the Book
of Kings the word *oni* appears with singular verbs, and thus seems to
have rather the meaning of "ship": "And the *oni* also of Hiram that
carried (*nasa*, sing.) gold from Ophir, brought (*hēvi*, sing.) from Ophir a
great plenty of sandalwood and precious stone" (1 Kings 10:11). As a
comparison of the two quoted verses shows, the tradition about the *oni*
sailing to Ophir was uncertain: first it says that the *oni* was made by
Solomon, but then it calls it "*oni* of Hiram." A little later the issue is
further confused by a statement speaking of two *oni*s that cooperated on
a regular basis: one of Solomon and one of Hiram: "The king [Solomon]
had at sea a Tarshish-*oni* with Hiram's *oni*: once every three years the
Tarshish-*oni* would come [*tavo*, sing.] carrying [*nos'ēt*, sing.] gold and
silver, ivories and apes and peacocks" (1 Kings 10:22).

This question aside, other biblical passages cast doubt on the building
of a ship (or a navy) by Solomon's men. According to 1 Kings 10:11, the
expedition to Ophir was undertaken by "the *oni* of Hiram," and 2
Chronicles 8:18 states explicitly that "Huram [Hiram] sent him [Solo-
mon] by the hand of his servants ships [*oniyoth*, pl.] and servants that had
knowledge of the sea, and they came with the servants of Solomon to
Ophir, and fetched from thence four hundred and fifty talents of gold
and brought them to King Solomon." That is, according to this version
of the Ophir expedition, Hiram sent to Solomon ships manned by his
own Phoenician crew, the ships took aboard "Solomon's servants," and
then proceeded to Ophir.

The major problem, however, with this version is that ships from the Phoenician Mediterranean port of Tyre could only reach Ezion-Gebher— a port on the Red Sea—if they circumnavigated Africa, and we have no knowledge about such undertakings by Phoenician seafarers in the days of Solomon, the tenth century BCE. If we rely rather on the version given in the Book of Kings, we must assume that timber from the port of Tyre was shipped by Hiram to some Mediterranean port in Solomon's kingdom, whence it was conveyed by Solomon's "servants" overland to the Gulf of Aqaba, and there the Hebrew workmen, supervised and directed by Phoenician experts, built one or more ships.

Whatever the manner in which Solomon's "navy" came into being, the Ophir expedition did not lead to development of a shipbuilding industry in either of the two Hebrew kingdoms into which Solomon's realm broke up after his death. The Bible says nothing about shipbuilding in the Mediterranean coastal cities of Judah and Israel, and as for Ezion-Gever, when it was again under Judean rule, and King Jehoshaphat "made Tarshish ships to go to Ophir for gold," the ships he had built "were broken at Ezion-Gever" (1 Kings 22:49; cf. 2 Chron. 20:36–37), either due to a storm or simply because they were inexpertly constructed.

The meaning of the expression "Tarshish ships" and the location of Ophir will be discussed in Chapter 13, dealing with the Red Sea ports.

In the biblical account, the visit of the Queen of Sheba to Jerusalem is bracketed between two references to Solomon's Ophir expedition (1 Kings 9:26–10:13; 2 Chron. 8:17–9:12). This makes is appear, without it ever being stated explicitly, that the country of Sheba was believed to be either identical with or a close neighbor of Ophir. The Bible says nothing about how the Queen of Sheba got from her country to Jerusalem, but this lacuna is filled in by the Aggada: the hoopoe took a letter from Solomon to the Queen of Sheba, in which the king invited her to visit him—actually to come pay homage to him. The queen assembled all the ships of the sea, and loaded them with the finest kind of wood, and with pearls and precious stones. Together with these she sent Solomon six thousand youths and maidens, all born in the same year, in the same month, on the same day, in the same hour—and all of equal stature and size, all clothed in purple garments. We must conclude that the legend envisages the arrival of quite a sizable fleet at the southern port of Solomon's domain. They bore a letter from the queen to Solomon as follows: "From the city of Kitor [where the Queen of Sheba resided] to the Land of Israel is a journey of seven years. As it is your wish and behest that I visit you, I shall hasten and be in Jerusalem at the end of three years." And so it came to pass.[1]

As she had come to visit Solomon with such a huge naval retinue, it was only meet that one of the riddles that the Queen of Sheba put to

Solomon should deal with a ship. She asked him: "There is something that when living moves not, yet when its head is cut off it moves. What is it?" Solomon, of course, had no difficulty in solving the riddle: "It is the ship in the sea."[2] The solution itself requires some explanation: it refers to a tree, which when alive, cannot move from its place, but when it is cut, and a ship's mast is made of it, moves all over the world.

But to return to information contained in the Bible itself: despite the apparent absence of first-hand experience with shipbuilding, the Hebrews of late monarchic times had some knowledge of how a seagoing vessel was constructed, equipped, and manned. This becomes evident from a prophecy of Ezekiel (late sixth century BCE) about (or rather against) Tyre, in which the prophet speaks of that great seafaring power as if she herself were a ship. In doing so, the prophet alludes to the manner in which a seagoing vessel was built:

> The word of the Lord came unto me, saying:
> And thou, son of man, take up a lamentation for Tyre,
> And say unto Tyre that dwelleth at the entries of the sea,
> The merchant of the people unto many isles:
> Thus saith the Lord God:
> O Tyre, thou hast said: I am the perfection of beauty.
> In the heart of the seas are thy boundaries,
> Thy builders have perfected thy beauty.
> Of cypress trees from Senir have they fashioned all thy planks.
> Cedar from Lebanon have they taken to make a mast upon thee.
> Of oaks of Bashan have they made thine oars,
> Thy deck have they made of ivory in larch from the Kittim's isles,
> Fine linen with broidered work from Egypt was thy sail,
> To be an ensign unto thee;
> Blue and purple from the isles of Elisha was thine awning.
> The inhabitants of Sidon and Arvad were thy rowers,
> Thy wise men, O Tyre, were in thee, they were thy pilots.
> The elders of Gebal and the wise men thereof were in thee thy calkers.
> All the ships of the sea with their mariners were in thee
> To exchange thy merchandise.
> Persia and Lud and Put were in thine army, thy men of war,
> The hanged shield and helmet in thee, they set forth thy comeliness.
>
> (Ezek. 27:2–10)

As we see, the prophet is not consistent in his imagery: when he says that "All the ships of the sea were in thee," what he evidently has in mind is not a ship but a port city, visited by many ships. Following this passage the prophet speaks of the city of Tyre itself, with all the various peoples inhabiting or visiting it, the great variety of merchandise found in it, and the trading partners in the Mediterranean islands and countries and in the Near East who were its "traffickers," including "Tarshish ships" that brought it supplies (Ezek. 27:11–25). Then, in the sequel, the prophet returns to the ship metaphor and speaks of the impending downfall of Tyre as if it were a ship on the high seas wrecked by a mighty storm:

> So wast thou filled and made very heavy in the heart of the seas,
> Thy rowers have brought thee into great waters,
> The east wind hath broken thee in the heart of the seas,
> Thy riches and thy wares, thy merchandise,
> Thy mariners and thy pilots,
> Thy calkers and the exchangers of thy merchandise,
> And all thy men of war that are in thee,
> With all thy company which is in the midst of thee,
> Shall fall into the heart of the seas in the day of thy ruin.
>
> (Ezek. 27:25–27)

At this point the prophet confounds the city itself and its ship image:

> At the sound of thy pilots' cry the waves shall shake,
> And down shall come from their ships all that handle the oar,
> The mariners and all the pilots of the sea,
> They shall stand upon the land,
> And cause their voice to be heard over thee,
> And shall cry bitterly,
> And cast dust upon their heads.
> They shall roll themselves in the ashes,
> And make themselves utterly bald for thee,
> And shall gird themselves with sackcloth
> And weep for thee in bitterness of soul
> With bitter lamentation.
> And in their wailing they shall take up a lamentation over thee:
> Who was there like Tyre, fortified in the midst of the sea?
> When thy wares came forth out of the seas,
> Thou didst fill many peoples.
> With the multitude of thy riches and of thy merchandise
> Didst thou enrich the kings of the earth.
> Now that thou art broken by the seas,
> In the depths of the waters,
> And thy merchandise and all thy company
> Are fallen in the midst of thee,
> All the inhabitants of the isles are appalled at thee,
> And their kings are horribly afraid,
> They are troubled in their countenance.

> The merchants among the people hiss at thee,
> Thou art become a terror, and never shalt be any more.
>
> (Ezek. 27:28–36)

Much has been said, and more remains to be said, about this remarkable chapter of Ezekiel, but the only thing we want to note here is that it contains a considerable vocabulary pertaining to shipbuilding, the parts of ships used by the Tyrian neighbors of Israel in the sixth century BCE, and the crew that manned them. It mentions the planks, masts, oars, decks, sails, awnings, towers, and shield (v. 11), and as to the members of the crew, it refers to mariners, oarsmen (rowers), pilots, calkers, and soldiers. We also learn from the text quoted that the materials that went into the building of a Tyrian vessel were supplied by Senir, Lebanon, Bashan, the Kittim isles, Egypt, the isles of Elishah, Sidon, and Arvad, while the crew came from Gebal, Persia, Lud, and Put.

One more point deserves mention. The prophet's reference to the attractiveness of the ship "perfected by its builders" (Ezek. 27:3–4, 11) indicates that he was well aware that the builders and owners of Tyrian "Tarshish ships" considered their vessels not merely means of transportation and warfare but also things of beauty, and that in the building and equipping of a ship esthetic considerations played a role. One way of "perfecting the beauty" of a ship that transported men of war was to have the men "hang their shields upon its walls round about" (v. 11). This description is illustrated by Oniyahu's seal (Figure 2 below) and by a Roman relief, both of which show ships with shields decorating their sides. The Roman relief (Figure 1) also shows a tower near the ship's prow, which can serve as an illustration of Ezekiel's statement that the Tyrian ship had towers (v. 11).

In addition to the material surveyed above, there are only two more passages in the Hebrew Bible that contain references to ships and seafaring, one in the Book of Psalms, the other in the Book of Jonah.

Psalm 107:23–32 contains a remarkable description of a storm on the sea, the deadly fright that grips the people in the endangered ship, and their relief upon seeing the tempest abate:

> They that go down to the sea in ships,
> That do business in great waters,
> These saw the works of the Lord,
> And His wonders in the deep;
> For He commanded, and raised the stormy wind,
> Which lifted up the waves thereof;
> They mounted up to the heaven, they
> Went down to the deeps,
> Their soul melted in trouble,

Figure 1. Two-level Roman galley, perhaps a quadrireme or larger, second half of the first century BCE. Relief found at Palestrina, now in the Vatican Museum.

> They reeled and staggered as if drunk
> And all their wisdom was swallowed up
> Till they cried to the Lord in their trouble,
> And He brought them out of their distress.
> He made the storm a calm,
> So that its waves were still.
> Then they rejoiced over the quiet,
> And He led them to their desired haven.
> Let them thank the Lord for His mercy,
> And for His wonders to the children of men!
> Let them exalt Him in the assembly of people,
> And praise Him in the seat of the elders!
>
> (Ps. 107:23–32)

No comment is needed on this powerful passage.

A storm on the sea and the sailors' reaction to it is described in some detail in the Book of Jonah, one of the twelve minor prophets. There we read that the Lord commands Jonah to go to Nineveh, the wicked city, and "proclaim against it." For reasons unstated, Jonah disobeys the divine command, and tries to "flee unto Tarshish from the presence of the Lord." He goes down to Jaffa, and there "he found a ship going to Tarshish; so he paid the fare thereof, and went down into it to go with them unto Tarshish." But Jonah did not reckon with the almighty power of the Lord. "But the Lord hurled a great wind into the sea, and there was a mighty tempest in the sea, so that the ship was like to be broken." Faced with mortal danger, the mariners resorted to both religious and practical measures: "they cried every man unto his god, and they cast forth the wares that were in the ship into the sea, to lighten it unto them."

Jonah, strange to say, was unaffected by the commotion and the pitching of the storm-tossed ship: he went down to the innermost parts of the ship, lay down, and fell asleep, and remained asleep until the shipmaster came and woke him, saying: "What meanest thou that thou sleepest? Arise, call upon thy God, if so be that God will think upon us, that we perish not." The rest of the story is related in some detail in Chapter 12, but from this introductory part of the Jonah story one can deduce a few details pertaining to seafaring in late biblical times: Jaffa was a port at which ships sailing to and from Tarshish put in; the ships took on merchandise in Jaffa, as well as paying passengers, who had to defray the fare in advance; the passengers were assigned places in the ship where they could sleep; the ship was propelled by oars (or perhaps had sails as well as oars), and when endangered by a storm the seamen tried to lighten the ship by casting the freight overboard.

Passing references to the role of the sea in transportation are contained in Kings and Chronicles. When Solomon requested Hiram king of Tyre to send him cedars from Lebanon for the building of the temple he planned to undertake in Jerusalem, and offered to send Hiram in exchange a considerable annual supply of wheat and oil, Hiram's response was positive:

> And Hiram sent to Solomon, saying: "I have heard that which thou hast sent unto me; I will do all thy desire concerning timber of cedar and concerning timber of cypress. My servants shall bring them down from Lebanon unto the sea, and I will make them into rafts to go by sea unto the place that thou shalt appoint me, and will cause them to be broken up there, and thou shalt receive them; and thou shalt accomplish my desire, in giving food for my household." So Hiram gave Solomon timber of cedar and timber of cypress according to all his desire. (1 Kings 5:22–23)

The parallel account in the Book of Chronicles adds some details to the agreement concluded between Hiram and Solomon, and specifies that Hiram said to Solomon: "We will cut wood out of Lebanon, as much as thou shalt need; and we will bring it to thee in floats by the sea of Jaffa, and thou shalt carry it up to Jerusalem" (2 Chron. 2:15). The Hebrew word for the "rafts" mentioned in Kings is *dovroth*, whereas in Chronicles the same assemblies of timber are called *rafsodoth*. From the reference to the "breaking up" of the rafts (the Hebrew word used is *nappes*) it is evident that the timber was actually sent down from Lebanon to Jaffa in rafts, that is in the form of tree trunks tied together into a sort of platform, and floated down the sea to Jaffa, where they were taken apart for transportation up the mountain to Jerusalem.

From an incidental reference to the manner in which King David crossed the Jordan, we learn that there were ferry boats (Hebrew sing. *'abharah*) shuttling back and forth between the two banks of the river (2 Sam. 19:19). The Prophet Isaiah seems to have had some information on water traffic in foreign lands, for he refers to "vessels of papyrus" (Hebrew *k'lē gome*) that plied the rivers of Ethiopia (*Kush*), as well as to an unidentified place where there are "broad rivers and streams, wherein shall go no galley with oars [*oni shayit*, literally 'rowing ship'], neither shall gallant ship [*tzi addir*, literally 'mighty ship'] pass thereby" (Isa. 18:1–2; 33:21). The author of Job was acquainted with "reed ships" (*oniyyoth ēveh*), which he refers to as symbols of swift transitoriness: "My days are swifter than a runner . . . they passed away as reed ships" (Job 9:26).

Even though the biblical references to ships and seafaring are extremely meager, this does not mean that sea traffic and sea trade played a correspondingly minor role in the life of the Hebrews in monarchic times. The paucity of references is rather due to the nature of the biblical books: their interest is focused on things spiritual and religious, on whether the people and their leaders did or did not do what was right in the eyes of the Lord. Seafaring was a religiously neutral occupation, and hence the biblical authors, chroniclers, poets, and prophets had little interest in it and little to say about it. This being the case, we are justified in assuming that, despite the paucity of biblical references, once their control extended to the Mediterranean coastline, the Hebrews engaged in shipping and fishing to no less an extent than the other peoples whose towns and villages bordered the Great Sea.

An unexpected corroboration of the role seafaring played in the life of the Hebrew people in the monarchic period became available in 1982, when the Israeli archaeologist Nahman Avigad published a paper in which he discussed a Hebrew seal depicting a sailing ship that dated (according to Avigad) from the eighth or seventh century BCE.[3] The photograph of the seal (Figure 2), whose original size is 18 by 15 millimeters, shows clearly the details of the vessel: in its middle there is a mast carrying a

Figure 2. Sailing ship on a Hebrew seal, eighth
to seventh centuries BCE.

yard and a broad square sail, supported fore and aft by two shrouds. It
has a rounded hull with raised prow and stern of equal height. The
curved prow terminates in the head of an animal, probably a horse. Avigad remarks that ships of this type were called by the Greeks *hippoi*,
"horses."[4] The stern is equipped with a rudder whose position, entering
the gunwale somewhat to the fore of the sternpost, shows that it is one
of a pair, but the artist was unable to show the other rudder in his miniature picture of the ship. The gunwale itself is screened along its total
length by round shields, in conformity with the custom referred to by
Ezekiel (27:11), and seen in the Roman relief (Figure 1). Since the ship
as shown has no oars, it could not be the picture of a warship but rather a
merchants' vessel, and the presence of shields along the gunwale indicates that this was either a decorative feature or else served as protection
for the vulnerable sides of the ship.

Most interesting is the name of the seal's owner: Oniyahu ben Merabh. Since Merabh appears in the Bible as a feminine name (the eldest
daughter of King Saul had this name, 1 Sam. 14:49), it appears that
Oniyahu is identified by a matronymic, which is rather unusual but not
unknown in the Bible (for example, Joab son of Ṣeruyah, Ḥanan son of
Maʿakhah, and so on). As for the name Oniyahu, it could mean "my
strength [*oni*] is Yahu [Yahweh]," in which case it would be in conformity with the many Hebrew names that have theophorous forms, such as
Adoniyahu, Yirm'yahu (Jeremiah), Zidqiyahu, and so on. The name, as
Avigad remarks, is that of a Judean, for in the northern kingdom of Israel
the name would probably have been spelled *Oniyau*. An abbreviated
form of this name, "On," appears in Num. 16:1, and its full form "On-

iyahu," occurs in a Hebrew tomb inscription from the eighth century BCE found at Khirbet el-Qom in the Hebron hills.[5]

The depiction of a ship on the seal seems to indicate, however, that the name "Oniyahu" was given another interpretation: the person so called probably took it to mean "Oni Yahu," that is, "the ship of Yahweh," or "Yahweh is my ship." Avigad, mentioning the possibility of this interpretation, remarks that "this, of course, does not make much sense."[6] I think it does make good sense: it belongs to the same category of theophorous names as Uzziyahu ("Yahweh is my strength"), Tzuriel (El is my rock"), Tzurishadday ("Shadday is my rock"), Ḥilqiyahu ("my share is Yahweh"), Uriyahu ("Yahweh is my light"), Ma'aseyahu ("act of Yahweh"), Susi (hypocoristic of Susiyahu, "my horse is Yahweh"), and so on. The ship was a symbol of strength and power in Talmudic literature (see Chapter 11), and appears in the Bible as a symbol of power (cf. *tzi addir*, "powerful ship," Isa. 33:21), and of beauty (cf. Ezek. 27:3–4, 10). Hence it seems likely that whatever the actual etymological origin of the name Oniyahu, it was taken by the owner of the seal in question as meaning "my ship is Yahweh."

In sum: this seal shows that the Hebrews in monarchic times were acquainted with large seagoing vessels, used either by the Hebrew people themselves or by their Phoenician neighbors, and that they prized such vessels highly. It is a valuable contemporary supplement to the data contained in the Bible on ships and seafaring.

As an addendum to this chapter on ships and seafaring in biblical times it might be of interest to include something contained about these matters in an unexpected outside source. We learned in the Introduction that in the sixth-century BCE mariners from the west coast of Asia Minor were rumored to have ventured out beyond the Straits of Gibraltar into the Atlantic along both the Spanish and the Moroccan coasts. This daring feat of striking out into unknown waters is dwarfed by what the Mormon tradition attributes to a group of Jews who lived in the days of King Zedekiah in Jerusalem, that is, in the early sixth century BCE (the same time in which the Phocaean skippers were supposed to have sailed through the Strait of Gibralter). According to Mormon tradition, their venture into unknown waters took place in the year 589 BCE, that is, three years before the destruction of Jerusalem by Nebuchadnezzar, and it was thanks to this extraordinary navigational feat that the American continent was populated by a remnant of biblical Israel.

In friendly response to my request, Dr. John M. Lundquist has summarized for this volume the Mormon version of the origins of the Mormons from sixty-century BCE Palestine, at which period, according to Mormon tradition, the biblical Hebrews had a highly developed seafaring trade (see Appendix).

Chapter 3

CONSTRUCTION AND PARTS

MUCH OF what the Talmudic sages had to say about the construction of ships, the parts of ships, types of ships, and seafaring in general they appended to biblical expressions or passages whose explication was one of their chief interests. Hence in coming now to present what we know about Jewish seafaring in the Talmudic age (ca. first century BCE to fifth century CE)—almost all of which is based on Talmudic and Midrashic literature—we shall inevitably have to refer to details already presented in Chapters 1 and 2.

To begin with, there has been much difference of opinion among Rabbinic commentators as to the meaning of the word *qinnim*, which in the biblical story of Noah's ark designates the cells or cabins into which the ark was divided. The majority favored the explanation that *qinnim* denotes the partitions between the cells; others, however, believed that it refers to the roofing or ceiling of these cabins. The modern Talmudic scholar Jacob Nahum Epstein was of the opinion that *qinnim* means beams, basing this interpretation on a Talmudic passage in which Rabbi Yosē bar Ḥanina, in answer to the question "what is ceiling [or roofing]?" says that *qinnim* means reeds or stalks.[1] Another Talmudic sage, Justine (or Justina), answers the same question by identifying *qinnim* with planks. These somewhat enigmatic opinions are elucidated by Rashi to the effect that the ceiling in question was made after the fashion of matting. If *qinnim* actually meant a ceiling made of matting, it could have been similar to the bamboo or palm-leaf matting used in modern Sri Lanka and India as the covering of cabins and cargo aboard canal and coasting vessels.[2]

A term similar to *qinnim* appears in the Elephantine papyri among the building materials used for shipbuilding; it is *ḥanan* (variant: *ḥananya*).[3] At the present time, well-constructed buildings in the Sudan are roofed with logs, overlaid with brushwood and clay. At Suakin the logs used in roofing are usually of mangrove saplings imported from Lamu and its neighborhood.[4]

The body of the Tyrian ship was built, according to Ezekiel, from planks made of cypress trees from Senir (Mount Hermon). The word for planks has the dual form in Hebrew *luḥotayim* (Ezek. 27:5), which evidently reflects the symmetrical form of a ship, in which each plank on one side has its counterpart on the opposite side of the hull. This was observed and pointed out by the medieval commentator David Kimhi (ad Ezek. 27:5). The medieval commentators differed with regard to the meaning of the term *qeresh* in Ezekiel 27:6: "Thy deck (*qarshekh*) they made of ivory." According to Rashi it meant the rudder, whereas David Kimhi considers the word to refer to the planking from which was made the superstructure or "castle" manned by fighting men. Whether it means rudder or planking, the statement by Ezekiel that it was made "of ivory" can only mean that it was decorated with ivory.

The sides of the hull itself were called *ḥomoth* (literally "walls," Ezek. 27:11) much as the English word "bulwark" denotes both a rampart and the planking around a vessel above the deck. The finest Egyptian ships were made of planking sawn out of Lebanese cedars, as were also the ships built in the Jewish colony on the island of Elephantine in the Nile.[5]

A ship with a mast at the center is depicted on a wall sketch in the Jewish catacombs of Beth Sh'arim near Haifa (Figure 3). The great Tyrian ships had two or more masts, made of the trunks of cedar trees from the slopes of the Lebanon hills. Ezekiel (27:5) refers to Lebanese cedars as supplying the masts of Tyrian ships.

The mast was stepped into a socket, called by Isaiah (33:23) *ken toren* or "mast stand." The word *ken* is also used in the sense of socket or stand elsewhere in the Bible (Ex. 30:18; Lev. 8:11; 1 Kings 7:31). The corresponding Greek term for mast stand was *hystopede*.[6] Close to the top of the mast, extending horizontally or slantwise, was the *nes*, yard, even though Ezekiel (27:7) uses this term to designate what the translations take as "ensign," a close synonym of *mifras*, sail. It is only from Isaiah 30:17 that we know that *toren* and *nes* were two kinds of poles. However, Isaiah also uses the word *nes* in the sense of "ensign" (Isa. 33:23).

The sail (Hebrew *mifras*, Ezek. 27:7) was hoisted and kept in place by ropes (*ḥavalim*) fixed to the mast and yard (Isa. 33:20, 23). The area at the top of the mast where the ropes met was called *rosh ḥibbel*, literally "roping head" (Prov. 23:34). It is clearly visible in Figure 3. If ever the ropes loosened or broke they no longer held the mast stand and the sails, and the ship was as good as lost—this is how Isaiah describes in a metaphor the impending fall of Zion (Isa. 33:23).

The Book of Proverbs compares the staggering of an inebriated person to the reeling to and fro of one sitting upon a roping head:

> Yea, thou shalt be as he that lieth in the midst of the sea,
> Or as he that lieth upon the roping head.
>
> (Prov. 23:34)

The reference is to a contraption with which the larger ships were equipped: in some Egyptian ships this took the shape of a basket lashed to the masthead for the purpose of accommodating a lookout. In Egyp-

Figure 3. Sketch of a ship on the walls of the Beth Sh'arim catacombs
near Haifa, second to fourth centuries CE.

tian warships, such as are shown on the sculptured walls of Medinet el-
Habu depicting a fight at sea between the navy of Rameses III and an
invading navy from the Greek islands, a fighting top can be seen at the
mastheads in which archers are stationed to fire upon the crew of the
enemy ships.[7] Such an accommodation for a lookout at the masthead is a
conspicuous feature in the present-day boats trafficking on the Upper
Nile.

   Some additional information about ancient ships that plied between
Palestine and other countries along the Mediterranean in the first century
CE can be gleaned from the description of Paul's voyage in a "ship of
Adramyttium," contained in Acts (27:1ff.). Adramyttium was a city on
the northwest coast of the Roman province of Asia (modern Turkey), and
a ship from that city was homeward bound when Paul and several others
boarded it in Caesarea. It was a relatively large ship, carrying 276 persons

(v. 37). From the account in Acts we learn that the ship had, in addition to the main sail or sails, a foresail (*artemon*, v. 40) as well. It had four anchors at the stern and additional anchors at the foreship (vv. 29–30). Its rudder (*pēdalion*) was held by means of bands (v. 40). It also had equipment for sounding the depth of the water (*bolys*, v. 28), and it had a lifeboat on deck, which could be lowered into the water by means of ropes (vv. 30–32). When encountering a storm the mariners tried to save the ship by casting overboard the cargo, the tackling (or furniture), and even the food (vv. 18–19, 38). Even if a ship did not founder in a storm, it could suffer serious damage that had to be repaired once it reached the safety of a haven. In the case of Paul's ship, after it had escaped the storm and reached the island of Cauda (modern Gaudos or Gozzo, about twenty-three miles south of Crete), they hoisted it up and, with the use of "helps" (*boetaia*), they "undergirded the ship" (v. 17). The "helps" mentioned seem to be identical with what are termed in other Greek sources *hypozomata*, long cables passed either underneath and around the hull vertically, or horizontally around the hull about or a little above the waterline to strengthen the structure and prevent the seams from opening.

More information about shipbuilding and the parts that went into a ship can be gleaned from Talmudic literature. The material that went into the construction of the ship's hull was in the main coniferous wood, either cedar or cypress. The planks of which the hull was constructed were called *dappim* (sing. *daf*). In case of shipwreck and the breaking up of the hull, these *dappim* could be the salvation of some of the crew or passengers who, by clinging to them, could occasionally reach shore.[8] The apocryphal Testament of Naphtali mentions (6:6) that shipwrecked sailors made use of such floating planks, or of the small boats carried by ships for communication with the shore, as the means of reaching safety.

The side walls of the ship were called in Talmudic Aramaic *dafna di-s'finta* (sing.), or else *m'hitzoth* (lit. "separations"), which, according to a Talmudic saying, were made to keep the water away.[9]

A picturesque term referring to the shape of a ship narrowing downward toward its keel is *s'finah roqedeth*, literally "dancing ship." This shape was well known to the sages, one of whom, Rabbi Yohanan, compares to it the shape of the loaves of bread offered up in the Temple. Rabbi Yohanan's laconic statement that the bread was shaped "like a dancing ship," is explained by Rashi: such a ship "has no brims, but is wide at the top and narrows toward the bottom until it has only the thickness of a finger. Its ends [that is, the stem and the stern] sharpen and rise upward and do not touch the water, and that is why she is called 'dancing,' because she dances along quickly."[10]

The question of how ship-shaped (V-shaped) loaves of bread could stand up without falling to the side is raised and answered in a passage in the Midrash: "The loaves were in the shape of ships, and therefore they had to be propped up with oblique supports . . . but the middle of the lowest loaf touched the table, for the loaf was like a dancing ship which is narrow at the bottom, broadening upward."[11]

The ancient Hebrew (or Aramaic) name of the keel has not come down to us, but from the description of the "dancing ship" it is evident that such a ship was built upon a longitudinal beam, the keel, which was either solid or slightly excavated, as is the case with the canoes of the Gilbert Islands.[12] This inference receives corroboration from the mention of the *ʿegel*, by which is designated in Talmudic literature the mass of iron used for ballast to increase the stability of the ship.[13] The *ʿegel* of old or disused ships was still valuable: it could be used for the making of pots.[14] According to the medieval commentator Rabbi Simson of Shanz, the *ʿegel* consisted of round iron bars placed in the ship as ballast beneath stones in order to give her stability in heavy weather.[15]

Under or around the *ʿegel* carried in the bottom of the ship's hold bilge water was apt to collect. According to Maimonides, there was a cavity or well in the hull for the reception of wash from the seams of the deck. Another medieval commentator, Obidiah di Bertinoro, was of the opinion that the *ʿegel* itself was a cavity at the bottom of the ship where water that entered through cracks in the hull would collect.[16] Another source of leakage of which the Mishnaic sages were aware was the seepage into the ship through the oar ports.[17]

The bilge water that collected in the bilge well had to be baled out, for which purpose a scoop or bucket, called *antlaya*, was used.[18] The term is derived from the Greek *antlía*, which means the hold of a ship as well as bilge water and the bailer used for emptying it overboard.[19]

The term *antlaya* is also used in Midrashic literature for a more complicated device utilized for the irrigation of fields. We are told that in "the wheel of the *antlaya* the full is emptied and that which is emptied is filled."[20] We may be justified in understanding this passage as referring to a contraption like the Persian waterwheel fitted with buckets or pots, attached in chain fashion to an endless rope, still in everyday use in the countries of the Middle East.[21]

Among the terms preserved in Rabbinic literature are *rosh ha-s'finah* (lit. "head of the ship"), meaning the forward part of the deck, and *aḥorē ha-s'finah* (lit. "back of the ship"), referring to the after part. The prow itself is called *ḥudah shel s'finah* (lit. "the point of the ship") in the Talmud. The Talmudic equivalent for the biblical *yark'thē ha-s'finah* (literally "hips of the ship," Jon. 1:5) is *safna*, derived from the same root as *s'finah*, ship. The bottom of the hold was called *garga'ith ha-s'finah*, or "the ground of the ship."[22] In the Aramaic papyri of Elephantine (several centuries older than the earliest layers of Talmudic literature), the deck is called *rega'*, and the hold *beṭen* (lit. "belly").[23]

The compartments below deck were called *battim* (lit. "houses"); they were used mainly for storing the cargo.[24] The cabins for the accommodation of passengers were in the superstructure, built upon the deck, that is, they were what today would be called deck cabins.[25] We have no record of the number of cabins usually carried, but a Talmudic legend tells of a ship with sixty cabins, built by the Emperor of Rome at the suggestion of R. Joshua ben Ḥananiah. That legendary ship was huge, for each of its sixty cabins had room for sixty chairs.[26] The number of sixty cabins, however, need not necessarily be considered an exaggeration, since Greek and Roman ships are known to have had a large number of cabins. It is recorded of the ship *Syracusia* of Hieron, for instance, that she had thirty cabins with four berths each, as well as a special *díaita* (quarters) for the shipowner and three major compartments or salons.[27]

Ships built as cargo vessels had no passenger cabins.[28] Perishable cargo had to be protected, and for that purpose the ship had *l'waḥin* ("boards," sing. *luaḥ*), with which to cover the fruits and other victuals carried on board.[29]

Temporary shelters for the poorer class of passengers could be set up in the free space on deck, exactly as is the custom to this day on certain Indian coasting steamers. On these the deck passengers spread their own bedding and sometimes erect temporary screens to obtain some degree of privacy, especially when their wives accompany them. The Babylonian Talmud tells us that on ships carrying passengers a light arched framework was often set up to afford this privacy. The arched supports were about one handbreadth (approximately three to three-and-a-half inches) in width, and were placed at about three handbreadths' distance apart. Over this framework mats were flung, and these constituted a useful awning and served as a temporary tent.[30] Comparable structures were also set up on some Egyptian ships, and were useful as shelters from the heat of the sun in the daytime and the cold at night.[31]

During the seven days of the Feast of Tabernacles, booths were erected on the foredeck.[32] It appears that in the Jewish view the forward part of the ship was considered the place of honor, whereas the Greeks preferred the after part.[33]

The prow of the ship was frequently adorned with the figure of a ram or, more often, of a ram's head, made of metal and seemingly sometimes of precious metal. The Babylonian Talmud tells us that on every ship there was a figurehead in the form of a ram; once, when this object was left by mischance on a sea cliff, it was found by Rabbi Akiba, who became rich through his find.[34] The commentators of the Talmud, who were unfamiliar with the custom of decorating the ship's prow with a sculptured ram's head, took the word *ayil* ("ram") to mean a sort of hollow receptacle in the form of a ram (ram's head?) in which the sailors kept their money. According to this fanciful notion, the receptacle was carved out of wood and given the shape of a ram in order to serve as an amulet and an omen that the ship should be as light in her movements as a ram.[35]

It seems probable that the ram's head on the prow of the ship was a relic of some half-forgotten religious belief. One manifestation of that belief was the custom of Arabian sailors in early pre-Islamic times of covering the prowhead with the skin of a sacrificial sheep or goat at the time of launching the vessel, as an offering to a protective deity. Traces of such a custom may underlie the procedure followed down to modern times in Spain and Portugal of affixing a tousled mop-head of rope yarn to the stem head.[36]

In the bow of the ship there were hawse holes, through which the anchor cables passed. In Talmudic times these holes were given the outline of an eye, and were called *ʿena* (Aramaic for "eye").[37] In later times the *oculus* (eye) became disassociated from the hawse hole, and was painted or carved close to it in a manner more or less resembling a human eye.[38] On the boats plying between the mouth of the Tagus and Cabo de Espichel, Portugal, in modern times, the eyes have become so stylized that they take a fishlike form. They are painted "so that the boats may see where they are going." Boats similarly painted and for the same reason are found at Malta, where they are supposed to be a legacy of Phoenician influence.[39]

In ancient times, these *ophthalmoi* or *oculi* were usual and conventional symbols on Greek and Roman ships: they were either painted on the bows or applied (nailed on) as wood or metal affixes. In time they became general all along the Mediterranean and other seas, from Cyprus to Spain and thence onward to Zanzibar and Madagascar (see Figure 4). Still, in several localities the combination of the eye and the hawse hole persists, as in the Italian trawlers working out of Adriatic ports: these boats work in pairs, towing their great *paranzella* net between them. Eyes could also commonly be seen on the boats of India, Southeast Asia, and China. The ostensible reason for their use is, as stated above, that the ships may be enabled thereby to see their way across the sea. At the same time the eyes serve as protective symbols against the dreaded effects of the "evil eye," a belief still extremely powerful among the seafaring peoples of the Mediterranean.[40]

The most important appurtenance on sailing ships is the mast. In Talmudic literature the mast is called either by its biblical name, *toren* (or its Aramaic form *turna*), or by one of several Aramaic terms. One of these is *makhuta*, according to medieval commentators; however, later critics

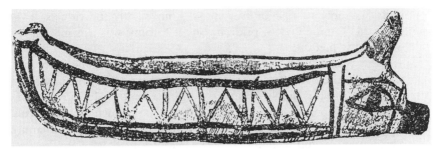

Figure 4. Clay model of a boat from the Island of Cyprus. The prow is decorated with the picture of an eye.

consider that *makhuta* designates a particular kind of boat (see Chapter 4). More frequently the mast is called *isqarya*, a term derived from the Aramaic verb *saqar*, meaning to view, to espy. Hence its literal meaning is "espying place," which would indicate that the term meant not mast but the lookout post on its top. However, since the biblical term for mast, *toren*, is also derived from a verb, *tur*, which means to espy, it is quite likely that in both cases, despite their derivation, the terms came to mean "mast." In fact, the Hebrew *toren* is explained in the Talmud as *isqarya*. When the Talmud speaks of the beauty of a mast as being a major asset for a ship, the term it uses is *isqarya*.[41]

The term *isqarya* appears in a story about Ilfa, a third-century CE Palestinian Amora (sage), who was a disciple of Rabbi Yehuda ha-Nasi. When, after a long absence, Ilfa returned to the academy, he found that his younger colleague, Rabbi Yohanan, had been appointed its head. He was told, "Had you remained here and studied, you would have obtained the position." Thereupon Ilfa, to prove his learning, "climbed up the mast-yard (*isqarya di-makhutha*) of a ship and said, 'If somebody can ask me anything of the teaching of R. Hiyya and R. Osha'ya [two editors of Tannaitic teachings after the completion of the Mishna] and I cannot authenticate it with a Mishna, I shall throw myself down from the mast of the ship and drown.'" When an old man came and asked him about the source of a rather obscure decision, Ilfa in fact had no problem in identifying its source.[42]

Although this act of Ilfa shows him as a man with a rather swollen ego, another anecdote about him presents him as a man of exceptional piety. Once there was drought in the land, and Rabbi Yehuda ha-Nasi decreed a fast, but no rains came. Thereupon Ilfa went up to the ark to lead the congregation in prayer, and when he pronounced the words, "He [God] makes the wind blow," a wind came, and when he said "He makes the rain fall" the rains came.[43] Such rainmaking power was ascribed in the

Talmudic age only to one or two most pious saintly individuals. Evidently, in the Talmudic view, pride in one's learning was not incompatible with saintly piety.

Since the name "Ilfa" is a common Talmudic-Midrashic term for "ship," one wonders whether his name had anything to do with the story attributing to Ilfa the highly dramatic gesture aboard a ship in demonstration of his superior learning. Did he, having grown up with this name, develop a special affinity to ships, a liking for ships, and a familiarity with ships, as did a thousand years before him that otherwise unknown Oniyahu ben Merabh, whose seal depicting a ship was found in an excavation (see Chapter 2)? It is certainly difficult to imagine the average sage climbing up to the top of a mast. If Ilfa was able to do this on the spur of the moment, it could not have been the first time he performed such a feat.

Yet another Aramaic term for mast was *diqla* (literally "palm tree").[44] One piece of information about the mast is that occasionally the name of the owner was inscribed on it, according to a Hebrew version of the apocryphal Testament of Naphthali.[45] On the other hand, we are told that Rabba bar Bar-Hana, the well-known author of many fantastic tales of the sea (see Chapter 12), used the picture of a mast as his signum instead of signing his name.[46]

The mast passed through the deck to be stepped in a socket or "shoe," as shown in the drawings of ships found in Mareshah and Beth Sh'arim (see Figures 5, 3). The masts of Egyptian ships were fitted in like manner.[47] Close to the top of the mast was hoisted the yard, as seen in the pictures of the ships in Beth Jibrin, Beth Sh'arim, the Madeba map, the Alexandrian grain ship seen on a Sidonian sarcophagus, and elsewhere. The biblical term *nēs*, "ensign" (Ezek. 27:7), was used in Talmudic literature in the sense of "yard," as well as mast.[48]

Those appurtenances of the ship that served the purpose of propelling or steering it were called by the collective term *manhigin*, "leaders." When a person sold a ship, it was taken for granted that the *manhigin*, such as the oars and the rudders, as well as the anchors, were included in the sale. Not included, however, were the slaves who manned the oars, the packing bags (*martzufin*), and the merchandise (*antēqē*, from the Greek *entheke*).[49] At the head of the mast there was a loop (*instrida*), bound by a permanent lashing to the mast itself.[50] This loop is clearly seen in the picture of the ship at Beth Sh'arim (Figure 3). To this masthead loop or loops, if they were similar to the fittings seen on Nile boats, the various shrouds and stays were roved or made fast as necessary. In place of this arrangement, many ancient Egyptian ships had a square wooden frame that functioned as a primitive set of pulleys or sheaves, through which the various ropes were roved.[51]

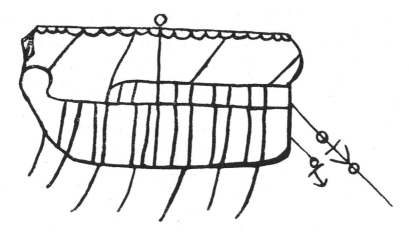

Figure 5. Sketch of a ship from Mareshah, a city southwest of
Jerusalem, about halfway to the seashore. It dates from the
third century BCE.

Rashi understood the term *instrida* differently. According to him, it
was made either of an *ʿeqel* (see above), or was a leather loop that passed
through the hawse hole in the ship's prow. When the ship had to be
moored in harbor or to the shore, this was done by means of a rope that
passed through the loop, and when the ship was ready to sail this rope
was cast off.[52]

According to a Rabbinic comment, which seems to be a landsman's
exaggeration and not based on anything but a superficial impression of
the large number of side stays on ancient vessels, "on ships coming from
Akharmania there were 365 ropes, corresponding to the number of days
in the solar year, and ships that came from Alexandria had 354 ropes,
corresponding to the number of days in the lunar year."[53] No locality by
the name of "Akharmania" is known, hence some scholars consider the
word a corruption of Carmania (in Persia), whereas others read *iyyē Bri-
tannia*, that is, "isles of Britain."[54] Alexandria is, of course, the great
Egyptian seaport city. An extraordinary number of shrouds and stays are
still used on the boats plying south of the fourth cataract on the Nile. In
one case a boat was seen with twenty-two shroud-stays on each side, a
number still insignificant in comparison with those mentioned in the
Rabbinic statement referred to.[55]

The tow rope by which boats were towed against the current on the
waterways of Babylonia was called *ashla*. The *ashla* was also used for
measuring distances in water, much as the surveyor's chain and the lead
line were used, respectively, for measuring distances on land and depths

in the sea. The rule on the Babylonian waterways was to keep the boat being towed at a distance of one rope's length from the shore.[56]

The usual Talmudic term for sail was *qelaʿ*.[57] The sail was generally made of sheeting (*sadin*), probably of linen, after the Egyptian custom.[58] When the ship came to its anchorage, the sail was furled (*m'qappel*),[59] as is shown on one of the Madeba pictures of a sailing boat. On the sketch of the boat at Beth Shʿarim (Figure 3) the vertical ropes (brails) by means of which the sails were furled are distinct. These ropes pass through loops attached to the sail in vertical rows. Similar arrangements can be seen on the relief of an Alexandrian grain ship found on a Sidonian sarcophagus contemporary with the Beth Shʿarim drawing (Figure 6), and on Roman and other depictions of ancient ships.[60]

It should not be left without mention that the term *qelaʿ* was also used in Rabbinic literature in the sense of sling, as well as rope.[61] In the latter sense it is used as a simile: the Evil Inclination is in the beginning as weak as a spider's thread, but in the end it has the strength of a ship's *qelaʿ* (rope).[62]

The Talmudic name for rudder is *murd'ya*. The Babylonian sages knew that on the narrow and shallow Babylonian canals a large rudder was indispensable.[63] Rashi explains that *murd'ya* is a wooden device—an implement by means of which the captain steers the vessel and keeps it away from the many dangers that beset those who go down to the sea in ships: he uses the French term for rudder, *gouvernail*.[64]

Ancient vessels had in general two rudders that were fitted abreast of one another on the quarters. This arrangement is frequently depicted in Egyptian ships, and can be seen clearly in the picture of the sailing vessel in the Beth Shʿarim catacombs (Figure 3). In a Hebrew version of the apocryphal Testament of Naphthali, Joseph is described as taking hold of both rudders, one on the right and one on the left. A pair of quarter rudders is also visible on each of two fragmentary pictures of boats on the Madeba mosaic map, dating from the sixth century CE (Figures 7, 8), which show boats sailing on the Dead Sea. One shows the figure of the helmsman standing, the other sitting. They also show the yardarm, one with the sail furled around it, in a manner familiar from other ancient pictures.[65]

An oar is called in Rabbinic literature *mashot* (plural *mashotot* or *mashotin*). The oars were considered integral parts of a ship, hence the rule that the sale of a ship included its oars.[66]

The term for anchor, *ʿogen* or *ʿogin*, is derived, according to the Babylonian Talmud, from the biblical verb *ʿagan*, which appears in Ruth 1:13 in the sense of "to shut oneself off."[67] The derivation is unlikely, as can be seen from the fact that in Palestinian Rabbinic sources the form of the word is *hogen*.[68] The term appears in a simile offered by Rabbi Shimʿon ben

Figure 6. Roman merchantman, as shown on a mosaic found in Rome.
The arrangement of the rudders and of the ropes vertically and
horizontally along the sail are identical with those depicted in the
Beth Sh'arim catacombs (Figure 3).

Yoḥai to illustrate the importance of adhering to the divine commandments:

> A *mashal* (parable): like a man who brought two ships and tied them with anchors (*hognim*) and weights (*'ashtoth*), and made them rest upon them, and built upon them a palace. As long as the ships are tied, the palace stands up; once the ships are loosed, the palace does not stand up. Thus Israel: when they do the will of God, they rise to heaven, and when they do not do the will of God, they sink down to earth.[69]

On the Sabbath a plank was thrust outboard from the side when there was need to draw water; on it a sailor would stand holding a bucket with

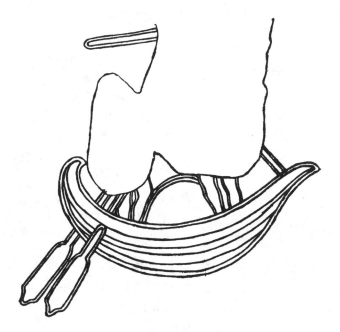

Figure 7. Picture of a ship on the Dead Sea, as shown on the mosaic map of Palestine found in Madeba, Jordan, in a sixth-century CE church. The crewmen are standing.

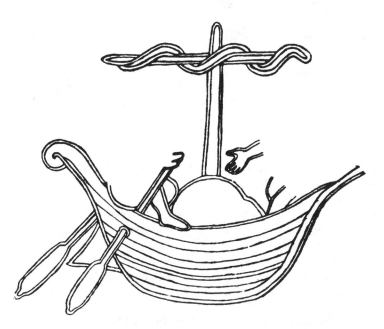

Figure 8. Another picture of a ship on the Dead Sea, from the same Madeba map.

which he would draw water from the sea. This outboard plank was called *ziz* or *neser*.[70]

An essential item in the ship's equipment was a large water tank containing drinking water. The water tank, called *bor* ("cistern") or *beth hamayim* ("house of water"), carried on board of the great Alexandrian ships, is described in the Mishna as "having rims and a capacity of more than forty *seah*." Smaller ships carried smaller water tanks. In any case, the water tank was an integral part of the ship, and thus was bought and sold together with her.[71]

A runged ladder was also considered part of the basic equipment of a ship. The Talmudic term for it is *askala* or *iskala*, derived from the Latin *scala*. The ladder was needed to reach the deck either from the shore or from a small boat. Greek and Roman ships also had ladders, which are often depicted in pictures of the classic age showing ships (such as that in Figure 9).

A landing bridge or gangway, pivoted on the gunwale and called *kebhesh*, provided easier access to or from the shore. The *kebhesh* did not rise as sharply as a ladder and had no rungs, but rather a smooth continuous surface.[72]

For the comfort of passengers, mattresses might be provided by the shipowner. These mattresses were called *yetzi'in* or *bistarqa*. Rashi explains the term *bistarqa* by the French word *tapete*.[73] In the Gospel of Mark it is said about Jesus that "he was in the hinder part of the ship, asleep on a pillow" (Mark 4:38). The ship referred to here was a small boat on the Sea of Galilee: "mattress" would probably be a better rendering than "pillow" here.

The meaning of the term *yeshiwin* is uncertain. One Talmudic dictionary explains it as cleats on which the ship's ropes are belayed; another, as the anchor or ballast stones.[74] The context affords no clue to the meaning, except that it refers to an appurtenance of a ship.

On board a ship there were to be found a number of strong poles, called *'ubhin*, which are explained as being *mareshoth*, joists or beams. These poles served a variety of purposes: for poling the ship in shallow water, for sounding the depths, and as boathooks.[75] Similar poles, called *kontoi* or *conti*, were carried aboard Greek and Roman ships.[76] Loose pieces of board, *l'wahin*, served to cover the food, vegetables, and pots on board.[77] Such boards were also found on Greek ships.[78] A small plank, called *gamla*, formed part of the equipment of a small boat.[79] Yet other planks were called *neser*, whereas the collective name of all sorts of ships' planks was *qursha di-s'finta*, or "planks of the ship."[80] These loose planks came in handy when a ship suffered shipwreck, just as did the *daf*.[81]

The apocryphal Testament of Naphthali contains a vivid description of the use of planks in case of shipwreck. The ship on which Jacob and his

Figure 9. The ship of the Argonauts, as depicted on a
Greek vase. The ladder shown was well known to
Talmudic literature.

twelve sons embarked in Jamnia (Jabneh) encountered a heavy storm,
and suffered shipwreck. Joseph escaped in a boat, and the other sons of
Jacob clung to nine planks and thus saved their lives. Judah and Levi
both held on to the same plank.[82] Bigger ships were, of course, equipped
with lifeboats, which were either placed on deck or towed astern. The
ship on which Paul sailed had a lifeboat fastened to it by ropes, probably
astern. When the sailors wanted to use the boat, they cut the ropes.
When the ship was about to break up, some of the sailors clung to
planks, some to other loose items from the ship (Acts 27:31, 44).

The cargo, as already mentioned, was called *antēqē* (from the Greek
entheke).[83] The most valuable items of the cargo were kept in a special
locker called *guza*.[84] Most of the merchandise carried by the ships was

stowed in sacks or leather bags, especially adapted for the purpose. They were called *martzufin* and, according to one statement in the Palestinian Talmud, they were used both at sea and on shore.[85] Other merchandise was contained in wrappings called *krēkhē di-zuzē*, literally, "wrappings of ships." Rashi explains this term as meaning mats for the covering of merchandise in the ship: "a pair of mats in which the merchandise in ships is wrapped. *Zuzē* is a dual form, for there were two of them made like a tent."[86] This method evidently differed from the dunnage mats used in present-day ships: such mats are placed beneath the merchandise to prevent it from being damaged by contact with bilge water or the "sweating" of the iron skin of modern ships.

A somewhat enigmatic instrument used aboard the ships was the *sh'fofereth*, a "tube" with which, according to one Talmudic passage, it was possible to distinguish objects at a distance of 2,000 cubits (3,000 feet), whether on land or sea.[87] What exactly this tube was is difficult to say; from its description it would seem to have been some primitive form of telescope, probably nothing more than a simple tube, which would indeed have some advantage over the naked eye when viewing distant objects.

A few references to the processes of shipbuilding have been preserved in Rabbinic literature. The manner in which a ship is built serves as the basis of a simile recorded in the name of Rabbi Shim'on ben Laqish, a second-century CE Palestinian sage:

> Rabbi Shim'on ben Laqish said: A flesh and blood [i.e. mortal] man, if he wants to build a ship, first he brings beams, then he brings ropes, then he brings anchors, then he places on it seamen; but the Holy One, blessed be He, created [heaven and earth] and their leaders [that is, the heavenly bodies that lead and direct the world] simultaneously, as it is written, "Thus saith God the Lord, He that created the heavens and stretched them forth" (Isaiah 42:5); this should be read not as "stretched them forth" (*notēhem*), but as "their sailors" (*nawtēhem*).[88]

Talmudic tradition was aware not only of the order in which the equipment of a ship was assembled but also of the fact that the various parts that went into building a ship originated from different localities: "Rabbi Yitzḥaq said: The nations of the world are likened unto a ship: Just as they make a ship's mast from one place and its anchors from another place, so King Salma was from Masrekah, Shaul from Rehoboth by the River."[89]

The final step in building the hull was to cover it with pitch. After the pitching, or perhaps before it, the ship was launched in order that, being in the water, the hull would be tightened (the Hebrew word used is *tzaref*). Under the influence of the water the planks of the ship's hull swelled at the seams, and every seam, split, or crack became tightly closed.[90] The construction of Egyptian ships was similarly brought to completion by this tightening process.[91] As for pitching, the hulls of Roman ships were smeared with pitch both on the inside and the outside.[92] Only after the ship had been treated in this manner was it considered fit to be launched (Hebrew: *hētzif*). The launching of ships was used as a means of divination, in a manner that can no longer be identified.[93]

Special craftsmen were employed to repair holes and cracks in the hull planking (cf. Ezek. 27:9). Some details about the repair of ships are preserved in a fifth century BCE Aramaic papyrus, which tells of the shipbuilding activity of the Jewish colony on the island of Elephantine in the upper Nile River. For the repair of ships (*ufshar s'finta*) cedar wood was used, together with brazen and iron nails of the length of three handbreadths; also brazen plates of twenty cubits in length, as well as sulphur (*kabrē, kabritha*), arsenic (*zarniqi*), and wool or cotton (*katan*). Other materials, too, are mentioned in the same papyrus, but linguistic difficulties make it impossible to understand what they indicate.[94] In a Midrashic source (a thousand years younger than the Elephantine papyri) to repair a ship is called "to heal the ship."[95]

A special skill sailors had to acquire was how to make knots in the ropes. These knots were termed by the collective name "sailors' knots."[96] Cables are also mentioned as used for securing ships in position, especially when lying in harbor. The laying out of these cables was effected with the aid of a small boat called *bitzit*, literally "swamp boat."[97]

Chapter 4

TYPES OF SHIPS

Considering the paucity of references to ships and seafaring in the Bible, it is surprising that several designations for sailing craft are nevertheless mentioned in the biblical books. Although one must be cautious in concluding from this relatively rich vocabulary that the biblical Hebrews had considerable interest in seafaring, one may be justified in assuming that it is indicative of at least a certain familiarity with the various types of vessels that were in use on the seas and the inland waters of the biblical Land of Israel.

To begin again with the ark of Noah, we have seen that this mythical vessel is called *tēbhāh*, a word whose original meaning was chest.[1] Although it is only from later Talmudic sources that we learn about its square, punt-like build (see Chapter 1), we may deduce from the biblical narrative itself that it was imagined as a flat-bottomed structure, for otherwise it could not have "rested"—which can only mean remain standing in an upright position—on Mount Ararat after the waters of the deluge abated (Gen. 8:4). No doubt the "ark of bulrushes" (*tebhat gome*, Ex. 2:3) that was improvised for the infant Moses by his mother (Ex. 2:2) was also flat bottomed, as are the ambatch canoes that have been in use among the Dinkas and Shilluks on the Upper Nile down to modern times.[2] These canoes are the lineal descendants of the papyrus canoes of Old Egypt, of which the ark of Moses was one miniature example.

From Isaiah (18:2) we learn that it was the custom in "the land that is beyond the rivers of Ethiopia" to dispatch "swift messengers" in "vessels of papyrus" (*klē gome*). The Bible translations of the Hebrew word *gome* are inconsistent: in the original Hebrew, the material of which both the ark of Moses and the vessels of these swift ambassadors are said to have been made is called *gome*; the word should be translated in both cases either as "bulrushes" or as "papyrus."

Another biblical term for reed vessels is *oniyyoth ēbheh*, literally "reed ships" (Job 9:26). Since in the context this vessel is mentioned as a simile for the swiftness with which the days of a human life pass, the translations render it as "swift ships," which is wrong grammatically, since *ēbheh* is a noun, and if it had anything to do with speed the expression should be translated as "ships of swiftness." In fact, *ēbheh* means reed, and is related to the Assyrian *abu*, which has the same meaning.[3] That is, what is said in the Job passage is: "My days are swifter than a runner, they flee away, they see no good; they pass away like ships of reed, as the vulture that sweepeth on the prey." The medieval commentator David Kimhi explains the expression correctly: "Ships made of bulrushes (*gome*) are light to sail on the water. And our master Saadia, blessed be his memory, wrote thus in the *Book of Faiths* and said that 'whosoever is in the land of Ethiopia will travel in boats of bulrushes (*'arēbhoth shel gome*) until he reaches Egypt, for in the upper course of the Nile a mountain rises out of the water [the reference is to the cataracts], and the fishing boats (*dugith*, sing.) cannot pass without being wrecked, but boats made of bulrushes which are coated with wax, should they ground when passing the mountain, are stranded but do not break.'"[4]

The papyrus boats of Egypt are well known from ancient Egyptian tomb reliefs and paintings, and from various Roman authors. An Egyptian relief from the tomb of Ptahhotep (sixth dynasty) at Saqqara shows the method of construction: four workmen are busy winding ropes around bundles of papyrus (Figure 10)[5] The Roman authors called these boats *papyraceae naves*.[6] It is probable that these papyrus boats were made watertight by bitumen coating, just as was the ark of Moses according to Exodus 2:3. As for the swiftness of these boats, it is again probable that they were equipped with sails, and if so, they must have been fitted with masts of the bipod type—two spars stepped in A-form with their upper ends lashed together. Sheer masts, which appear very early in Egyptian history, certainly not later than the fourth dynasty, could not be used in papyrus boats, since the latter have no thwarts or deck beams to support the legs of a straddle mast—the only possible support is that afforded by the side bundles. (This arrangement could be seen until the present time in the reed canoes that fish and trade on Lake Titicaca in Bolivia and Peru: the lower ends of the bipod mast are tied to the side bundles in such a way that there is no danger of the mast heels working their way through the bottom of the craft.)[7]

The most common biblical term for ship is *oniyyah* (Judg. 5:17; 1 Kings 22:49; Isa. 2:16, 23:1; etc.). This word always denotes a single ship, whereas its short form, *oni*, either can denote a single vessel or is a collective noun designating a fleet of ships (1 Kings 9:26–27; 10:11, 22). A synonym of *oni* is *tzi* (*ṣi*), which, too, can denote either a ship or a fleet (Isa. 33:21; plural: Num. 24:24; Ezek. 30:9; Daniel 11:30). A third designation of ship is *s'finah* (Johan 1:5, etc.). Large seagoing vessels were called "Tarshish ships" (1 Kings 10:22; 22:49; 2 Chron. 9:21; 20:36), the name possibly being derived from that of Tartessus in southern Spain, which was the farthest destination of ships sailing from the ports of the Levant coast. A ship propelled by oars was called *oni shayiṭ* (Isa. 33:21),

Figure 10. The construction of a papyrus boat as shown on an Egyptian wall painting. Such boats were known to the biblical Hebrews, who called them *oniyyoth ēbheh* (Job 9:26) and also *k'li gome* (Isa. 18:2).

whereas a large ship was termed *ṣi addir* (ibid.), literally "mighty ship." Merchant's ships were called *oniyyoth soḥer*; it was known that they sailed to great distances (Prov. 31:14).

A raft used on the river Jordan was called *'abharah* (2 Sam. 19:19), literally "crosser." Rafts made of logs tied together were called *dobhroth* (1 Kings 5:23) or *rafsodoth* (2 Chron. 2:15). Such rafts were used for transporting large logs from one port to another along the Levant coast of the Mediterranean. They are still used on the rivers of Iraq, where they go by the name of *kelek*.[8]

RABBINIC SOURCES

Turning to Rabbinic sources, we are rewarded by a rich flow of information concerning the types of vessels used by or known to the Jews of Palestine and Babylonia in the Talmudic era (ca. first century BCE to the fifth century CE). The general designation for ship was still the biblical word *s'finah*, either in its Hebrew form or in the corresponding Aramaic forms *s'fina'* and *s'finta'*. (This term, incidentally, is used also in Arabic in the form of *safinah*, or in the collective form *safin*.) To this basic term various adjectives are appended to designate different types of ships. A distinction is made between a *s'finah g'dolah* ("big ship") and a *s'finah q'tanah* ("small ship").[9] The question, "What is the characteristic feature of a big ship?" is answered by Rabbi Yehuda to the effect that a big ship is one "that cannot be shaken by one person."[10] As one can see from this statement, the Tannaitic concept of a "big ship" was a rather modest one. Just as in biblical times big seagoing vessels were called "Tarshish ships," so in Talmudic times they came to be known as "Alexandrian ships."[11] They were so called because they plied between Alexandria, at the time the largest port in the eastern Mediterranean, and the other trading centers on the coasts of southern Europe, particularly Rome, to which they carried cargoes of wheat and other food supplies from Egypt.

A ship narrow at the bottom and gradually widening upward from a keel was called, as already mentioned above, *s'finah roqedeth*, literally "dancing ship."[12]

The Roman warships were known to the Jews of Palestine by their Latin name, *liburna*.[13] In several passages in Rabbinic literature the biblical term *tzi* (*și*) is explained, or rather translated, as *liburna*.[14] The Latin *liburna* itself is derived from the name of the country of the Liburnians, an Illyrian people between Istria and Dalmatia on the Adriatic coast, who were the first to use this type of swift and light vessel. The *liburnin g'dolah*, "big liburna," was the largest ship known to the inhabitants of Palestine in Talmudic times.[15] The expression used by Isaiah (33:21) *și addir* ("mighty ship"), is rendered in the Aramaic translation of Jonathan as *burni rabtha*, which is an abridged or distorted form of *liburni rabtha*, "large liburna." Other Aramaic translators render *și* as *dromon*, from the Greek *dromōn*, a light vessel.[16]

By a fortunate chance we have some data in the Talmud that help us to calculate the capacity of the ships mentioned. In the Babylonian Talmud we read that if a person hires a ship and overburdens it by one *kor*, he becomes responsible for any loss or damage that this may occasion. According to Rabh Papa, the addition of one-thirtieth of the normal burden must be regarded as an overloading; hence, one *kor* must be considered as one-thirtieth of the ship's normal cargo capacity. From this he concludes that "the capacity of an ordinary ship is thirty *kor*."[17] Various scholars have calculated the value of a *kor*: the mean of their calculations is 350 liters.[18] Taking this as the basis, we arrive at a capacity of about ten tons for an ordinary vessel, and about thirty-one tons for a "big liburna." For comparison we may mention that Cicero refers to ships having a capacity of about eighteen and a half tons, and Pliny mentions "Indian ships" of some twenty-eight tons. The average Roman ship had a burden of about sixty-eight tons.[19]

Some information can also be elicited from Talmudic sources concerning the height of ships between the deck and the water line. In Palestinian sources we read that if a ship is higher than ten handbreadths, it is forbidden on the Sabbath, the day of rest, to move anything from the ship into the sea or vice versa.[20] It is therefore evident that some of the ships that put in at Palestinian ports were higher, others lower, than ten handbreadths (or roughly thirty-six inches). For comparison we may mention that the height above the water line of the *dieris* of Samothrace was 1.6 meters or about sixty inches.[21]

Talmudic sources term the distance between the water level and the bottom of the ship "the depth of the ship," the equivalent of the modern "ship's draught." This, too, is given as about ten handbreadths, or thirty-six inches.[22] The draught of the Greek *trieris* was about the same.[23] In the Babylonian Talmud it is expressly stated that a ship can only sail safely in water that is at least ten handbreadths deep.[24]

Much feared on the high seas, as well as all along the Mediterranean coast, was the *s'finah shel piratin*, "pirates' ship."[25] A simile transmitted by Rabh Huna in the name of Rabbi Binyamin ben Levi runs as follows:

> A king said to his son, "Go out and engage in business." The son answered: "Father, I am afraid of highwaymen on the road, and at sea of pirates." What did his father do? He took a staff, engraved it and put an amulet (*qame'a*) on it, and said to him: "Let this staff be in your hand, and you have to fear no living being." Likewise the Holy One, blessed be He, said to Moses: "Say to Israel: My children, devote yourselves to the Torah, and you have to fear no nation."[26]

The same Rabh Huna was familiar with the Greek term for ship, *naus*, and used it in an observation in which he summed up what he considered the primacy of Greece over Rome: "In three things did the kingdom of Greece precede this evil kingdom [i.e., Rome]: in seafaring (*nausin*), in palaces, and in language."[27]

In addition to references to the biblical "bulrush boat," Talmudic literature mentions two other kinds of vessels that derived their names from the material of which they were made. *S'finoth shel heres* ("ships of clay") are mentioned in both Palestinian and Babylonian Rabbinic sources.[28] A clay model of a boat has been found in Cyprus (Figure 4). Juvenal also refers to river craft on the Nile being made of clay.[29] In modern times earthenware pots have been used in India as supports when fishing in rivers or in irrigation pools, or when crossing rivers, and also in Egypt to buoy up small rafts of wood employed by people to ferry themselves across irrigation channels.[30]

"Large copper ships" are also mentioned, but this expression was probably used to designate vessels with hulls covered with plates of copper, such as those referred to in the Elephantine papyri.[31]

Repeated reference is made in Rabbinic literature to a large seagoing ship called *ilfa*, at the top of whose mast there was a seat for a lookout (*q'bharnit*, from the Greek *kubernetes*, helmsman).[32] No other detail as to the character of this ship can be derived from the references to it.[33]

A small boat used on the River Jordan was called *s'finath haYarden* ("Jordan ship"). This is described as "being loaded on dry land and then launched into the water." In Palestinian sources this boat is called *'arebhath haYarden*, literally "Jordan trough."[34]

'Arebhah boats were used also on the coast of Palestine, and there too the loading and unloading took place on dry land.[35] Hence one can deduce that they were of small size and light draught. They may have been similar to the *bellum* still used on the rivers of Iraq; these are imported from the Malabar coast of India, where their name is *ballam*.

The Rabbinical sources differentiate between the large and the small *'arebhah*,[36] but as to their burden only that of the average *'arebhah* can be deduced from the fact that the adding of one *ardab* was regarded as an unreasonable overload for it. The *ardab* was a Persian and Egyptian dry measure, and the capacity of thirty *ardab* for an *'arebhah* would result in a ship of one and a half tons.[37]

Even smaller boats were the *n'didaya di-Ashq'lon* ("rocking boats of Ashkelon"), which were used as lighters for vessels of larger size, and were drawn half out of the water for loading and unloading.[38]

The *arba* was a Babylonian cargo boat, coated with pitch, as we learn from a passage in the Babylonian Talmud that speaks of "seven pieces of pitch from seven *arba*s."[39] It may have been either like the basket-shaped *quffa*s or a canoe-shaped structure made of light branches, such as ambatch stems or date palm leaf-stalks, as still used in modern times in the Iraqian bitumen-coated *shasha*. The *arba* was regarded as a valuable property, and the question of its ownership often occasioned quarrel and judicial litigation. At times the *arba* was sold together with its cargo and, for reasons no longer clear, it required a special mooring place.[40]

Among the merchandise shipped by the *arba* were wine and wheat; however, it was also used to transport passengers. Of several sages it is stated that they traveled together on an *arba*.[41] The duties of the crew of an *arba* included loading the craft.[42] The *arba* also served as support of pontoon bridges, as mentioned in the Babylonian Talmud, and shown on the Madeba mosaic map (Figure 11).

Dugith was the Palestinian name for a small boat or dinghy attached to a ship for communication with the shore and similar duties.[43] In Babylonia the same type of boat was called *bitzith* (*biṣith*) or *butzith* (*buṣith*).[44] This, and especially the type used on the river Mēshan in Babylonia (called *butzitha di-Mēshan*, or "Mēshan boat"), was a small boat, elongated, narrow on the bottom but widening upward, so that at a height of three handbreadths (about ten inches) its beam attained a width of four handbreadths (twelve to thirteen inches) or more; evidently, at the gunwales its width was greater. In order to give the bottom a flat surface on the inside of the hull, a quantity of reeds and bulrushes was put in to level it.[45]

The name *bitzith* is derived from *bitzah*, marsh, so that it signifies a "marsh boat." *Dugith* is derived from *dug*, to fish, and hence its primary meaning was "fishing boat." However, the boats proper to professional fishermen were called *s'finath tzayyadin*, literally "fishermen's boats."[46]

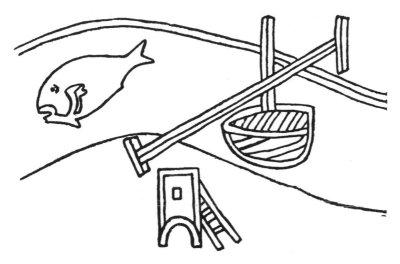

Figure 11. Picture of a pontoon bridge on the Jordan from the Madeba map. The bridge is shown supported in the middle by a ship.

Another kind of small boat was the *isqofa*, which belonged to the equipment of a bigger vessel, and was towed after it.[47] The term is borrowed from the Greek *skafe*, a light boat or skiff; it has also a close and significant resemblance to the Arabic *quffa*, the circular basket boat of Iraq, which is often used as a tender to large river craft, to carry passengers and cargo to and from the shore.

The three biblical terms for rafts did not survive into the Talmudic language. In it the rafts were called either *asdah*, or *askadya*, *asqadya*, *aksadya*.[48] In one passage it is explicitly stated that these terms are identical with the biblical *rafsodoth*.[49] The word *askadya* seems to be derived from the Greek *skhedia*, raft or float.[50] The medieval commentator Obidiah di Bertinoro explains that "*askadya* are logs that are bound together and floated on rivers and the sea, and in the Bible are called *rafsodoth*."[51]

Ferryboats used for crossing the rivers of Babylonia were called *mabbara* (a contraction of *ma'bara*, "crossing boat"). They seem to have been of flimsy construction and hence prone to accidents. By way of precaution, Rabbi Yannai was accustomed to inspect the ferryboat each time before crossing a river on it.[52]

An unusual device used by swimmers is mentioned in a Tannaitic source: the swimmer's barrel. This was, according to the explanation appended to the passage by Bertinoro, "a sort of hollow closed barrel; it is not provided with any opening in order that it should not sink in the water. A swimmer rests upon it while learning to swim."[53] Although swimming floats are known from many parts of the world in various forms and made of various materials (such as wooden blocks, inflated skins, large open-mouthed earthenware pots, and so on) this particular form (a closed barrel) has no parallel elsewhere.[54]

Chapter 5

THE CREW

Biblical Data

Only a very few incidental pieces of information about the crews of ships are contained in the Bible. In King Solomon's time the sailors were called *anshē ha'oniyyah* ("men of the ship") or *yod'ē hayam* ("knowers of the sea") (1 Kings 9:27). Later they were referred to as *mallaḥim* (literally "salties") or *ḥobhlim* ("ropers") (Ezek. 27:27; Jon. 1:5). All persons who ventured to set sail on the sea were called *yordē hayam ba'oniyyot*, literally "the descenders of the sea in ships," poetically rendered in the Bible translations as "they that go down to the sea in ships" (Ps. 107:23; cf. Isa. 42:10), using no fewer than five words for the single Hebrew word *yordē*.

The captain was called *rabh haḥobhel* ("master roper") (Jon. 1:6). The captain of the ship on which Paul sailed for Italy was called the "master of the ship" (Acts 27:11). In the Hebrew version of the apocryphal Testament of Naphthali the captain is called *manhig*, that is, "leader."[1] The oarsmen were called *shatim* ("rowers"), or *tofsē mashot* ("oar holders") (Ezek. 27:26, 29). A passage in Proverbs (23:34) indicates that its author was familiar with the task of the lookout who sat at the top of the mast to watch lest the ship suffer damage from a collision or by running aground.[2]

Rabbinical Data

In Talmudic times the captain was called *q'bharnit*, from the Greek *kubernetes*. From various passages in Rabbinical literature referring to the captain, one can deduce that it was generally known that the captain of a ship had to be a highly qualified person, versed in all the diverse duties required aboard a ship. He also had to possess much experience in the ways of the sea. He had not only to take charge of all that concerned his ship but also to shoulder the difficult task of setting and keeping a correct course from port to port.[3] The very life of the ship, the crew, and the passengers depended on the captain. Hence, "Woe to the ship that lost its captain!"[4] This is how Rabh, a leading second-century CE Babylonian sage, refers to the death of Abraham, which left the world leaderless. Rabh lived for several years in Palestine, and the term he uses for captain, *q'bharnit*, shows that the saying was of Palestinian origin. Again, no greater misfortune can befall a ship and its crew than to have a bad captain: the sages say to Rabban Gamliel: "Woe to the ship of which you are the captain!"[5] In case of an emergency, it was the duty of the captain to try and save the people in the ship. If someone fell overboard, the captain threw him a rope, saying, "Catch hold of this rope, and do not let it go, for if you let it go you have no life."[6]

Ranking above the captain of an individual ship in the Roman fleet that anchored off the shores of Palestine was the admiral, called in a Rabbinic source "head of all the liburnas."[7]

An important member of the crew was the *gashosha* ("sounder"), whose task it was to stand on the bow of the vessel, holding the sounding pole, *gashosh*, to fathom the depth of the water as the ship approached the shore.[8] The figure of such a pilot is seen on an ancient Egyptian painting that shows the fleet of Queen Hatshepsut (Figure 12).[9]

One of the Talmudic names for sailors, *notim* or *nawtim*, was derived from the Greek *nautai*. When a man completed the construction of his ship, "he set upon it *notim*."[10] Another Talmudic term for sailors, *arrabha*, was derived from the Aramaic name for a ship, *arbha*.[11] The biblical term *mallaḥ* appears in Talmudic literature in the Aramaized form of *mallaḥa*.[12] In one instance, at least, this term seems to mean not sailor but dealer in sailors' outfitting. Rabbi Abbahu was such a *mallaḥa*, and he used to steep the sails he offered for sale in water to improve their appearance.[13] The boatmen who towed the boats along the shores of the Babylonian rivers and canals were called *naggadē* (singular: *naggada*), literally "draggers."[14] The owner, or the man in charge, of a ferry (*mabbara*) was called *mabbora*, ferryman.[15] Sometimes the sailors are referred to as ʿabhadim, slaves.[16]

Far commoner than any of these designations was the name *sappanim*, derived from the usual Talmudic term for ship, *sᵉfinah*.[17] A *sappan* might be either the owner of a ship or a hired sailor.[18] When the ship was about to set sail and leave port, it was the task of the *sappan* to cast off the mooring ropes.[19]

Before the eyes of the *sappan*, who sails to distant lands, "the world is open."[20] The usual length of a sea voyage was six months, and hence the sailors would return home and unite with their wives once in six months.[21] It might, however, happen that a sailor would remember his home and his wife, and the longing would be so overwhelming that he would hurry home immediately.[22]

The Talmudic sages found much interest in talking to the sailors who had visited foreign lands and seen many strange sights. Some of the conversations that took place between sages and sailors are summarily recorded in the Rabbinic sources. In these accounts the sailors are frequently designated by the term *neḥutē yamma*, which is the precise

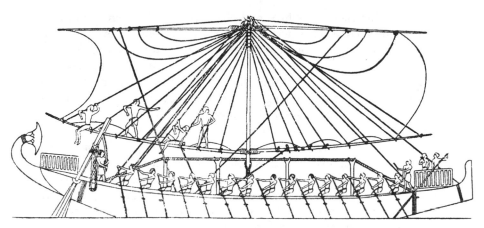

Figure 12. A ship in the fleet of Egyptian queen Hatshepsut (sixteenth century BCE). The ship is shown equipped with both sail and oarsmen. In the prow (right) in a boxlike structure stands a sailor holding a sounding pole.

Aramaic equivalent of the biblical *yordē hayam*, "descenders of the sea." When the sages were in doubt as to the exact meaning of a term denoting something foreign, they would consult the sailors. It is reported of Rabban Shim'on ben Gamliel that when the sages could not decide what was meant by the Mishnaic term *kalakh*, he said, "I made the rounds of all the sailors, and they said it is called *kulka*."[23] This is recorded in the Palestinian Talmud. In the Babylonian Talmud, the same inquiry was made by Shemuel, another leading second-century CE Babylonian sage, and the sailors he consulted gave him the same explanation: "It is called *kulka*," which term is then explained by other Babylonian sages as meaning raw silk.[24] Despite this unanimity between the Palestinian and the Babylonian sailors' explanation of the term, modern scholars cannot agree on the meaning of *kulka*. Levy and Goldschmidt accept the Talmudic explanation of raw silk, but Jastrow interprets it as cisseros blossoms.[25]

Shemuel was fond of gathering information from sailors. He asked them the meaning of *shemen qiq* (ricinus or castor oil), and was told that there was a bird in "the cities of the sea" (that is, oversea cities), which is called *qiq*.[26] It so happens that this explanation is erroneous, for *qiq* is definitely the name of a plant.[27] On another occasion Shemuel asked the sailors what *ashleg* was. They answered him: "It is called *shalga*, and it is found in the holes in which the pearls sit, and is scraped out with an iron nail."[28] The term *ashlag* is known from other Talmudic passages to have meant a kind of alkali, or mineral used as a soap.[29]

Shemuel was a physician, and he spent many years of his life in Pal-

estine as the physician of Rabbi Yehuda ha-Nasi.[30] While there, he probably visited the coastal cities and had occasion to converse with sailors.
Another piece of information he may have received from them concerned
the word *dar* (Esther 1:6) translated variously as *pinninos lithos* (Sep-
tuagint), "yellow marble," "mother of pearl," or "shell." Shemuel, however, found out that "there is a precious stone in the cities of the sea and
its name is *dara* . . . and it shines like the noonday."[31]

It was only natural that such friendly relations with the sailors should
sometimes result in business connections between them and some sages.
Of Rabbi Akiba, for instance, it is told that he once gave four *zuzim*
(silver coins, worth one quarter of a *sheqel*) to some sailors, saying:
"Bring me something." But the sailors found nothing suitable, so finally
they brought him a chest they had found on the seashore, and when he
opened the chest, he found it full of denarii.[32]

Rabbi Gamda had a similar experience with sailors. He too once gave
them four *zuzim* so that they would bring him something. Again the
sailors found nothing suitable, and finally bought him a monkey. The
monkey escaped from them and hid in a hole; when they tried to dig him
out, they found that he was sitting on pearls. And so, the story continues,
these extraordinarily honest sailors brought the whole treasure of pearls
to Rabbi Gamda.[33]

Not always were the relations between the sages and the sailors as
friendly as it appears from these two anecdotes. It also happened that
quarrels broke out between them. Thus we are told of a sharp exchange
of words between a non-Jewish ferryman and Rabbi Yehuda ben Ilai. The
ferryman saw that the face of Rabbi Yehuda "was radiant" (flushed?), and
remarked caustically: "This man must be one of three things—either he
loves to drink wine, or he lends money for profit, or he raises pigs."
Rabbi Yehuda, overhearing his remark, said to him: "May that ferryman's
soul depart! For not one of the three is true of me." Thereupon the
ferryman said to him: "Then why is your face radiant?" And he answered:
"It is the Torah that makes my face radiant."[34]

In times of danger, when a gale threatened to wreck the ship, the
sailors were wont to make vows. In the Book of Jonah we are told that
the sailors offered vows after the sea quieted down (Jon. 1:16). From
Talmudic sources we learn that sailors made vows while endangered by a
storm: they pledged to do certain things if their lives should be spared. A
Talmudic legend has it that in fulfillment of such a vow sailors once
brought to the sick Rabbi Eliezer ben Rabbi Shim'on sixty slaves carrying
sixty bags, and prepared for him sixty different kinds of food.[35]

Thanks to Russian performers, *Ey ukhnyem*, the song of the Volga
boatmen, has become famous all over the Western world. By a lucky
chance the Talmud has similarly preserved the words of a rhythmic chant

sung by the boatmen (trackers) who towed the cargo boats along the shores of the Babylonian rivers and canals, or by the longshoremen while loading and unloading the vessels in the Palestinian ports. The words are given by Rabh, who seems to have learned them in Palestine. The chant went as follows:

Hilni hiyya holla - w'hilloq holya.[36]

The words have no meaning and, like other chants of this kind, their popularity was due to their rhythm. The ancient Greeks had a similar sailors' cry in which the words were, "*ō op, ō opop, rhyppapai.*"[37]

The songs of Jewish boatmen are also referred to elsewhere in the Talmud. After the destruction of the Temple of Jerusalem (70 CE), when the sages felt that all gaiety was out of place and forbade the singing of songs, they made an exception for boatmen and cattle drivers: they were allowed to continue to chant their habitual songs.[38]

Although some non-Jewish sailors are described as almost saintly in their piety and honesty, others had the reputation of being ruthless and evil. A story recorded in a Midrash reminds one of more recent accounts of the cruelties committed by pirates:

A merchant sailed with his son in a ship, and he had with him a bundle full of denarii. The sailors gave them a place in a dark part of the ship. The merchant happened to overhear the sailors talking among themselves and saying: "When we reach the *pelagos* [that is, the open sea], we shall kill the merchant and his son. We shall throw them into the sea, and take their bundle of denarii." What did that merchant do? He pretended to be quarreling with his son, and took hold of the denarii and flung them into the sea, so that they should not be killed. When they reached the shores of Caesarea in Palestine, the merchant went and lodged a complaint against the sailors with the proconsul of the city. The proconsul arrested the sailors and ordered them to repay the merchant his loss.[39]

It may have been that some such unfortunate experience influenced the Talmudic sage who includes the trade of the sailors among those occupations that he warns Jewish fathers not to let their sons learn: "Let a man not teach his son to become a donkey driver, a camel driver, a potter, sailor, shepherd, or shopkeeper, for their trade is the trade of robbers."[40] Why the pursuit of precisely these trades was considered robbery is difficult to understand, and would require a special investigation of their conditions and activities in Talmudic times.

On the other hand, Talmudic sages knew many a tale and legend in which non-Jewish sailors appear in a much brighter light, as people who recognize the power of God. These tales are so interesting and important for the light they throw upon the imagination of sailors and seafarers that they deserve a special chapter (see Chapter 11).

Jewish sailors were, on the whole, well thought of by the sages of the Talmud. In a Mishna we read that although most donkey drivers are wicked, and most camel drivers reasonably good, "most sailors are righteous men."[41] Another opinion has it that although all camel drivers are wicked, some donkey drivers are wicked and some virtuous, but all sailors are virtuous. Rashi explains that sailors live in constant danger, and therefore their hearts are inclined toward their Father in Heaven; they travel to places of much danger and are always trembling at the perils that beset them.[42] This view is consonant with that of Rabbi Yehuda, who states, basing his conclusion on Psalm 107:23, that in view of the constant danger to which seamen are exposed they must not fail to praise God after they reach the shore in safety.[43] More on the sailors' reactions to the dangers of the sea will be said in Chapter 11, dealing with sailors' tales.

Chapter 6

MARITIME TRADE

EXPORT-IMPORT

Merchant vessels bringing their varied wares from distant lands were a familiar sight on the shores of the land of Israel in biblical times. In the Book of Proverbs the good housewife is praised by comparing her to such vessels: "She is like the merchant ships, she bringeth her food from afar" (Prov. 31:14).

In Talmudic times the chief merchandise brought by ships to be sold in the markets of Palestine and Babylonia was still foodstuffs. We hear of a Palestinian merchant of victuals, Baithos ben Zunin by name, who imported dried figs on a ship that also carried wine.[1] Among the goods brought to the ports of Palestine and Babylonia are mentioned apple wine and edible locusts,[2] fruit of the caper bush, leeks, fruit in general,[3] wheat,[4] and wine.[5] Rabh Dimi of the Babylonian city of Nehardea was engaged in transporting by ship dried figs from the place where they were produced to another city where he sold them.[6] The sages were aware that ships carrying foodstuffs often housed mice.[7] The ships sailing on the Mediterranean, and especially those coming from Rome, had a cargo of all kinds of merchandise.[8]

The ships that came to Acre—one of the chief ports of Palestine in Talmudic times—brought wine offerings from Jews in Qiliqya (that is, Cilicia, a district in the southeast of Asia Minor) or, according to a variant version, from Sicily. The recipient of the shipment, a certain Shim'on ben Kahana, wished to drink the wine in Acre, but since it was the rule that no *t'rumah* (religious offering) was allowed to enter the Land of Israel from abroad, the local rabbis in charge ordered him to drink his wine aboard the ship, that is, outside the borders of the country.[9] To Acre came also ships loaded with *muries* (brine, pickle, a Latin loan word), a preparation containing chopped fish in a heavy solution of salt, to which wine was sometimes also added. If the muries was prepared by a gentile professional cook, its consumption was permitted, because it was known that professional cooks would put no wine in it. (To drink wine prepared by gentiles was ritually forbidden.) A variety of muries was the *ḥēleq* (another Latin loan word, from *allec* or *hallec*), a sauce prepared from small fish, which also was declared kosher even though prepared abroad by gentile producers. The fact that both pickled fish products were known among the Palestinian Jews by their Latin names indicates that they were imported from Italy. Some of the ships arriving in Acre carried nothing but muries, which must have been a popular food item in Palestine.[10] Fish entrails and fish roe were brought to the port of Caesarea from Pelusa (Pelusium) and Aspamia (Spain).[11] Of a ship belonging to the house of Rabbi Yehuda ha-Nasi it is recorded that it once brought more than three hundred barrels of pickled fish.[12] From this incidental piece of information we learn that the head of the Jewish community of Palestine in the second century CE was, among other things, a shipowner and an importer of merchandise from overseas. In connection with another ship that brought muries we are informed that in order to make sure that no tampering with the muries would take place, Rabbi Abba of Acre put guards aboard.[13]

Wheat was brought to Palestinian ports from Alexandria. Some of these wheat cargoes would inevitably get wet from the bilge water that collected at the ship's bottom.[14] Again, from Rome were brought lumps of salt called in the Talmud *salqundrith* salt, a term derived from the Latin *saliginarii* or *saliquiarii*, that is, "salt of the bakers." According to another opinion it was called *sal conditum*, that is, "salt of condiment."[15] Items transported by boat on the River Jordan included water to be used for purification.[16] Ritual meals were also transported by ship.[17]

Various kinds of clothes and cloth for making garments were brought in ships to the shores of Palestine from oversea countries. Thence came the *birsin* (from the Greek or Latin *birrus*), a cloak of thick woollen material, and the even thicker *bard'sin* (Brundisian) cloaks, the *dalmatiqin* (Dalmatian) long undergarments of Dalmatian wool, and the *pinon* (Greek *pilos*, Latin *pilleum*) felt shoes.[18] Roman linen was regarded as an especially luxurious item.[19] The much prized scarlet-colored garments also came from Rome.[20] Overseas countries were the place of origin of the so-called *olyarin* or *olarin* (Latin *aularis*), white court cloaks.[21]

In Babylonia, too, barrels containing pickled fish were an important merchandise, transported on the river ships.[22] We also hear of sesamum transported on the Babylonian river Malka.[23]

Palestinian Jewish merchants not only imported merchandise from overseas but also exported local products to the Roman market. Jewish traders seem to have had storehouses of their own in Rome. At any rate, it is certain that they stored their merchandise in that city.[24] Evidence of the presence of Jewish merchants is afforded by two Greek inscriptions found in Rome, dating from the second century CE, according to which merchants from Tiberias and Claudiopolis (a city in Syria Palaestina) had a *statio*, that is, a society and a club house of their own, in Rome.[25]

The Talmudic sages were acquainted with three foreign ports of great importance, of which they knew some details. Regrettably, they do not state where the ports were located. What they say is that two of them were Roman and one Persian. The two Roman ports supplied corals (called *k'sitha* and *almog*), whereas the Persian port, called the Port of Mashmahig, supplied pearls. The way in which the corals were obtained is described in an exaggerated, semilegendary manner as follows:

> Six thousand men ballast a great *liburna* with sand during twelve months, or, as others say, twelve thousand men during six months. It is being ballasted until it settles on the bottom. [Evidently, the operation is imagined as taking place in shallow water.] Then a diver goes down and ties ropes to the corals and makes them fast. Then they throw the sand overboard, and the higher the ship rises the more the corals are lifted up out of the water. In exchanging them for silver, one obtains double their weight.[26]

Although the numbers of the men and the months mentioned, and indeed the whole operation, are fantastic, the method itself may well have been employed: some modern methods of raising sunken ships are conducted on a similar principle.

These bits and pieces of Rabbinic information on Jewish maritime trade are supplemented by references made by contemporary Hellenistic writings. The earliest among these is the apocryphal Letter of Aristeas, a Jewish-Alexandrian literary composition, written in Greek by an anonymous author probably in the second century BCE. In it the author sings the praises of Jerusalem and its country, and states that the Arabs bring to it a great variety of spices and precious stones and gold, for the land is good and suited for trade, and the city is rich in crafts, and there is no lack of anything that is brought by the sea. It has ports suitable for the import of merchandise in Ashkelon and Jaffa and Gaza, and even in Talmaida (that is, Ptolemais, the Greek name of Acre), which was founded by the king (that is, Ptolemy II Philadelphus), and which is located between the places mentioned, at no great distance from them.[27] The geography of Aristeas is faulty: the proper order of the three ports he mentions should be Gaza, Ashkelon, Jaffa; Acre is located not "between them" but at a great distance to the north of Jaffa. He is also inaccurate in stating in the sequel that "around the land flows the river called Jordan"—the Jordan only flows at the eastern borders of Palestine; nor does it, as Aristeas says, connect with another river that flows into the sea.

Strabo (ca. 64 BCE–ca. 21 CE), the Greek geographer and historian, says that "the Jews who come down to the sea use Jaffa as their port," and also reports that on the river Jordan cargo boats used to sail, even upstream.[28] Boats sailing up the Jordan must have been either rowed or towed by the crew walking along the bank.

Philo (ca. 20 BCE–ca. 50 CE), the Alexandrian Jewish philosopher, mentions that among the Jews of Alexandria there were a number of shipowners, which can only mean that they were engaged in trading with overseas countries.[29]

What Flavius Josephus (ca. 38–ca. 100 CE), the Jewish historian, says about Jewish maritime trade is ambiguous and self-contradictory. In his apologetic treatise *Contra Apionem* he asserts roundly, "We do not dwell in a country situated on the seashore, and we have no part in the maritime trade or in any other trade."[30] The first part of this statement is so patently at variance with the facts that one must assume that for the sake of argument Josephus here purposely asserted something he knew was untrue. He wished to explain why it was that the ancient Greeks were not aware of the existence of the Jewish people, notwithstanding the fact that the Jews too were an ancient people: he argues that the Greeks knew only those foreign peoples who had ports and engaged in maritime trade, while the Jews had not and did not.[31]

The assumption that in this passage Josephus deliberately distorted the truth is confirmed by the information he himself gives elsewhere on Jewish maritime trade. It is from Josephus that we know of the important seaport of Caesarea built by Herod the Great, of the important role Caesarea had as a trade center of Judea, and as a hub of economic and political life under Herod's successors. Most of the merchandise brought from overseas countries to Palestine passed through Caesarea, and it was from this port that most of the export trade left the country. Within a short time after it was built, Caesarea became a serious competitor not only of the ancient Palestinian ports of Gaza, Ashkelon, Dor (Dora), and Acre, but also of the Syrian harbors of Tyre, Sidon, and Arvad. The royal income derived from Caesarea was enormous. Less, but still considerable, was the income Herod derived from the customs levied in the three other ports under his jurisdiction: Gaza, Anthedon, and Jaffa.[32] These concrete details supplied by Josephus himself show that, in contrast to his assertion in his *Contra Apionem*, maritime trade did play a vital role in the life and economy of the Jewish state for at least several generations before his own lifetime.

IN THE MIRROR OF LEGEND

More about the importance of maritime trade in the life of the Jews in Talmudic times can be learned from the Aggadic material contained in Rabbinic literature. Legends, homilies, similes, parables, religious views, and observations often touch upon maritime trade and activities connected with it.

In general, sea trade was looked upon by the Talmudic sages as a hazardous affair. One of the sayings in which this view is reflected runs as follows: "Money that comes from an overseas country has no blessing in it, for not every day does a miracle occur."[33] Evidently, the chances of shipwreck or mishap were considered so great that a merchant whose ship came in had to consider it a miracle.

During the last decades of the Jerusalem Temple (destroyed in 70 CE) it was still customary among the Jews of the Land of Israel to make vows to the Sanctuary. These vows would be expressed in such phrases as "I vow my own value . . . ." The amount a man had to pay the Temple in fulfillment of such a vow depended on the value of the property he owned at the time he made the vow, and not at the time he fulfilled it. It is in this connection that we get a glimpse of the changing fortunes of those who entrusted their capital to the treacherous waves. If a man, a Tannaitic source informs us, makes a vow at a time when his ships are at sea, it is better that he fulfill his vow right away at the valuation of a poor man, rather than wait for a future date to do so as a rich man.[34] The same view of the tricky turns of fortune at sea was in the minds of the Mishnaic legislators who laid down the rule that if a man makes such a vow, and before he fulfills it his ship comes in and brings him "tens of thousands of denarii, the Sanctuary will have naught of it."[35] What the sages in both cases express is the view that it is better for the Sanctuary to obtain the amount of the vow while the man who made it is poor, rather than wait in the hope that he would become rich, since he may lose his ship and with it the ability of paying anything at all. From the comments appended to the Mishna in question by the Babylonian Talmud we learn that merchants or mariners sometimes chartered ships from their owners.[36]

It occasionally happened that a little mishap prior to embarkation prevented a merchant from boarding a ship that subsequently sank. Reference to such an occurrence is made by Rabbi Joseph in his explanation of the verse "O Lord, I will praise Thee: though Thou wast angry with me, Thine anger is turned away, and Thou comfortedst me" (Isa. 12:1). Rabbi Joseph said: "What is this verse referring to? To two men who set out on a business voyage, but a thorn got lodged in the foot of one of them [so that he could not sail], and he began to curse and imprecate. Some days later he heard that the ship of his fellow merchant sank in the sea, whereupon he began to give thanks and to praise."[37]

One circumstance that made some sages look down upon maritime trade was that the merchants engaged in it devoted themselves entirely to their business, and that consequently no Torah (learning) could be found among them.[38]

The Aggada, the legendary and homiletic explications attached by Talmudic sages to verses of the Bible, reflect the conditions of their own times. Since maritime trade played a definite role in the life of the society within which the sages lived, they discovered hidden references to sea trade in biblical passages. Although these explanations cannot serve as information concerning the conditions in biblical times, yet they are of interest as shedding light on the situation prevailing in the age in which they were written, that is in about the first century BCE to the fifth century CE.

The so-called "Blessing of Jacob" states: "Zebulun shall dwell at the shore of the seas, yea he shall be a shore for ships, and his border shall be unto Sidon" (Gen. 49:13). This passage is amplified by the Targum, the Aramaic translation-paraphrase of the Bible: "Zebulun shall dwell at the shore of the seas, and he shall conquer districts by ships, and he shall eat the richness of the sea, and his boundary shall reach unto Sidon." The apocryphal Testament of Zebulun (6:1–3) has Zebulun boast of his knowledge of navigation, which he learned from God: "I was the first to make a boat to sail upon the sea, for the Lord gave me understanding and wisdom therein. And I let down a rudder behind it, and I stretched a sail upon another upright piece of wood in the midst. And I sailed therein along the shores, catching fish for the house of my father until we came to Egypt."[39]

In the Rabbinic explanation of the same blessing of Zebulun, the fishing activities of Zebulun are transformed into maritime trading. In the Tannaitic Midrash Genesis Rabba the question is raised: why does the blessing of Zebulun precede that of Issachar, even though Issachar was older than Zebulun? The answer given is: "Zebulun occupied himself with *praqmatya* (trade, from the Greek *pragmateia*), and Issachar occupied himself with the study of the Torah. Zebulun came and fed him, and for this reason he preceded him. . . . Issachar sat indoors [studying] and Zebulun would bring [wares] in ships and sell them and bring him all his needs."[40] The same explanation is given elsewhere in Midrashic literature: "Zebulun sets out on the seas and returns and fills the mouth of Issachar, and thus learning is augmented in Israel."[41] And again: "Was not Issachar older than Zebulun? But because Zebulun withdrew from settled life and occupied himself with trade and came and filled the mouth of Issachar, therefore he received a reward for his pains."[42] "Zebulun shall dwell by the seashore—he made ships and sailed and went on the sea."[43]

Reference to the trading activity of Zebulun was read by the Midrash into the Blessing of Moses as well. The words, "Rejoice, Zebulun, in thy going out" (Deut. 33:18) are amplified by the Midrash: "Zebulun was a go-between for his brethren; he would take from his brethren and sell to the gentiles, and [take] from the gentiles and sell to his brethren."[44]

The role of Zebulun as a maritime merchant continued to interest the medieval commentators of the Bible. According to Rashi, the blessing given to Zebulun meant that "he would always be found at the shore of ships, at the harbor place where the ships bring merchandise. For Zebulun used to trade and thus to provide food for the tribe of Issachar."[45]

Another medieval commentator, Abraham ibn Ezra, remarks: "Ships are unable to abide in a place exposed to winds," and that is why they have to shelter in ports. Likewise, R. 'Ovadya Sforno, yet another medieval commentator, observes that "Zebulun used to go outside his country to the shore of ships with all kinds of merchandise."

The Blessing of Moses, referred to above, continues: "[Zebulun] shall suck of the abundance of the seas, and of the treasures hidden in the sand" (Deut. 33:19). The traditional Talmudic explanation of this verse is that the tribe of Zebulun made its fortune through the purple snail (*ḥilazon*), the manufacture of white glass, and various rare things that came out of the sea and were found in the territory of Issachar and Zebulun.[46]

In the Song of Deborah two other tribes are associated with the sea: "and Dan, why doth he sojourn by the ships? Asher dwelt at the shore of the sea, and abideth by its bays" (Judg. 5:17). The traditional comment on this passage has it that in the hour of danger Dan took to his boats with all his belongings and fled across the Jordan for safety.

Still, in Talmudic tradition the tribe of Zebulun continued to be regarded as the seafaring tribe par excellence. It is curious to note that at that time, when tribal divisions had already sunk into oblivion, it was a current opinion that anyone who would manifest a special liking for the sea and the seashore must be descended from the tribe of Zebulun.[47]

The tradition that Zebulun was devoted to sea trade left its traces in a number of Aggadic details. One of them relates that this trade was indicated also by his stone in the High Priest's breastplate, each of whose twelve stones stood for one of the twelve tribes of Israel. Zebulun's stone was a white pearl, for the pearl is drawn from the sea and Zebulun drew his sustenance from the sea with his merchant ships. The pearl also has the quality of bringing its owner sleep, and it is all the more to the credit of the tribe of Zebulun that they nevertheless spent the nights in commercial ventures to maintain their brother-tribe Issachar which lived only for the study of the Torah. Furthermore, the pearl is round, and as such it is symbolic of the changeability of fortune that turns around and around like a wheel, and thus it served to remind the wealthy tribe of Zebulun of the fickleness of fortune.[48]

The seafaring proclivity of Zebulun was attested also by the name of its prince, Eliab son of Helon (Num. 1:9, etc.), which the Aggadic source interprets as meaning "Ship, son of the Sand." This name indicated that the tribe of Zebulun spent its life on ships, seeking "treasures hidden in the sand." In fact, Zebulun was blessed with three kinds of sea treasures: the purple snail, pickled fish (*tarith*), and white glass. Zebulun's connection with seafaring was also expressed in his flag: it was white, like the color of the pearl, and was decorated with the picture of a ship.[49]

Chapter 7

IN THE HARBOR

LOADING AND UNLOADING

To reach a safe harbor was the goal of every voyage undertaken by a ship. Once safely anchored in the harbor, the disembarkation of the passengers and the unloading of the cargo was effected by means of the *kebhesh*, the landing bridge.[1] Before preparing "the cities of the sea" for the next voyage, the crew would have time to enjoy the amenities offered by the port city. One of the things most attractive to men who had spent a long time at sea on a meager and monotonous diet was the rich variety of food and drink obtainable in port. But those who could not afford to buy the tantalizing wares did better to stay on board and avoid setting eyes on them, so as not to arouse cravings they had no means of satisfying.[2]

Those passengers who went on to the next destination of the ship had to be careful when going ashore at an intermediary port of call to be back aboard in time before the ship departed. It could happen that while a passenger was still ashore his ship set sail. To prevent such an unpleasant occurrence, the merchants who were used to sailing adopted the habit of arranging with the captain how long they intended to be gone before they went ashore.[3]

A late moralizing parable, recorded in *maqamah* style by the Spanish-Jewish philosopher and scientist Shem-Tov Falaquera in the thirteenth century, but probably going back to an older prototype, tells about the behavior of five types of passengers when their ship reaches a most desirable island. The first group does not leave the ship at all, for they say, "If we leave the ship, a wind may come and carry the ship away, and we shall be left behind. . . . Thus we may lose all our money on board and may be left behind on the island and perish." The second group leaves the ship and goes ashore, but spends only a little time there. They promptly return to the places they left on board, and settle down at ease. The third group goes ashore and enjoys itself until the wind comes and the sailors wish to raise anchor and depart; the latter blow trumpets, as is their wont when they set out. When the people of the third group hear the trumpet, they begin to fear for their lives, hasten back to the ship, and have to be satisfied with whatever places they can find aboard, sitting crowded and crushed together. The fourth group, when they hear the trumpet, say: "Even though the trumpets have sounded, they will not leave until they have stepped the mast." When the mast has been stepped, they say, "They will not leave until they have raised the flag." When the flag is raised, they say, "They will not leave until the sailors have eaten." Thus they remain on the island enjoying its luscious fruit and getting drunk with the wine of their desire. When they see that the ship is leaving, they run to the shore, fling themselves into the water, and risk their lives until they reach the ship and clamber aboard. They find very little space on the ship and have to sit crowded together in great discomfort. The fifth group remains on the island eating and drinking, and not even thinking of returning to the ship. They stay on the island, and when the warm weather passes, they suffer from the cold. Soon wild beasts appear and attack them. Now they weep and mourn, regretting that they did not go back to the ship, but it does not help in the least, and soon all of them are lost. Falaquera tells this story to illustrate his thesis that the sooner a person repents the better, and that too late a repentance may be of no avail.[4] The details he gives about the preparations made aboard before the vessel is ready to depart show that he (or his source) had a certain familiarity with Mediterranean shipping.

Returning to Talmudic times, we learn from a Tannaitic source that while the ship was in harbor merchants from the town would come aboard to buy the merchandise brought by the ship, especially all sorts of grain. This was customary in the Palestinian ports of Jaffa and Caesarea.[5]

The loading and unloading of ships was a troublesome task, requiring much manpower. Small boats were drawn ashore halfway out of the water and were there loaded or unloaded, afterward to be launched once more into the water.[6] Bigger boats and ships would anchor off the shore where the depth of the water was about ten handbreadths (about three feet).[7] When nearing land, the pilot (*gashosha*) had to be particularly careful lest the ship run aground on a rock or sandbank. This was a responsible and difficult task, since ships had to be brought as close as possible to the shore in order to facilitate the loading and unloading. As a rule the ship was brought so close in that its keel very nearly touched bottom (the term used is *goshesh*).[8] The pilot, or "leadsman" as we would now call him, stood at the prow of the ship; according to Rashi he sounded the depth of the water with a pole, and did not allow the ship to advance unless the water was deep enough.[9] Water less than ten handbreadths in depth was called *r'qaq mayim*, literally "spittle of water," used in the sense of shallow water. The Talmud reports that when nearing port ships could move even in the *r'qaq*.[10]

When the ship reached the minimum depth at which it was still able to float, the anchors were let go, and the unloading or the loading, as the case may be, began. The stevedores entered the water and waded to the ship carrying merchandise to or from the shore on their heads and shoulders. This must be the meaning of the Tannaitic religious ruling that on the Sabbath, the day of rest, it is forbidden to move anything from the ship to the sea and vice versa, if the ship is more than ten handbreadths high.[11] In the same way, the ships of the ancient Greeks generally anchored so near the shore that men could wade to the ships.[12]

Another method of loading and unloading was to set up a chain of men stretching from the shore to the ship. The man standing on the ship would hand the load to the man standing in the water next to the ship, or would fling it to him if the distance between the men were greater; the second man passed it on to the third, and so on until the last would set it or fling it ashore. To load the ship the process was reversed.[13] If rocks projected above the water between the anchoring ship and the shore, as is common along the Mediterranean coast of the land of Israel to this day, the stevedores might use them as a temporary resting place for the merchandise while loading or unloading.[14] If several ships were anchored near one another, the merchandise would sometimes be flung from one ship to the next.[15] It happened at times that the sailors or the stevedores themselves had to jump from one ship to the next.[16] Ships sometimes might even be lashed together.[17]

Loading and unloading frequently caused serious damage to the ship, so that special legislation was enacted to meet such cases.[18] On the rivers of Babylonia, where in Talmudic times the Jews had an active part in shipping, it was found that the heavier the load the greater the strain upon the tow ropes, causing them to wear out more quickly.[19]

EMBARKATION

As we have seen earlier, when Jonah embarked on the ship in Jaffa, he paid the fare in advance (Jon. 1:3). As to the exact amount of the fare, no biblical information is available, and the Talmudic data are legendary in nature. One passage has it that Jonah paid the price of the whole ship to the amount of four thousand gold denarii.[20] A more realistic piece of information tells us that the fare (the term used is *s'khar ha-s'finah*, "fee of the ship") could be paid not only in cash but also in grain.[21]

A special term was employed to designate the passengers who were embarked on board the ship: they were called *p'rushim*, literally, those who had drawn away, or had separated themselves.[22] When all the passengers had embarked and the loading of the ship was completed, the owner of the ship (or the captain) would give orders to the sailors: "Loosen the ship!"[23] In the Babylonian rivers and canals, where the level of the water was apt to fluctuate a great deal, it often happened that the boat found itself stranded in a small bay and was unable to get afloat again until the water level had risen.[24] Along the coasts of Palestine between Tyre and Acre the ships had to sail with great care, for they were liable to run into bays formed by protruding rocks or into shallow pools created by melting snows.[25] Rashi understands this passage as referring to boats towed along the shore by ropes.

Where there were no port facilities the ship was anchored off the shore, and when it was ready to sail again it was only necessary to raise the anchor.[26] Such anchoring places along the shore were the private property of the owners of the adjoining sections of the shore.[27]

Despite the many dangers the ship has to face on high seas, its departure from port was an occasion for general rejoicing. This was observed by the Talmudic rabbis, who used it as a simile to illustrate the difference between the day of birth and the day of death:

> The day of a man's death is greater than the day of his birth. Why? Because on the day of his birth a man does not know what awaits him in his life, but on the day of his death his deeds are made known to everybody. Rabbi Levi said: a parable. It is like two ships sailing the great sea. One was leaving port (*limen*), the other was entering the port. All those aboard the ship that was about to depart were rejoicing; those aboard the ship that was entering the port were not rejoicing. A wise man was there, and he said: "I see here reversed things. Those aboard the ship that is about to depart should not be rejoicing, for they don't know what fate awaits her, what seas she will encounter, and what winds she will meet; those aboard the ship that is entering the port should rejoice, since they know that she entered the sea in peace and came out in peace." Thus a man, when he is born, his days are counted until he dies, and when he dies, he is heading for [eternal] life. It is of him that Solomon said: "A good name is better than precious oil, and the day of death than the day of one's birth" (Eccl. 7:1).[28]

Sailing ships had to wait for a favorable wind to help them leave the port. In another Rabbinic parable we read: "Two ships stand in the harbor. One awaits a north wind, and one awaits a south wind. Can one wind drive both of them at the same time? No, either this one, or that."[29]

The ship "rises and sinks" even while standing in the harbor or anchored off the shore,[30] yet only when it reaches the *pelagus diyamma*, "the open sea," do the waves become really strong, until it seems to the passengers that the sea is rocking them to sleep, or that the ship itself is sleeping in the midst of the billows.[31]

Chapter 8

ON THE HIGH SEAS

SAILING SEASONS

Because of the small size and frailty of the ancient ships, every departure from the harbor was considered fraught with danger. To sail across "the great sea" and arrive at one's destination safely was, in the eyes of the Talmudic sages, nothing short of a miracle. Were it not for special divine dispensation, they said, "every man who goes down to the sea would die at once."[1] Therefore, those who land safely after a sea trip must thank God.[2] According to a popular belief, the malevolent activities of Satan are greatest in times of danger: he does his worst on three occasions: when a man walks alone on the roads, when he sleeps alone in a dark house, and when he sails on the great sea.[3]

Even within the inevitable dangers of the high seas, however, there were gradations: in the summer it was less dangerous to go down to the sea than in the winter. This experience was expressed in the statement that "the paths of the sea" were open only in the summer. The words of Isaiah (43:16), "Thus saith the Lord, who maketh a way in the sea and a path in the mighty waters . . ." were explained by the sages to mean that from Shabhu'oth (Pentecost) to Sukkoth (Tabernacles)—that is approximately from May to October—there was a way in the sea open for ships, whereas from the Feast of Tabernacles until Hanukka (December) there was only a path in the mighty waters, that is, sailing in this period was more dangerous than in the summer.[4]

When Rabh Nathan Kohen, a third- to fourth-century Palestinian Amora (Talmudic sage), planned to sail on the great sea, he said to his brother, R. Ḥiyya, "Pray for me!" But his brother answered: "What is the point of my praying for you? Don't you know the saying, 'When you tie your *lulabh* [the palm branch used in the Sukkoth ritual], tie your feet.'" According to another version of the same anecdote, Ḥiyya said to him, "When you tie your *lulabh*, tie your ship. If you go up to the synagogue and hear that they are praying for rain, you should no longer rely on my prayer."[5]

The rainy season, which in the land of Israel starts about November, was not only dangerous for the ships, it was also a time of discomfort for the passengers. Those who nevertheless ventured aboard suffered from the rain.[6] Philo, who lived in the great Egyptian port city of Alexandria, states that at the beginning of the autumn sailing is still permissible, but in the course of the autumn itself all ships return to their harbor.[7]

The Greeks and the Romans also set similar limits to the seafaring seasons. According to Livy, the vernal and autumnal equinoxes (March 21 and September 22–23) mark the beginning and the end, respectively, of the sailing season.[8] Hesiod states that seafaring was safe for fifty days after the summer solstice (June 21 or 22).[9] That is, he considered seafaring hazardous after about August 10. Varro held that sailing was safe from the rise of the Pleiades until the rise of the Arcturus, that is, from May 27 to July 14; therafter it was unsafe until November 11, and from that date until March 10 the seas "were closed."[10] From the comments of several Greek, Hellenistic, and Roman authors we know that the prevailing view was that only the most daring set sail in winter, and that they often had to pay for their temerity with their lives.[11]

Such an outcome is related in a Midrash about a certain Rabbi Joshua, the son of Rabbi Tanḥuma. Some urgent business prompted him to sail from the city of 'Asia, better known by its biblical name of Ezion Gebher (see Chapter 13). The season was late autumn, between Sukkoth and Hanukka. A matron said to him: "At this time of the year you want to sail? I am surprised!" In a dream his father came to him and said: "[I see] my son without a burial!" Despite these warnings, Rabbi Joshua sailed—and was lost with his ship. In a parallel account, the sage about whom this is related is called Rabbi Yose, the son of Rabbi Tanḥuma.[12]

Once a ship was wrecked and sank, most of her passengers were regarded as lost.[13] Hence to curse somebody with the words, "May your ship sink!" was the equivalent of wishing him dead. This curse was once hurled by a woman at Rabha, whereupon, in order to render the curse ineffectual, the clothes of Rava were sunk into water. But this ruse was of no avail, and Rava met his death by drowning.[14] Of the merchant who escaped death by drowning because a thorn lodged in his foot kept him from embarking, we have heard above (Chapter 6).

Because of the dangers that ships represented in the imagination of the people, the shadow of a ship was counted among the shadows that harbored evil spirits.[15] Notwithstanding all this, we also find the view expressed that "Many sail on the sea, and most of them return; only a few are those who go and do not return."[16]

Seasonal differences in sailing practices were also observed on the rivers and waterways of Babylonia. In the spring, in the month of Nisan, when the rivers were swollen with the melting of the snows in the Taurian mountains, ships were wont to sail at a distance of one rope's length from the shore. In the autumn, in the month of Tishri, when the waters of the rivers were shallow after the dry summer, the ships sailed at a

distance of two ropes' length from the shore, to be sure to have a sufficient depth of water for their draft.[17]

LIFE ABOARD

As long as the weather was favorable, life aboard was not without its
attractions. The ship itself was made as pleasant as possible, even to the
point of providing it with decorative features, such as palm branches.[18] A
trip from one end of the Mediterranean to the other, what with lying in
harbor during the winter, took many months. According to one Mishnaic
statement, the voyage from Palestine to Spain took a whole year.[19] Hence
adequate food was a prime requisite for those embarking on a voyage.
Fresh water, perhaps even more important than food, was provided by
the ship, stored in a special tank aboard (see Chapter 3). Food, on the
other hand, had to be supplied by the passengers themselves. A parable
in the Mishna asks, "If a man does not prepare while on shore, what will
he eat at sea?"[20] Among the victuals brought along were, first of all, bread
and flour,[21] which were also the basic staples aboard the Roman ships.[22]

An anecdote told in the Babylonian Talmud illustrates the manner in
which, in case of need, passengers who were friends shared the food they
had brought along for the long voyage, and, incidentally, allows us also a
glimpse of the astronomical knowledge of some of the sages. The story is
about Rabban Gamliel II, the rich and autocractic *nasi*, head of the Palestinian Jewish community, toward the end of the first century CE, and
Rabbi Joshua ben Ḥananiah, one of the leading sages of the period. Rabban Gamliel had considerable astronomical knowledge,[23] which, however,
was far exceeded by the expertise of Rabbi Joshua in mathematics and
astronomy. At the same time, Rabbi Joshua was a poor man, who made a
living as a blacksmith, and, for reasons not entirely clear, had to sail frequently.[24] On one occasion this is what took place between them:

> Once it happened that Rabban Gamliel and Rabbi Joshua sailed together in
> a ship. Rabban Gamliel had bread with him, and Rabbi Joshua had both
> bread and flour. Rabban Gamliel's bread gave out, and he had to partake of
> the flour of Rabbi Joshua. He said to him: "Did you know that we would be
> delayed, that you also took flour along?" Rabbi Joshua answered: "There is a
> star that appears once in seventy years, and leads astray the ships, and I said
> to myself, it could appear and lead us astray." Rabban Gamliel said: "You
> know all this, and nevertheless you must travel by ship [to seek a living]?"
> Rabbi Joshua answered him: "While you wonder about me, I wonder about
> two of your students, whom you have on land, R. Eleazar Hisma and R.
> Yoḥanan ben Gudgada. They know to calculate how many drops of water
> there are in the sea, and yet have no bread to eat and no garb to wear."

Thereupon Rabban Gamliel decided to give them high positions. After he landed, he sent for them, but they did not come [out of modesty]. He sent for them again, and they came. He said to them: "You think I want to give you mastery; what I want to give you is rather servitude, as it is written, 'And they spoke to him [to King Rehoboam], saying: If thou wilt be a servant unto this people this day . . .'" (1 Kings 12:7).[25]

The star Rabbi Joshua referred to was probably Halley's Comet, which was reliably observed as early as in 240 BCE, and which in actuality has a nearly seventy-six-year periodicity.

It may be mentioned here, by the way, that although the Jews in Talmudic times had a good knowledge of astronomy, they used it primarily for the purpose of determining the months and leap years in order to be able to fix the dates of the new moon and the annual holy days. Shemuel, a leading Babylonian sage, said of himself: "The paths of heaven are known and clear to me as the paths of Nehardea [the city in which he lived], except one luminous star, whose nature I do not know."[26] Talmudic literature contains no statement referring to the observation of stars for the purpose of guiding a ship in crossing the open sea. This absence of reference may be due, however, to the nature of the extant Rabbinic sources rather than to an actual lack of knowledge. Other peoples living around the Mediterranean had a good knowledge of navigating with the help of stars, for which reason the sailors of Tyre and Sidon often chose to sail by night rather than by day.[27]

To return to the food consumed aboard ships: in order to have meat on the long voyage, passengers took along live fowl or even cattle, which were ritually slaughtered when the need arose.[28] Jewish religious precepts demanded that the blood of slaughtered animals be covered with earth; to be able to do this aboard ship, some earth was carried especially for this purpose.[29] A method of providing fresh vegetables aboard ship was to plant certain quick-growing kinds in boxes of earth carried on deck. A sufficient amount of earth was carried on board for this purpose, as well.[30] Yet there were always passengers who could not afford to supply themselves with sufficient food for the long voyage; to give nourishment to such persons was considered a highly meritorious charitable act.[31] Only in case of the gravest danger was food flung overboard to lighten the ship.[32]

WHEN STORMS STRUCK

When the wind increases and the waves grow stormier, it seems to the mariners that their ship is veritably "dancing" on the sea.[33] Yet to the passengers, watching the waves beat against the side of their ship, it appears as if the ship itself is standing still and it is the water that is moving past.[34] Trailing behind the ship was its wake, as though the ship were "ploughing great furrows" on the surface of the water. According to a Midrash, Noah attached the *re'em*, the huge legendary animal that had no room in the ark, to the outside of the ark, and the *re'em*, trailing after the ark, "ploughed furrows as great as the distance from Tiberias to Susitha," two towns on the opposite shores of the Sea of Galilee.[35] The picture of the huge animal ploughing the sea must have been based on the observation of the wake a ship leaves behind it.

A detailed account of the measures taken by the sailors to save their ship in a stormy sea is given in the Acts of the Apostles. When the Alexandrian ship in which Paul was sailing reached a well-protected haven near Lasea, a city along the south coast of Crete, the fast (the Day of Atonement, September–October) was already past, and Paul admonished those escorting him to put the ship into harbor and not to endanger her and the passengers by continuing to voyage at a dangerous time of the year. The ship's officers, however, had set their minds upon spending the winter in a more commodious and pleasant harbor of the island of Crete, and insisted on sailing on toward Phoenix, a safe harbor near the western end of the south shore of Crete.

> They weighed anchor and sailed along Crete close in shore. But after no long time there beat down from it a tempestuous wind, which is called Euraquilo ("northeaster"), and when the ship was caught and could not face the wind, we gave way to it and were driven. And running under the lee of a small island called Clauda, we were able, with difficulty, to secure the boat. And when they had hoisted it up, they used helps, undergirding the ship, and fearing lest they be cast upon the Syrtis,[36] they lowered the gear and so were driven. And as we labored exceedingly with the storm, the next day they began to throw the freight overboard, and the third day they cast out with their own hands the tackling of the ship. . . .
>
> But when the fourteenth night was come, as we were driven to and fro in the sea of Adria [the Adriatic], about midnight the sailors surmised that they were drawing near to some country, and they sounded and found twenty fathoms, and after a little space they sounded again and found fifteen fathoms. And fearing lest haply we should be cast ashore on rocky ground, they let go four anchors from the stern, and wished for the day. And as the sailors were seeking to flee out of the ship and had lowered the boat into the sea, under color as though they would lay out anchors from the foreship, Paul said to the centurion and to the soldiers, "Except these abide in the ship ye cannot be saved." Then the soldiers cut away the ropes of the boat, and let her fall off. . . .
>
> And when it was day they knew not the land, but they perceived a certain bay with a beach, and they took counsel whether they could drive the ship

upon it. And casting off the anchors they left them in the sea, at the same time loosing the bands of the rudders, and hoisting up the foresail to the wind they made for the beach. But lighting upon a place where two seas met they ran the vessel aground, and the foreship struck and remained unmoveable, but the stern began to break up by the violence of the waves. And the soldiers' counsel was to kill the prisoners lest any of them should swim out and escape, but the centurion, desiring to save Paul, stayed them from their purpose, and commanded that they who could swim should cast themselves overboard, and get first to the land, and the rest, some on planks and some on other things from the ship. And so it came that they all escaped safe to the land. (Acts 27)

A plank or a board from the ship was often used, according to Talmudic sources as well, by the crew and the passengers to save themselves from drowning after a shipwreck.[37] In fact, it was such standard procedure to throw things overboard in order to save a ship caught by a storm that the passage in Ecclesiastes (3:6), "A time to keep and a time to cast away," was rendered in the Targum, the Aramaic paraphrase-translation: "A time to keep merchandise ['isqa], and a time to cast merchandise into the sea at the time of a great storm."[38]

Practical measures were not always considered sufficient to save a ship from being wrecked by a storm. At times esoteric methods were added or substituted. One of these was to blow the shofar horn and thus to awaken the compassion of God.[39] To blow the shofar was considered a well-tried means of drawing divine compassion and thus save people from various misfortunes.[40] In the story of Paul's shipwreck quoted above we are also told that the sailors fasted, evidently in order to awaken divine compassion toward their plight (Acts 27:21, 34). Paul's opposition to this measure (v. 34) was in accordance with the position of the Talmudic sages, who held that people in serious danger must not fast lest they weaken themselves: "A town surrounded by a foe, or flooded by a river, also a ship in distress on the sea, and again a man pursued by gentiles or robbers or by an evil spirit, are not allowed to afflict themselves by fasting so as not to impair their strength.[41] Moreover, all those mentioned as being in trouble are instructed to break the law of the Sabbath rest in order to save their lives.[42] In another source we find the reassurance that God will help those Children of Israel who are on a ship in distress at sea.[43]

Some years after Paul's ship was wrecked in the Adriatic Sea the ship on which Flavius Josephus sailed from Palestine to Rome was overtaken by the same fate in the same sea. Josephus reports in his autobiography: "our ship was drowned in the Adriatic Sea; we that were in it, being about six hundred in number, swam for our lives all the night . . . upon the first appearance of the day, and upon our sight of a ship of Cyrene, I and some others, eighty in all, by God's providence . . . were taken up into the other ship." Thus he escaped, and reached "Dicearchia, which the Italians call Puteoli."[44]

As we see, the ships plying the Mediterranean in the days of Paul and Josephus were of a fair size: Paul's ship carried 276 persons, Josephus's about 600.

When a storm struck, the duty to save the ship and with it the lives of the crew and the passengers superseded the observance of the Sabbath laws of rest, which were taken, at least by some extremely religious Jewish seamen, to mean that on the Sabbath, as long as the ship was in no danger, they were not allowed to touch rudder or sails. Permission to do whatever work was needed to save the ship in a storm was in accordance with the general principle that "the duty of saving lives supersedes the Sabbath laws."[45] In an account of a voyage given by Sinesius, bishop of Corynna, in the year 404 CE, we happen to have an illustration of the religious dilemma a storm on the Sabbath meant for pious Jewish seamen. From another source, the Codex of Theodosius (dated 390 CE), we know that in the fourth century CE the Jews had an active share in seafaring based on Alexandria, Egypt, and even had a shipmasters' guild (*corpus naviculariorum*) of their own.[46] It was aboard the ship of one of these Jewish shipmasters, Amarantus Navicularius by name, that Bishop Sinesius sailed from Alexandria to Corynna. Captain Amarantus, despite his Latin name, which seems to indicate a degree of assimilation to the dominant Alexandrian culture of the fourth-fifth centuries CE, was an observant Jew (today he would be called ultra-orthodox)—this becomes clear from the account Sinesius gave of his voyage after the ship weathered the storm that almost wrecked it. Incidentally, Sinesius paints a lively picture of life aboard the Jewish-owned and Jewish-manned ship, and of the behavior of the Jewish seamen:

> All the sailors of the ship, their number being twelve, and together with the captain thirteen, were Jews, the children of that accursed nation which thinks that it is doing a good deed by causing death to the Greeks. . . . They were all deformed in one or another part of their bodies. As long as we were not in danger they amused themselves by calling one another not by their proper names but by their bodily defects: Lame, Ruptured, Left-handed, Squint, and so forth. . . . We too amused ourselves with them a good deal. We were about fifty passengers on board; among us a third part were women, mostly beautiful and charming. But, nevertheless, you should not envy me. Even Priapus himself would have behaved piously in a ship steered by Amarantus, who did not allow us even one short hour of pleasure in which to be free of mortal fear. . . .

[Sinesius is not aware that he contradicts himself: if the passengers had not even one short hour free of mortal fear, how could they amuse themselves a great deal with the sailors?]

On the day which the Jews call the sixth day, a great storm arose. The Jews believe that on that day the evening already belongs to the following day, on which it is forbidden to them to do any work. When Amarantus perceived that the sun had gone down, he dropped the steering rudder from his hands. The passengers believed that he had done thus because of despair. When it became known to them what the real reason was, namely, the keeping of the Sabbath, and all their requests that he should return to the rudder were in vain—because as we entreated him to save the ship from danger he only continued to read his book—they tried to threaten him. One brave soldier— there sailed with us a few Arab horsemen—drew his sword and threatened to cut off the man's head unless he instantly took the rudder again into his hands. But the captain, like a true Maccabean, could not be moved to transgress the commandments of his religion. Later, however, at midnight, he returned to the rudder voluntarily, saying, "Now our law permits it to me, because there is a danger of life."

The book that Amarantus read must have been either a prayer book or a copy of the Bible. If Sinesius's account is correct, the Jewish captain allowed his vessel to drift for several hours, from sunset to midnight. What he more likely did was to tie down the rudder and thus make it immobile, so that the ship should keep its course without his having to touch the rudder. In later passages of his letter, Sinesius tells of the further events of the voyage until they reached Asarius. Reaching that port, Amarantus was happy and confident, for he hoped that after completing the voyage successfully he would be able to save himself from the hands of his creditors by repaying his debts from the fares he received from his passengers.

The ship of Amarantus seems to have been in a rather neglected state of repair. Despite the strong wind, it sailed with all the sails set, for the loops and rings did not work, and although the sailors, with the help of the passengers, tried all they could to haul on the ropes, they were unable to furl the sails. Neither could the sails be changed, for the ship carried no spare sails. When it came to anchor the ship, it transpired that it had only one single anchor left, for the other anchor had been sold, and the ship had never had more than two. Later, when the ship sailed again, a second storm broke out, the ship drew near the shore, whence one of the "peasants" (acting as a pilot?) came aboard and took the rudder in his hands, while the "Syrian" (that is, Amarantus) willingly let him have this honor. Finally, all of them went ashore at Asarius.[47]

Despite the unsatisfactory condition of his ship, Amarantus evidently had no trouble in finding passengers; probably the other ships available were in no better repair. The indebtedness of Amarantus, too, must have been a situation common to the owners of small ships—we cannot imagine that Amarantus was able to obtain loans unless this was a general practice among shipowners. In any case, Sinesius's report gives us an idea of the circumstances of Jewish seamen in Alexandria about 400 CE.

A late legendary trace of the twofold efforts to save a storm-tossed ship by the practical measure of throwing cargo overboard and by the religious method of repentance and confession is contained in the so-called *Mishle Shuʿalim* ("Fox-Fables") of R. Berechiah haNaqdan. R. Berechiah, as his name ha-Naqdan ("the Punctuator") shows, was a scribe specializing in copying and perhaps establishing the correct details of the "punctuation," that is, vocalization, of the Masoretic text of the Bible; he probably lived in the thirteenth century in France. In his best-known work, the *Fox Fables*, he collected a large number of animal tales and other fables from both Jewish and non-Jewish sources, and presented them in his own freely restyled versions.[48] One of his tales, from which animals happen to be absent, is the one (no. 100) about "The Devil and the Ship," which runs as follows:

> Once the Devil and his mother were walking up and down the earth, until they reached the seashore. There they saw a ship full of people and horses. The ship was tossed about by a storm, and was about to founder amid the raging waves. As the tempest increased, the desperate passengers and sailors cast forth all their wares, including their most precious things, into the stormy sea, and confessed their sins and iniquities. Observing the plight of the ship and its passengers, the Devil said to his mother: "If you were in the foundering ship with those unfortunate people, they would say that you were the cause of all these woes and troubles. Usually they reproach you with all their misfortunes, making fallacious accusations against such an innocent person as you." The devil's mother, however, plucked up courage and replied: "Do not forget, my son, that even when I am not present in the sea during a raging tempest, I always see to it that my envoys, disciples, and apprentices carry out my sinister orders, and put into effect my pernicious designs."[49]

The very brevity of the reference to the sailors' and passengers' actions in trying to save themselves from the storm indicates that at the time of Berechiah (or his source) it was generally known that these were the measures typically taken by people threatened by shipwreck.

Chapter 9

NAVAL WARFARE

ALTHOUGH THE BIBLE contains no data on the use of ships by the Hebrews as instruments of war, it refers repeatedly to the warships of the neighboring peoples.

The Tyrian ship described by Ezekiel (Chapter 2) was a warship: he speaks of "Persia and Lud and Put" as supplying the fighting men for the Tyrian ship, as well as of "the men of Arvad and Helech" and "the Gammadim" (Ezek. 27:10–11). What the prophet evidently refers to is a navy carrying a fighting force of mercenaries recruited from many countries.

Persia is well known. Lud cannot be definitely identified, but it would seem either that it was located in North Africa or else was Lydia in west-central Asia Minor.[1] The identification of Put is likewise debated: Somalia and Libya have been suggested, with the latter considered more likely.[2] Arvad is the modern Ruad; it was the northernmost Phoenician city, located on an island adjacent to the coast. Soldiers from Arvad are mentioned among the opponents of Shalmaneser III in 853 BCE.[3] Helekh (or Helech) is probably the Assyrian Hilakku, the original "Cilicia," in southeast Asia Minor. Mercenaries from Hilakku are mentioned in the records of Shalmaneser III.[4] Gammadim (that is, "those of Gammad") have tentatively been identified with the Kumidi known from the Amarna Letters and other sources, and with the place *qmd* or *kmt* appearing in the Karnak topographical list of Seti I, a locality between Byblos and Arvad.[5] Several of these countries or peoples are known to have supplied mercenaries to various foreign armies in antiquity.

In the passage referred to, Ezekiel mentions towers and the hanging of shields upon the walls, meaning either the bulwarks of the ship or, dropping the metaphor, the walls of the city of Tyre itself. Towers were built on Roman warships: usually two towers on each ship.[6] As for hanging shields on the bulwarks, this was customary in the ancient Assyrian warships, one of which was found depicted in the palace of Sennacherib (Figure 13).[7] A picture of a Tyrian warship with the shields hanging on its side has also been preserved.[8] Roman warships, too, are shown with shields covering their sides (see Figure 1).

Balaam's eschatological prophecy predicts that

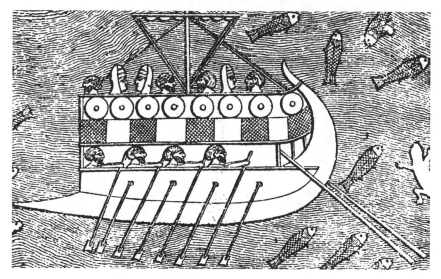

Figure 13. Assyrian warship, depicted in the palace of Sennacherib (ruled 704–681 BCE). The shields of the soldiers are hung along the ship's flank.

> Ships shall come from the coast of Kittim,
> And they shall afflict Asshur and afflict Eber
> And he shall also come to destruction.
>
> (Num. 24:24)

This ancient prophecy is echoed in Daniel: "For ships of Kittim shall come against him, and he shall be cowed. . . . And at the time of the end shall the king of the south push at him; and the king of the north shall come against him like a whirlwind, with chariots and with horsemen, and with many ships" (Dan. 11:30, 40). The name Kittim is apparently derived from that of the town Kition, near modern Larnaca, on the south-central coast of Cyprus, but in biblical usage was expanded to cover the entire island. Subsequently its meaning underwent further expansion, and came to designate Macedonia, the Greek Peninsula, Rome, Italy, and even China (Cathay).[9]

Egyptian warships, too, are referred to in the Bible, even though only indirectly. In the blessings and curses pronounced on Mount Gerizim and Mount Ebal, among the plagues with which the Children of Israel are threatened if they disobey the Lord is this: "The Lord shall bring thee back into Egypt in ships (*oniyyoth*), by the way whereof I said unto thee, 'Thou shalt see it no more again'" (Deut. 28:68). The only way in which the biblical author could have imagined the "bringing back" of the Children of Israel in ships to Egypt was in Egyptian warships.

As for Babylonian naval power, that is referred to in a Midrash in which we are told that Nebuchadnezzar made copper (copper-sheathed?) ships, and used them in his wars.[10]

The first piece of information about maritime power employed by the Jews themselves dates from Maccabean times. In the second century BCE, when the Hasmonean rulers liberated their country from foreign domination, they also opened up access to the sea. Both Jonathan and Simon had a part in conquering Jaffa and in making it a "gateway to the islands of the sea" (1 Macc. 10:76; 12:32; 14:5). In commemoration of his conquest of Jaffa, Simeon had seven pyramids built upon the graves of his father, his mother, and his brothers in Modiin, surrounded by columns that were visible to seafarers from afar, and were decorated with reliefs of ships (1 Macc. 13:27–30). Since Modiin was located next to Lod (Lydda), at a distance of some ten miles from the sea,[11] the columns must have been tall indeed to be visible from the sea.

Jewish coastal expansion continued under Alexander Jannaeus, who subjected to his rule the whole coastline of Palestine, from Raphia in the south to Acre in the north (see Chapter 13). He conquered no fewer than seven seaports, as a result of which the Jews were in a position to take an active part in maritime trade in competition with the Greeks and the Phoenicians.[12]

That the Hasmonean kings were not content with peaceful sea trade but also tried their hand at piracy may be learned from a passage in Josephus, which describes how Aristobulus, the last of the independent Hasmonean kings, was accused by his brother Hyrcanus before Pompey: "that the piracies that had been at sea, were owing to him."[13] Since Josephus neither refutes nor confirms this charge, we may conclude that it had a foundation in fact, although neither the form nor the extent of these "piracies" can be assessed.

That naval affairs played a considerable role under the Hasmonean kings as well as under their successors of the house of Herod is distinctly shown by the coins struck by these rulers. Coins of Alexander Jannaeus, of his grandson Alexander Yannai II, and of Herod bear the picture of an anchor (see Figures 14, 15). Herod's son, the ethnarch Archelaus (ruled 4 BCE–6 CE), had coins struck showing pictures of an anchor and a trident. One of his coins shows a warship with oars and a cabin on its deck, and its prow and stern curved high (Figure 16). Another shows a ship with oars, the same highly curved prow, and fitted with a mast, yard, and shrouds (Figure 17).[14] The presence of ships and other naval symbols on these coins can have only one meaning: that the later Hasmonean and the earlier Herodian rulers had fleets of their own, and could, moreover, pride themselves upon significant naval exploits, some of which may have been of piratical character.

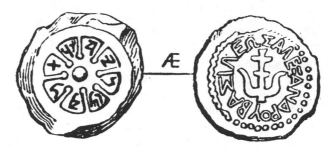

Figure 14. A coin of the Hasmonean king Alexander Jannaeus (ruled 103–76 BCE). The Hebrew inscription reads *Y'honathan hamelekh*, that is, "Jonathan the king," and the obverse reads in Greek *Alexandrou basileos*, that is, "King Alexander." Alexander Jannaeus brought under Hasmonean rule most of the Mediterranean coast of Palestine, and the coin with the anchor indicates that he sponsored Jewish seafaring activity.

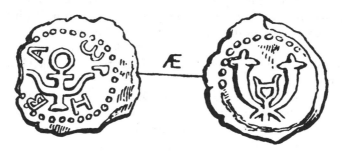

Figure 15. A coin of Herod, king of Judea (ruled 37–4 BCE), showing an anchor. Around it are the Greek initials of the name "King Herod."

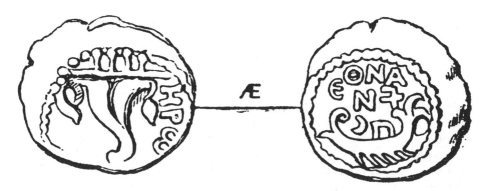

Figure 16. A coin of Archelaus (ruled 4 BCE–6 CE), ethnarch of Judea, son of Herod, showing a warship with oars and a cabin. The inscription is in Greek.

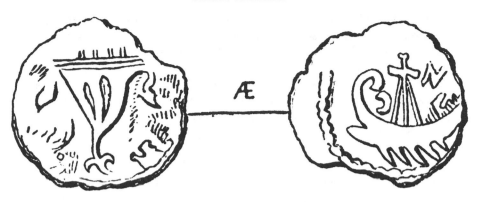

Figure 17. Another coin of Archelaus, showing a warship with oars.

This inference is strengthened by the fact that some decades later, during the Jewish war (66–70 CE), which resulted in the destruction of Jerusalem, the Romans had to fight the Jews not only on land but also on the sea, as well as on the inland waters of Palestine. After Flavius Josephus was nominated by the central authorities in Jerusalem to be governor of Upper and Lower Galilee, the city of Tiberias revolted against him while he sojourned in Taricheae, another city on the shores of Lake Kinnereth (see Chapter 14, under Magdala). Josephus, however,

> contrived to circumvent the revolters by a stratagem, and in the first place ordered the gates of Taricheae to be shut so that nobody might go out and inform those of Tiberias for whom it was intended what stratagem he was about: he then got together all the ships that were upon the lake, which were found to be two hundred and thirty; and in each of them he put no more than four mariners. So he sailed to Tiberias with haste, and at such distance from the city that it was not easy for the people to see the vessels, and ordered that the empty vessels should float up and down there, while himself, but seven of his guards with him, and those unarmed also, went so near as to be seen. But when his adversaries who were still reproaching him, saw him from the walls, they were so astonished that they supposed all the ships were full of armed men, and threw down their arms, and by signals of intercession they besought him to spare the city.

In the sequel Josephus relates how he succeeded in carrying off in his ships no fewer than 2,600 men from Tiberias, and putting them in prison in Taricheae.[15]

Some time later this Galilean Jewish fleet, the crews presumably reinforced, tried to make a stand against the Romans, but suffered a crushing defeat. The Jews of Taricheae, Josephus tells us, "had a great number of ships gotten ready upon the lake, that, in case they were beaten at land, they might retire to them; and they were so fitted up that they might undertake a sea fight also." In the event, the defenders of Taricheae were defeated by the Romans, and those of the Jews who had fled to the lake, upon seeing the city taken, sailed as far as they possibly could, and still reach the Romans "with what they threw at them, and then cast anchor, and brought their ships close, as in a line of battle, and thence fought the enemy from the sea, who were themselves at land."[16]

Titus, Vespasian's son and aide, at this point exhorted his army in a lengthy speech, which Josephus, as is his wont, purports to quote verbatim,[17] whereafter the Romans threw themselves at the city and took it. Some of the defenders tried to get away in ships (it seems that the first group of defenders who took to their ships did not take out all the ships tied up in the harbor), but they were slain by the Romans before they could get away. Next day, Titus "commanded that vessels should be fitted up, in order to pursue those that had escaped in the ships. These vessels were quickly gotten ready accordingly, because there was plenty of materials, and a great number of artificers also."[18]

Josephus goes on to describe in detail what happened next. His account of the sea fight that developed between the Roman and the Jewish fleets is unique in the annals of Jewish history, and hence of sufficient interest to be quoted in full:

> But now, when the vessels were gotten ready, Vespasian put upon ship board as many of his forces as he thought sufficient to be too hard for those that were upon the lake, and set sail after them. Now these which were driven into the lake could neither fly to the land, where all was in their enemies' hand, and in war against them, nor could they fight upon the level by sea, for their ships were small and fitted only for piracy; they were too weak to fight with Vespasian's vessels, and the mariners that were in them were so few that they were afraid to come near the Romans, who attacked them in great numbers. However, as they sailed round about the vessels, and sometimes as they came near them, they threw stones at the Romans when they were a good way off, or came closer and fought them; yet did they receive the greatest harm themselves in both cases. As for the stones they threw at the Romans, they only made a sound one after another, for they threw them against such as were in their armor, while the Roman darts could reach the Jews themselves; and when they ventured to come near the Romans, they became sufferers themselves before they could do any harm to the others, and were drowned, they and their ships together. As for those that endeavoured to come to an actual fight, the Romans ran many of them through with their long poles. Sometimes the Romans leaped into their ships, with swords in their hands, and slew them; but when some of them met the vessels, the Romans caught them by the middle, and destroyed at once their

ships and themselves who were taken in them. And as for such as were drowning in the sea, if they lifted their heads up above the water they were either killed by darts, or caught by the vessels; but if, in the desperate case they were in, they attempted to swim to their enemies, the Romans cut off either their heads or their hands; and indeed they were destroyed after various manners everywhere, till the rest, being put to flight, were forced to get upon the land, while the vessels encompassed them about [on the sea]: but as many of these were repulsed as they were getting ashore, they were killed by the darts upon the lake; and the Romans leaped out of their vessels and destroyed a great many more upon the land: one might then see the lake all bloody, and full of dead bodies, for not one of them escaped. And a terrible stink, and a very sad sight there was on the following days over that country; for as for the shores they were full of shipwrecks, and of dead bodies all swelled; and as the dead bodies were inflamed by the sun, and putrefied, they corrupted the air, insomuch that the misery was not only the object of commiseration to the Jews, but to those that hated them, and had been the authors of that misery. This was the upshot of the sea-fight. The number of the slain, including those that were killed in the city before, was six thousand and five hundred.[19]

Here, as throughout his *Wars of the Jews*, Josephus plays down the role of the Jews in confronting the Romans, and emphasizes the Roman superiority in arms, in tactics, and in fighting ability. Reading this account, one gets the impression that the Jews were not armed, that they were inept as fighters, and were totally incapable of inflicting any damage on the Romans: all they did was ineffectually throw stones at the Romans, against which the Romans were well protected by their armor. Among other improbabilities contained in this account is the supply of stones the Jews happened to have aboard when they fled from the city into their ships, and their suicidal move in approaching the Roman ships and exposing themselves to the Romans' spears and arrows. It is also peculiar that although Josephus states that the Romans killed 6,500 Jews in and around Taricheae, he says not a word about Roman casualties, thus making it appear that the Romans suffered none.

Soon after the Roman massacre of the inhabitants of Magdala-Taricheae, a Jewish community again developed in the city. After the destruction of the Temple (70 CE) the priestly family of Ezekiel settled there, and in the third century CE several Amoraim (Talmudic sages), including Resh Laqish, R. Isaac, and R. Judah, lived there.

After the Romans "pacified" Galilee, they proceeded to the south of Palestine, where again many Jews sought refuge in ships on the Dead Sea (called Lake Asphaltitis by Josephus). The Romans put "soldiers on board ships, and slew such as had fled to the lake."[20]

Although Josephus has sympathy for the Jews of Galilee, some of whom fought the Romans under his command, he has none for the Jewish effort to oppose the Romans on the Mediterranean. He gives no details of those activities, but his attitude is clear from the very fact that he calls the Jewish armed vessels "piratical ships":

> They [the Jews of Jaffa] also built themselves a great many piratical ships, and turned pirates upon the seas near to Syria and Phoenicia and Egypt, and made those seas unnavigable to all men. Now as soon as Vespasian knew of their conspiracy, he sent both footmen and horsemen to Joppa [Jaffa], which was unguarded in the night-time; however, those that were in it perceived that they should be attacked and were afraid of it; yet did they not endeavor to keep the Romans out, but fled to their ships, and lay at sea all night, out of the reach of their darts.[21]

In the opinion of modern researchers, the purpose of the armed Jewish ships in the eastern Mediterranean was not piracy but to destroy the grain ships sailing from Egypt to Rome, and thus to weaken the Roman power at this vulnerable point by cutting off the source of an essential food supply.[22] It is also noteworthy that the Jews repeatedly sought safety aboard their ships on Lake Kinneret, the Dead Sea, and the Mediterranean; this indicates that the Romans, at least in the earlier phase of their war against the Jews, were not equipped with a sufficient naval force to make all Jewish naval resistance to them futile. However, in the port of Jaffa, the Romans were helped by a violent storm. Josephus reports:

> Now as those people of Joppa were floating about in this sea, in the morning there fell a violent wind upon them; it is called by those that sail there the "black north wind," and there dashed their ships one against the other, and dashed some of them against the rocks, and carried many of them by force, while they strove against the opposite waves, into the main sea; for the shore was so rocky, and had so many of the enemy upon it, that they were afraid to come to land; nay, the waves rose so very high that they drowned them; nor was there any place whither they could fly, nor any way to save themselves, while they were thrust out of the sea, by the violence of the wind, if they stayed where they were, and out of the city by violence of the Romans. And much lamentation there was when the ships dashed against one another, and a terrible noise when they were broken to pieces; and some of the multitude that were in them were covered with the waves, and so perished, and a great many were embarrassed with shipwrecks. But some of them thought that to die by their own sword was lighter than by the sea, and so they killed themselves before they were drowned; although the greatest part of them were carried by the waves and dashed to pieces against the abrupt parts of the rocks, insomuch that the sea was bloody a long way, and the maritime parts

were full of dead bodies, for the Romans came upon those that were carried
to the shores and destroyed them; the number of the bodies that were thus
thrown out of the sea was four thousand and two hundred. The Romans also
took the city without opposition and utterly destroyed it.[23]

Although this destruction of the Jewish fleet at Jaffa could not be ascribed to the power of Roman arms, the fact remains that the events
described by Josephus put an end to Jewish presence in the Mediterranean, at least for several decades. Nor did the Romans refrain from claim-
ing naval victories over the Jews and from commemorating them in the
triumphal procession arranged by the Roman Senate in honor of the victorious Vespasian and Titus. In the procession, which also served as an
exhibition of the spoils taken, "a great number of ships" were carried.[24]
These ships could not have been too large if groups of captives were able
to carry them, whether on their shoulders or mounted on wheels.

Moreover, both Vespasian and Titus, as well as Domitian, the younger
son of Vespasian, who followed Titus on the Roman throne, struck coins
inscribed *Victoria navalis.* One of these coins shows Titus Caesar holding
in his right hand the figure of winged victory, while his right foot is
placed on the prow of a Judean ship. In front of Titus stand vanquished
Jews with their arms stretched out in a posture of supplication. A palm
tree in the background symbolizes the land of Palestine (Figure 18).[25]

Figure 18. A coin of Titus commemorating his victory over
Judea (70 CE). It shows Titus placing his foot on the bow of a
captured Judean ship, holding in his right hand a statue of
victory, while defeated Jews plead for mercy. A naval victory
of Judea was evidently considered an important
part of Titus's triumph.

When, some six decades later (132–135 CE), the Jews, led by Simon Bar Kokhba, revolted against the Romans, the latter sent against them not only several legions from the neighboring Roman province but also the *classis Syriaca*, that is, the Syrian fleet. After the suppression of the revolt, the commander of this fleet was honored with high rewards.[26] The necessity for bringing the Syrian fleet into action against the Jewish rebels would seem to indicate either that some naval forces were improvised by the Jews or that the Romans had found it necessary to impose a naval blockade on the Judean ports.

With the defeat of Bar Kokhba and the loss of Judean independence, the possession of naval forces remained beyond the horizon of whatever Jewish social aggregates continued to exist in Palestine, Babylonia, Egypt, or elsewhere. However, in Jewish imagination and folklore ships continued to have a role in warfare, and the defeat of one nation by another with the help of a mighty navy became incorporated into legendary historical traditions down to the Middle Ages.

The most important source from which traditions of this type are known to us is the *Sefer haYashar*, an anonymous work written in all probability in the twelfth century, and containing heroic Midrashim loosely connected to biblical figures and episodes. A remarkable section of this book tells about the struggle that took place between the kingdom of "Africa" (that is, Carthage) and that of the "Sons of Kittim" (that is, Italy).

Angias king of Africa died in those days, and his son Azdrubal [Hasdrubal] ruled in his stead. And in those days Janius, king of the Sons of Kittim, died, and they buried him in his palace that he had built for himself as a seat on the Plain of Kanfania, and Latianus ruled in his stead. In the twenty-second year of the rule of Moses over the Children of Kush, Latianus ruled over all the Children of Kittim, for forty-five years. And he too built for himself a very great and mighty tower, and built within it a beautiful palace for his seat, to conduct his kingdom lawfully. In the third year of his rule he let word pass to all his wise men, and they made him many ships. And Latianus gathered his whole army, and they came in the ships, and went to fight Azdrubal son of Angias, king of Africa. And they came to Africa and waged war with Azdrubal and his army. And Latianus prevailed over Azdrubal, and Latianus captured from Azdrubal the water canal which his father Angias had brought from the Sons of Kittim when he took Yania daughter of ʿUṣṣo [Utzo] to wife, and Latianus destroyed the bridge of that canal, and smote the whole army of Azdrubal with a great blow. And the other brave men of Azdrubal took strength, and their heart became filled with zeal, and they desired death, and waged more war against Latianus king of Kittim. And the war became strong over all the men of Africa, and they all fell victim to Latianus and his people, and also Azdrubal the king perished in that war.

And Azdrubal had a very beautiful daughter, and her name was Uspiziona. And all the men of Africa embroidered her likeness upon their garments, she was so beautiful. And the men of Latianus saw Uspiziona, and praised her to Latianus their king. And Latianus commanded, and they brought her to him, and Latianus took Uspiziona to wife, and he turned around and went back to Kittim.

And it came to pass after the death of Azdrubal, when Latianus returned to his own country from the war, that all the inhabitants of Africa arose and took Anibal [Hannibal], Azdrubal's younger brother, and made him king over all the land of Africa. And it came to pass when he ruled that he considered to go to Kittim to wage war against the Sons of Kittim, to avenge the death of Azdrubal his brother and the vengeance of the inhabitants of Africa, and so he did. And he made very many ships, and took in them his whole army, and went to Kittim.

And Anibal fought the Sons of Kittim, and the Sons of Kittim fell victim before Anibal and his army, and Anibal avenged the death of his brother. And Anibal fought the Sons of Kittim eighteen years, and Anibal dwelt in the land of Kittim, and encamped upon it many days. And Anibal struck the Sons of Kittim a mighty blow, and he killed their great ones and their princes, and of the rest of the people about eighty thousand men. And it came to pass at the end of many days and years that Anibal turned around and returned to the land of Africa, and ruled in safety in Africa.[27]

This excerpt can serve as an example of how historical events are reflected in the mirror of folk tradition. Of the great sea battles that took place between the Carthaginian and the Roman navies, the author of *Sefer haYashar* knows nothing.[28] In his account the navies are used solely for the transportation of troops, and the battles themselves take place on dry land. Nor is there any mention of the defeat of Hannibal: he is said to have held sway over Italy (Kittim) for eighteen-years (actually Hannibal waged war on Roman soil for fifteen years), and then returned home to Africa to rule over his country in peace and safety. The *Sefer haYashar* story places the Roman-Carthaginian wars that took place in the third century (264–201 BCE) into the days of Moses, that is, the thirteenth century BCE, which, of course, is but an indication of the lack of historical grasp on the part of the author. Incidentally, the heroic deeds of Moses are a favorite theme of the *Sefer haYashar*, which has a lot to say about the role of Moses as king of Ethiopia, in which capacity he was supposed to have served for many years before he became the liberator of the children of Israel from the Egyptian captivity. Nor is the author of the *Sefer haYashar* very accurate when it comes to the predecessors and ancestors of Hannibal. Hannibal was not the son of Angias, but of Hamilcar Barca. The Hasdrubal who succeeded Hamilcar Barca was not the brother but the brother-in-law of Hannibal. Hannibal did have a brother, also called Hasdrubal, but he was only the commander of the Carthaginian army in Spain. I am unable to identify any of the women mentioned by the *Sefer haYashar*. And, needless to say, Rome had no king at the time of the Punic wars, but was a republic. Nor, for that matter, was Carthage a kingdom: it was headed by two elected *suffetes* (cf. Hebrew *shofet*, judge). It is also curious that the author calls the country of Azdrubal and Anibal "Africa," and not Carthage (derived from the Phoenician *qarta ḥadta*, that is, "New City"), as one would have expected.

I am puzzled by the reference to the "water canal" (in Hebrew *t'alath hamayim*) that Angias had brought from Kittim to Africa, and to the "bridge of that canal" (in Hebrew *gesher hat'alah hahi*) that Latianus destroyed. Perhaps some experts in engineering history can throw light on these statements.

Chapter 10

LAWS OF THE SEA AND
THE RIVER

THE IMPORTANT ROLE seafaring and river faring played in the economic life of the Jews in Talmudic times in Palestine and in Babylonia made it inevitable that the legal acumen of the sages should be applied to issues raised by the ownership, purchase and selling, renting, and using of ships, whether on the sea or on the waterways.[1] And since a focal interest of the Talmudic sages was the application of religious laws to situations and problems that arose in the environment in which they lived, it is little wonder that much of their legislative work regulating Jewish seafaring and river faring activity dealt with its religious aspects. In this chapter we shall examine first the commercial laws and then the religious laws relating to seafaring and river faring.

COMMERCIAL LAWS

Talmudic law devotes considerable attention to the legal side of commercial transactions concerning ships, seafaring, and shipping. The purchase of a ship was concluded either by duly signing a contract or, presumably in the case of smaller craft, by the traditional act of taking movable property into possession, namely, by pulling: the buyer pulled the ship toward himself, and thus his ownership became legally established.[2]

Several passages in Tannaitic and Amoraic sources specify the parts of the ship and the gear that went with the hull in case of purchase. If a person sold a ship, it was understood that he sold with it the mast, the yard, the anchor, the oars, the rudder, the ladder, the water tank, and, according to the opinion of some sages, also the small boat (*dugit* or *bitzit*) that was part of its equipment.[3] Several other items of the equipment, however, remained the property of the seller: the ballast rods or stones (*yeshiwin*), the poles (*'ubhin*), the mattresses (*y'tzi'in*), the dunnage bags (*martzufin*), and the little boat called *isqofa*. The cargo that happened to be aboard the ship, as well as the slaves who manned the ship, also remained the property of the seller.[4] If the intention of the shipowner was to sell the ship together with all these items and the personnel, he had to state explicitly at the time of the sale, "I am selling you the ship and all that is in it."[5]

The right of ownership of ships was often the subject of litigation. The Babylonian Talmud records that once two men argued over an *arva*, a boat. Each of them claimed that the craft belonged to him alone. One of the two went to court and requested it to foreclose on the boat in order to prevent the other from selling it until he was able to produce witnesses to establish his claim. The decision of the court in this case was not to interfere, that is, not to foreclose on the boat. In another similar case the court declared itself willing to foreclose, whereupon the litigant who requested the foreclosure set out to find his witnesses, but was unable to locate any. He thereupon returned to the court and requested the judges to cancel the foreclosure in order to enable the two contesting parties to try their luck in seizing the boat by force. However, the decision of the court concerning this second request was not to annul the foreclosure. The only case in which the court allowed the two parties to use force against each other in trying to seize the boat was when each of them argued that he inherited the boat in question from his father.[6]

Information on the price of ships is scanty. One statement, quoted in the Babylonian Talmud in the name of Rabbi Romanos, to the effect that the price of a ship was no less than 4,000 golden denarii,[7] is not very helpful, since we are left in the dark about the size of the ship in question. We are likewise left uninformed concerning the fares charged passengers by boatowners. From a statement in the Mishna it appears that some owners or operators of ships accepted fruits or vegetables from the passengers as payment of the fare.[8]

In Babylonia, where the rivers and canals served as the main thoroughfares for the transportation of all kinds of cargo, owners of cargo boats would charter their vessels to merchants for the shipping of their goods. Some shipowners, however, served as their own skippers.[9] If somebody chartered a ship, he had to pay the charter money in advance or upon completion of the voyage, when he handed the ship back to its owner.[10] If a person seized another man's ship and made use of it for his own purposes, the owner of the ship could claim either payment for the hire or compensation for wear and tear.[11] The Talmudic rabbis were so familiar with the chartering of ships that they used it as the basis for a simile: "There are men who own ships but the merchandise in them is not theirs, and men who own the merchandise but the ship is not theirs. Not so the Holy One, blessed be He, who owns both the earth and everything that is in it."[12]

Legislation was necessary to regulate the relationship between the lessor and the lessee of a ship. The general rules as to their rights and obligations were laid down by the Tannaim (the Talmudic sages who lived in Palestine prior to 200 CE), and they were later amplified and refined by the Amoraim (the Talmudic masters of the third to fifth centuries) of Babylonia. Several of these rulings deal with problems of damages arising from the loss of ship or cargo. According to Tannaitic legislation, for instance, if a person hired a ship and it was wrecked and sank in the course of the voyage, the following rules applied: if he had paid the charter money, he was not entitled to demand its refund; but if he had not yet paid it, he was not required to do so. The Amoraim approached this ruling from several legal angles, and came to the conclusion that it was valid only in case the lessor and the lessee had contracted concerning a definite ship for the transportation of a definite cargo, for in that case, if the ship sank together with the cargo, neither the lessor nor the lessee was able to fulfill his agreed-upon obligation. On the other hand, if they had contracted concerning a ship without specifying one particular vessel, and the contract concerned an unspecified cargo, the ruling was that the lessee had to pay the lessor half of the fee due for the voyage actually made by the ship.[13]

Again according to the Tannaim, if somebody hired a ship to transport cargo to a certain destination but then unloaded the ship when it had covered only half the distance, he had to pay the lessor only the fee due for half the way.[14] The Amoraic elaborations of this ruling are too lengthy and complex to be quoted here in full; while trying to define the exact cases to which this ruling applied, they discussed such technicalities as the wear and tear on the ship, any change in its route, and the relationship between any increase of the cargo and the number of ropes worn out. From the context it becomes clear that the owner of the ship sailed with his ship, probably in the capacity of skipper, or as supercargo. The sailors, in general, had the status of hired laborers.[15] When ships entered or left port, they had to pay customs dues.[16] From a Midrash it appears that occasionally these customs dues were so severe that they caused ruin to the merchants.[17]

Considering the great risks connected with sea trade, it is not surprising that merchants who engaged in it were often in need of loans. In such cases the merchants would apply for a loan first to the shipowners as persons most likely to be interested in the success of their enterprises. Since, however, biblical law prohibited the taking of interest on loans (Lev. 25:35–37), without the incentive of an increased return the shipowners could not be expected to run the risk of losing their money in addition to their ship. This obstacle was overcome, not only in the case of sea trade but also in other similar cases, by offering the owner a higher rent, or freight rate, than originally stipulated, in consideration of a loan to be used to improve his property. A tenant, for instance, might offer higher rent for a field on condition that the owner of the field give him a loan that the tenant was bound to use for improvements. The loan was, in this case, regarded as a loan without interest, for the higher rent paid by the tenant to the owner was considered due to him owing to the improvements in the field, and consequently in its yield, made possible by the loan.[18] The same sort of agreement might also be entered by the owner of a ship and the merchant who hired it from him. Talmudic law, however, expressly stipulates that no higher rent may be charged by the owner of a ship if the merchant used the loan for buying merchandise or for any other investment into his business. Only if he made use of the loan to improve the ship was he allowed to offer, and the owner to accept, a higher rent, because in that case the ship would bring greater gain to the merchant.[19]

One form of loan used by maritime merchants was called *qalito shel yam* (literally, "suction," or "gorge of the sea"), which largely corresponded to the Greek *tokos nautikos*, or the Roman *fenus nauticum*.[20] The Palestinian Talmud explains: "What is *qalito shel yam?* If somebody advances a certain amount of denarii to his neighbor in the manner of those who give goods to the men who sail to the isles,[21] at a share of two or three sextarii, this is not usury but *tarsha*."[22] To understand this ruling, one must explain the terse language of the Talmud. "A share of two or three sextarii" means payment of this amount per each modius of profit earned by the merchant. A sextarius was one sixteenth of a modius, so that the two or three sextarii taken by the lender per each modius earned by the merchant represented an interest of one-eighth or three-sixteenths, respectively, on the money lent. This type of interest was termed by the Talmudic sages *tarsha*, that is, silent interest, which was considered permissible. The principle underlying the tarsha was the higher price charged in case of deferred payment. Rabbi Yehuda ha-Nasi (second century CE), who owned several merchant ships plying the Mediterranean, was interested in legalizing the *qalito shel yam* type of hidden interest, but he was overruled by the sages.[23]

In Babylonia, where cargo transport on the rivers and canals was a highly developed business, shippers used to undertake the responsibility for the transport of a given cargo to a certain port, and for discharging it there. Such responsibility covered even cases of force majeure. Rabh Papa and Rabh Huna, two Babylonian Amoraim of the mid-fourth century CE, once bought a load of sesamum seed on the banks of the Old King's Canal, and hired sailors to track it to its place of destination. The sailors undertook to be responsible in case of any accident that might occur. It so happened that the canal became blocked, whereupon the two merchant-rabbis demanded from the sailors that, having undertaken the responsibility in case of any accident, they hire donkey drivers to carry the cargo to its destination. The sailors, however, objected, and when the case was brought before Rabha, the head of the Jewish academy of Mehoza, he absolved the sailors, finding that it was a most unusual occurrence for that big canal to become blocked.[24] Incidentally we learn from this case that the shippers who dragged the ship in question along the Old King's Canal were Jews—otherwise they would not have submitted their case to a Jewish law court.

Talmudic law regulates the responsibility of the owner of a boat, of the sailors who charter it from him, and of the passengers, in case the boat suffers damage. If a man charters a ship, he has to pay its hire when he takes over the ship, and has to pay damages if the vessel suffers shipwreck.[25] This ruling can be compared to paragraph 236 in the Code of Hammurabi, preceding the Talmudic legislation by at least two millennia: "If a seignior let his boat for hire to a boatman, and the boatman was so careless that he has sunk or wrecked the boat, the boatman shall make good the boat to the owner of the boat."[26] According to Talmudic law, if the boatman who has hired a boat overloads it by at least one-thirtieth of its usual load, he becomes responsible for any damage suffered by the vessel.[27]

In cargo shipping there were usually three parties involved: the owner of the boat, the boatman or boatmen who hired the boat from him, and the owner of the merchandise who hired the boatmen. We may thus take it for granted that the boatmen were responsible to the owner of the cargo not only for transporting the cargo to its agreed-upon destination but also for the safety of the cargo itself. The Code of Hammurabi rules (paragraph 237), "When a seignior hired a boatman and a boat, and loaded it with grain, wool, oil, dates, or any kind of freight, if that boatman was so careless that he has sunk the boat and lost what was in it as well, the boatman shall make good the boat which he sank and whatever he lost that was in it."[28]

The carelessness or carefulness of the boatmen was considered a decisive factor in Talmudic legislation in connection with the significant institution of mutual insurance that played an important role in the commercial shipping practices of both Palestinian and Babylonian Jews some fifteen centuries before Lloyd's Underwriting Association. The idea of mutual insurance seems to have originated among the Jewish sailors of Palestine, who in sailing the Mediterranean must have suffered many more accidents than their Babylonian colleagues on the quiet canals and rivers of their country. Tannaitic legislation gave its approval:

> The sailors are permitted to say, "Whosoever loses his ship, we shall supply him with another in its stead." If, however, he lost his ship through negligence [busya or bisya], they are not bound to supply him with another ship. Only if his ship was lost not due to his own negligence are they bound to supply him with another ship. If he sailed to a place where people do not usually sail, they are not bound to supply him with another ship.[29]

The Babylonian sages adapted this Palestinian rule to the Babylonian conditions and interpreted accordingly the phrase "if he sailed to a place where people do not usually sail" as follows: It was the usage on the Babylonian waterway, as has been said, to sail in the spring, when the water level was high, at a distance of one cable-length from the shore, while in the autumn, when the rivers ran low, they sailed at a distance of two cable-lengths from the shore. If a boatman did not follow these rules, he was regarded as having been negligent, and if as a consequence his boat was wrecked, it did not have to be replaced by another boat.[30]

In the canals of Babylonia collision between two boats was an ever-present danger. Two millennia before the Talmudic age, the Code of Hammurabi considered such contingencies, and ruled (paragraph 240), "If a rowboat rammed a sailboat and has sunk it, the owner of the boat that was sunk shall in the presence of the god set forth the particulars regarding whatever was lost in his boat, and the one in charge of the rowboat which sank the sailboat shall make good to him his boat and his lost property."[31]

The Talmudic sages went into greater detail in their legal provisions concerning such damages, and even enacted preventive measures in the form of traffic regulations: Two ships sailing in opposite directions on a river meet; if both continue to sail, they will collide, and both will sink. If one of them draws near the shore and lets the other pass, no harm will befall either of them. The question thus arises, which of the two ships has to give way to the other? The Talmudic ruling is that if one of the ships is empty and the other loaded, the empty one must draw aside and let the full one pass. Or, if one of them is nearer the shore and the other farther away, the one nearer the shore must let the other pass. If both of them are at equal distance from the shore, they have to come to an agreement, and the one that wishes to pass has to pay the other for the right of passage.[32] This ruling is contained in the Babylonian Talmud, and is concerned with conditions on the Babylonian rivers. However, like the rules governing mutual insurance, it goes back to an older, Tannaitic, Palestinian prototype: "Two ships that sail toward each other, one empty and one loaded, the empty one must give way to the loaded one; if both are empty, or both are loaded, they must come to an understanding."[33]

To appreciate the importance of these regulations, especially for Babylonia, one must remember that in Babylonia boats were in many cases towed along narrow irrigation canals (*nigrē*, sing. *nigra*), so that for a boat to pull aside and let another boat pass involved considerable additional work, as well as much loss of time. Although the smaller canals or channels were the private property of the landowner through whose fields they passed, he was obliged to leave their banks free of cultivation to a width of at least four cubits (about six feet) so that the vegetation should not obstruct the passing of the boats that were towed from its banks. The larger canals and their banks were considered public property, and they too had to be kept free of all growth to a width of four cubits. Rabbi Ammi bar Nathan, an outstanding Palestinian Amora of the third century CE, who lived for some years in Babylonia, decreed: "Cut down [the vegetation] on both banks of the river to the width of the shoulders of the *naggadē* [the draggers of the boats]."[34]

Once it happened that one of the sages gave orders to cut down the trees bordering a river to a width of sixteen cubits (twenty-four feet), whereupon the enraged owners of the trees thus destroyed fell upon him and beat him.[35] From the Talmudic stories it becomes evident that the availability of free passageways along the riverbanks was considered such a basic public right that when the paths were found obstructed by trees or other vegetation, the sages, in their capacity as community leaders, felt justified in ordering the removal of the obstructions, even without the consent of the landowners.[36] On the other hand, one must understand that trees in Babylonia, especially if they were date palms, were extremely valuable property, as they are to this day in Iraq, which explains the outrage felt by the owners at their destruction.

Since the Babylonian canals tended to become obstructed with sediment, it was necessary from time to time to dredge them. Talmudic legislation provided that this should be carried out by the owner of the land that adjoined the silted-up stretch of the canal. He was to be helped by the owners of the lands that lay lower down along the banks of the canal, for they would suffer from any diminution of the water needed for irrigation. However, the owners of the adjoining land higher up along the canal were not expected to help, since they only benefitted from accumulation of water caused by the obstruction of the canal lower down.[37] On occasion, major repairs had to be undertaken: canals had to be cleaned up by digging a course through a sandbank, or in some other manner. This repair was considered so essential for the general public that its performance was permitted even on a half-holiday.[38] The details contained in the Babylonian Talmud about this issue allow us, incidentally, an insight into the social conditions of the Jews in Babylonia in the Talmudic age. We get a picture of a society in which the Jews were landowners, shipowners, merchants, river farers, and manual laborers employed in the cutting down of trees and in earthwork, and which was governed and controlled by formal religio-legal institutions headed by sages.

In Palestine, where navigation was mainly maritime, the sailors suffered much from storms. One of the most common methods of trying to save a ship caught in a storm was, as we have seen in Chapter 8, to jettison the cargo or part of it. Rabbinic legislation dealt with the legal aspects of such rescue maneuvers. It decreed that if a number of merchants sail on a ship, each with a certain amount of merchandise with him, and the need arises to jettison the cargo, then each of the merchants has to take his share in the sacrifice in relation to the weight and value of his merchandise. If, on the other hand, several merchants jointly charter a ship for the transportation of their wares, each of them has to pay his share according to the weight of his merchandise, without regard to its value.[39] But these Talmudic rulings are accompanied by the warning "One does not, however, deviate from the usage of the sailors."[40] That is, local custom must be regarded as taking precedence over the rabbis' rules.

RELIGIOUS LAWS

As mentioned above, a major part of Talmudic legislation concerning ships and shipping deals with religious issues, and comes to grips with the problems encountered in trying to observe the prescriptions and prohibitions of the Halakhah, the traditional religious rules, aboard ship, in situations very different from those in which those rules developed and for which they were intended.

Prayers

The fulfillment of the basic Jewish religious duty of reciting prayers three times a day could not be interrupted even when setting out on a sea voyage. On the contrary, as soon as a person came in sight of the sea (that is, the Mediterranean), he had to recite a special benediction, "Blessed be He who created the Great Sea."[41] When aboard any vessel, a man must direct his heart toward the Temple of Jerusalem, and say the obligatory prayers.[42] This rule, evidently, dates from before 70 CE, when the Temple of Jerusalem was destroyed.

At times passengers had to embark very early in the morning, even before dawn, in which case they had to recite the *Shaḥarith* (morning) prayer prior to embarkation, even though it was still dark; and later, on board the ship, they had to recite the *Sh'ma'* prayer ("Hear, O Israel . . ."), the part of the morning prayer that can be said only after dawn.[43] Once the traveler had happily reached his port of destination, he had, according to Rabbi Yehuda, to say a special grace for having been saved from the perils of the sea.[44]

An inscription from the second century CE shows that the Egyptian Jews of that period occasionally expressed their gratitude to God for having saved them from a storm in the sea in a more permanent form. The inscription, found in the Temple of Pan at Apollonopolis Magna (Edfu) in Upper Egypt, reads in Greek: "Thanks to God, the Jew Theodotos son of Dorion was saved from the sea."[45] That the names of the Jew and of his father were Greek, and that he placed his inscription in the Temple of Pan, indicate that he was the scion of a thoroughly Hellenized Jewish family, who nevertheless retained enough of his ancestral faith to feel that he owed thanks to the (Jewish) God for saving him from the sea. At the same time we learn from this inscription that Jews living in Egypt far from the sea nevertheless, occasionally at least, undertook sea voyages.

Jews who died outside the land of Israel often expressed the wish to be buried in the ancestral land, and their bodies were transported by ship to a Palestinian port. The large Beth Sh'arim necropolis near Haifa contains hundreds of inscriptions testifying to the burial there of Jews from all parts of the Diaspora, beginning with the second century CE.[46] The depiction of sailing ships on the walls of the catacombs may be a reference to the way in which the dead were transported from the places in which they died to the shores of Palestine. Since in Jewish law the proximity of a corpse causes defilement, if the body of a deceased was transported on a ship, it was put in one corner of the ship, and when the time for prayers arrived the passengers and sailors retired to another corner to be able to recite the prayers at a distance from the source of impurity.[47]

In addition to reciting the obligatory daily prayers, Jewish sailors and passengers used to pray frequently and spontaneously. It seems to have been customary to say a prayer before setting out on a sea voyage, and to request a friend or relative who had the reputation of great piety to pray for the voyager. Such a request addressed by Rabh Nathan Kohen to his brother Rabbi Hiyya was referred to above.[48] From the apocryphal Wisdom of Solomon (date uncertain) it appears that among the pagans of antiquity, too, it was customary to pray before setting out on a voyage on the sea.[49]

If a ship was caught in a storm, both Jew and gentile aboard would pray, each to his own god. The earliest evidence of this is found in the Book of Jonah (Jon. 1:5), discussed earlier. A Tannaitic source tells of a wise Jewish child who admonished the gentile sailors to pray not to their idols but to "Him who created the sea," and of the Jewish sailors' custom of fasting and blowing the shofar in the hour of danger on high seas.[50] In Numbers 10:9 the Talmudic sages see an allusion to the effect that God will help those of His people who are in danger on the sea.[51] It was well known to the sages of the Mishna that the day on which a gentile reached his destination after a sea voyage was celebrated by him as a feast day with prayers and thanksgiving offerings.[52]

The Sabbath

Sea voyages in ancient times usually lasted many days, and thus Jewish sailors and passengers were compelled to spend the day of rest, the Sabbath, on board. In this connection a number of regulations were promulgated by the sages in order to define precisely what was allowed and what was forbidden to a Jew sailing on the Sabbath. Since riding or sitting in any vehicle on the Sabbath was forbidden, precautions had to be taken to avoid even the suspicion that one embarked on a ship with the intention of spending the Sabbath aboard. Hence it was ruled that one had to board the ship at least three days prior to the Sabbath, that is, not later in the week than on Wednesday. Only if the purpose of the voyage was to perform a religious or pious act was it permitted to embark later in the week, even on a Friday.[53] Moreover, according to one Tannaitic opinion, it was necessary to come to an agreement with the skipper to the effect that he would break the voyage for the Sabbath, even though one knew that such an agreement was not likely to be kept.[54]

In order to give an outward indication of observing the Sabbath rest on board the ship, the more strict among the sages remained put during that whole day within a space of four cubits, which they occupied before the onset of the Sabbath. Tannaitic sources record that once (in the second century CE) four leading sages sailed from Brundisium (Brindisi) in southern Italy to Palestine. Such a trip inevitably involved spending the Sabbath aboard. During the day of rest, two of the sages, Rabban Gamliel and Rabbi Eleazar ben Azarya, walked about freely on the ship, while the two others, Rabbi Joshua and Rabbi Akiba, who wanted to observe the Sabbath rest as strictly as possible, did not move outside of their four cubits.[55] The Halakhah (traditional religious law) was fixed according to the more liberal spirit of Rabban Gamliel and Rabbi Eleazar ben Azarya.[56]

Another problem that had to be solved by religious legislation was whether it was permissible to disembark on the Sabbath. Again, the Halakhah was fixed according to what is reported as an actual event. A ship on which Rabban Gamliel and several other sages sailed reached port shortly after sunset on Friday, that is, after the onset of the Sabbath. His companions asked Rabban Gamliel, "Are we permitted to go ashore?" His answer was, "You are permitted to disembark, for I observed that we had already reached the Sabbath limits [reckoned from the port] before it became dark."[57] That is to say, the ship was within two thousand cubits of the port before the Sabbath began. The Halakhah was fixed accordingly: "When a ship enters port,[58] the passengers may disembark only if it was within the Sabbath limits before it became dark."[59] If the landing gangway was put out especially for a Jew on the Sabbath, he was not allowed to go ashore by it; if, however, it was run out for the convenience of non-Jews, he was permitted to cross by it to the shore.[60]

With regard to the Sabbath laws, the cabins of a ship were equated with the private homes on dry land: the carrying of objects within them was permitted, just as one was permitted to carry about objects within one's own home. The deck of the ship, on the other hand, was equated with a courtyard common to several houses: hence carrying objects on it was prohibited.[61] In addition, it is expressly stated that it was forbidden to carry about on the Sabbath any wooden part of the ship.[62] On the other hand, it was permissible to move the anchor,[63] probably because it was deemed essential for the safety of the ship and its passengers. It should be noted that all these rules are contained in Tannaitic sources, that is, they were promulgated in Palestine not later than the second century CE. They thus reflect the reactions of Palestinian sages to religious problems that arose in connection with sailing on the Mediterranean, which evidently was an activity often engaged in by the Jewish community for which the Tannaites acted as religious legislators. The laws discussed below are also of the same provenance.

If a ship stood in the water higher than ten handbreadths (about 36 inches), it was prohibited to remove anything from it or to bring anything aboard on the Sabbath.[64] However, one was permitted to throw any object from the sea to the shore or vice versa, or from the sea into a ship, or from one ship into another.[65] These rules were ad hoc applications of the general Sabbath laws that prohibited the carrying of anything on that day from one house to another, or from a private property to a public domain, that is, from a house to a street or to a courtyard, and vice versa. To avoid the considerable inconvenience caused by these rules, a legal fiction was resorted to: a symbolic act was performed by which a continuity or commonality was created among the dwellings that surrounded a common courtyard. It consisted of preparing a dish of food to which all families who lived in the homes in question contributed a share. The dish was then deposited in one of the dwellings, and by this act, called *'eruv*, all the houses around the courtyard became a common dwelling, and thus the carrying of objects among them was permissible. A similar *'eruv* was used to make the carrying of objects from one ship to another permissible on the Sabbath, if the ships were lashed to one another with cables. If, however, the ships were not lashed together but anchored alongside one another, even if they touched each other, the resort to such an *'eruv* remained ineffective, and the carrying of objects from one of the ships to another remained prohibited.[66]

Since it was forbidden to fetch anything from the sea to the ship on the Sabbath, the question arose whether it was allowed to draw water from the sea on that holy day of rest. To make that permissible, it was ruled by Tannaitic sages that a plank should be run out from the deck over the water, and then the water that lay under the plank was considered part of the ship and could be drawn aboard.[67] Also, it was permitted to pour waste water over the side of the ship, whence it flowed down into the sea.[68]

The knotting of ropes was an important part of the sailors' skills, and conditions encountered by the ship made it necessary to make knots when and as the need arose. The sages (we are again dealing with Palestinian Tannaites) decreed that it was forbidden on the Sabbath to make a permanent "sailor's knot"; a temporary knot, however, which was frequently slipped and knotted again, might be made on the Sabbath.[69] This ruling made it impermissible on a Sabbath to bind the rigging loops to the head of the mast, since that was done by a permanent lashing. On the other hand, it was allowable to pass ropes through these loops, for that had to be done each time anew.[70] As to the mats used as awnings to protect the cargo, the opinions of Rabh and Shemuel, two leading third-century CE Babylonian sages, were divided: according to Shemuel it was permitted to move them on the Sabbath, while according to Rabh it was forbidden.[71] As we have seen above (Chapter 8), some Jewish skippers interpreted the religious prohibitions of doing any work on the Sabbath so strictly that they would not even touch the rudder on that day. It certainly was not easy to be an observant Jew and a sailor at the same time.

There was no difference of opinion among the sages, nor among the Jewish sailors, as to the liberty to violate the Sabbath in order to save the ship from being wrecked in a storm,[72] in accordance with the general principle that "the duty of saving life supersedes the Sabbath laws."[73] What this meant in practice we saw in the case of the ultra-pious Jewish skipper Amarantus, who was captain of his ship and plied the Mediterranean about 400 CE (Chapter 8).

Holidays

Passover. If a person set out on a sea voyage within thirty days before the Feast of Unleavened Bread, he had to remove from his house everything containing leavened substance—an observance ordinarily carried out on the eve of the Pesaḥ (Passover)—for he could not count on being able to return home from his voyage before the feast.[74] Rabbi Yehuda (a Palestinian Tanna of the early second century CE) tried to forbid sailing on the five days of the half-holiday intervening between the first and the last (the seventh) days of the holiday of Passover, but this was not accepted and did not become part of the Halakhah. Only the inhabitants of Mesha, a locality in northern Galilee, undertook voluntarily to observe this stricture.[75] Some time later, however, their descendants found that it was too difficult for them to follow the usage of their fathers, and they approached Rabbi Yehuda ha-Nasi, the head of the Palestinian Jewish community in the second half of the second century CE, who incidentally was a pupil of the aforementioned Rabbi Yehuda, and asked him, "Our fathers refrained from sailing on the Great Sea [the Mediterranean] on the Passover half-holiday, now, as for us, what are we to do?" Rabbi Yehuda's response was, "Seeing that your fathers took upon themselves this prohibition, do not deviate from the usage of your fathers."[76] Apart from the religious issue, what is interesting for us in this exchange between Rabbi Yehuda and the people of Mesha is that the inhabitants of a small Galilean town in the late second century CE were so involved with seafaring that not to sail on the five days in question was for them a deprivation from which they tried to be released.

The religious duty to sell before Passover all the *hametz*, foodstuff containing leavened substance, also had to be observed by Jews sailing in ships. A Tannaitic source discusses the situation in which a Jew and a gentile travel in a ship on the day before Passover. The ruling is that the Jew must sell the gentile all his *hametz*, or else give it to him as a present; then, after the seven days of the Passover, he can buy it back from him.[77] A Jewish passenger also had to comport himself aboard ship exactly as was incumbent on him in his own home: he had to search his quarters on the ship and collect any *hametz* he might find. In his home the next step was to burn the *hametz* ritually; aboard the ship he had instead to grind it into dust and cast it overboard.[78]

The Jewish calendar was regulated by the phases of the moon. The day on which the new moon was first sighted was taken to be the first day of the new month. The fixing of this day was of great religious importance, because on it depended the date of the holy days: Passover started on the fifteenth of the month Nissan, New Year's day was on the first of the month Tishri, and so on. The fixing of the day of the new moon was the prerogative of the central religious authorities of Palestine, who then sent fire signals or messengers to all parts of the country to inform the people of the date and to enable them to celebrate the ensuing feasts on the proper days.[79] Such signals or messengers could, of course, not reach Jews sailing on the high sea, who therefore remained uncertain as to the correct date on which the Passover began. To solve the problem, Rabbi Nahman[80] advised the Jewish seafarers: "Since you do not know which day has been fixed as that of the new moon, burn the *hametz* as soon as you see that the moon shines until dawn."[81] In the sequel to this passage, the Talmud states that, although on land the moon is visible until dawn only on the fifteenth day of the month, at sea, where the sailors have an unobstructed view of the entire horizon, they can see the moon until dawn as early as the fourteenth day of the month, and thus they are able to observe the burning of the *hametz* on that day, as demanded by the Halakhah.

Tabernacles (or *Sukkoth*, "Booths"). The ritual of this feast, celebrated in the autumn from the fifteenth to the twenty-first day of the month of

Tishri, consisted of reciting, on each day of the feast, the prescribed benediction over the festal wreath, the *lulabh*. Moreover, for the duration of the feast one had to dwell and take one's meals in a booth built especially for the feast and covered with a roofing of green branches. Even though sailing at this time of the year was considered inadvisable, occasionally Palestinian Jews did venture out to the sea in the days of this feast.[82] If they did so, they would provide themselves in advance with *lulabhs*,[83] and also would build themselves booths on the foredeck. On one occasion Rabbi Akiba built himself a *sukkah* (booth) on the foredeck of a ship, but the next day a strong wind blew away his structure.[84]

Purim. Even though this feast fell at the end of the winter season (fourteenth of the month of Adar, February–March), when the sea was considered "closed" to maritime traffic, it nevertheless happened that urgent business overseas forced Palestinian Jews to brave the inclement weather of this season. In that case it was their religious duty to celebrate the feast of Purim on board ship by reading the Book of Esther in the same manner they did on land in the synagogues of their home towns.[85]

Rabbinical sources contain no information as to whether Jews sailed on the other holy days of their ritual year, and if they did, how they observed them on board ship.

Ritual Purity

The question of ritual purity and impurity played an important role in Jewish religious life in Talmudic days. There were objects that might become ritually impure, whereas others were not subject to ritual defilement even if brought into contact with a ritually impure object. Ships in general were regarded as immune to ritual impurity,[86] but certain small boats were susceptible to it. Among the latter were the small Jordan boats called ʿarebhath haYarden, as well as small vessels made of clay.[87] When a ship was launched the first time, in order to make its hull watertight (see above, Chapter 3), the same water that caused it to be wet could also make it susceptible to ritual impurity.[88]

The principal source of ritual impurity was the human corpse. One need not even touch a corpse directly to become ritually impure; it was sufficient to enter a room in which there was a corpse, and immediately the ritual impurity of the dead body communicated itself across the empty space of the room. However, the application of this rule to a ship would have caused undue hardship to everybody; hence the sages ruled that as long as the ship sailed on the sea, it did not render the passengers ritually impure. But as soon as the ship was made fast to the shore, or its anchor was dropped, it did communicate ritual impurity to all the passengers aboard.[89] The same held good not only for ships in general but also for individual cabins aboard ship.[90]

Moreover, although houses in general were liable to become ritually impure through what was called in biblical legislation a "plague of leprosy in a house" (Lev 14:34–57),[91] cabins built on board ships or rafts remained ritually pure even though they exhibited signs of such "leprosy."[92]

A water tank of an "Alexandrian ship" that contained at least forty *seahs* (or about 120 gallons) of water and had a flat bottom transmitted ritual impurity to a person or object if the latter remained underneath it together with a corpse.[93] This ritual ruling indicates that such a big water tank stood on legs, so that a person as well as a corpse could find space beneath it. The water tank itself, however, was not liable to becoming ritually impure.[94] On the other hand, the water tank of a small ship was liable to become ritually impure either from a corpse or from "leprosy," since such a tank contained less than forty *seahs* of water.[95]

The sails of a ship were also liable to ritual impurity.[96] The packing bags aboard a ship, if they became loosened and opened, could become ritually impure if an impure person trod on them.[97] Similarly, implements or vessels made out of the *ʿeqel* (the ballast; see Chapter 3) of a ship were liable to become ritually impure.[98] On the other hand, the water that entered the ship through the oar ports or collected in the bilge well could not render any object wetted by it ritually impure.[99] The baked-clay "swimmer's barrel," probably used by swimmers as a float, was itself liable to becoming ritually impure.[100]

On board ship many people met who knew nothing of one another, and therefore the danger was always present that a person could become ritually polluted by the touch or proximity of an impure person. Talmudic legislation lays down the rules covering such ritual contagion on board ship. If a ritually pure person finds himself on board a big ship together with a *zabh*, a man suffering from a discharge (gonorrhea?), and hence ritually impure, he does not become impure.[101] Other rules deal with such problems as the possible defilement caused by menstruating women to ritually pure persons or vessels on board;[102] the pollution of wine owned by Jews and transported on a ship if a gentile should touch it;[103] the effect of a wave that sweeps overboard and wets objects found there and thereby renders them liable to ritual impurity.[104]

In order to be able to partake of meat on board a ship during a long sea voyage, Jewish passengers would take with them live animals to be ritually slaughtered and consumed. Since ritual slaughter required the covering of blood with earth, they were obliged, as already mentioned, to carry along some earth for this purpose. If, however, they had no earth at hand, they were allowed to slaughter the animal in such a manner that its blood would flow directly into the sea, or else cover the blood with earth as soon as they reached land. According to one Palestinian Tannaitic opinion, however, the covering of the blood with earth was so indispensable that the slaughterer was enjoined to burn his *tallith* (prayer shawl) and cover the blood with its ashes if he had no earth available.[105]

Missing Persons and Tithing

Talmudic legislation relating to seafaring also deals with the legal position of a woman whose husband was missing at sea. As long as there was no definite proof that the husband was actually dead, his wife was regarded as a married woman with all the obligations and rights this status entailed.[106] In order to spare the woman the complications attendant to this situation, a man would give instructions before embarking on a sea voyage that his wife should be given a *get*, a letter of divorce, in the event he failed to return home.[107] Talmudic legislation also discusses the status of a woman whose husband was seen falling into water but was not seen reaching shore. The ruling was that in such a case, if the body of water in question was small, so that all its shores were visible, and it could be observed that the man did not emerge from it anywhere, he was presumed to have drowned, and his wife was considered a widow, and could remarry. If, however, that man fell into "water that had no end," that is, into the sea, whose shores could not be seen, there was always the possibility that he reached shore somewhere unobserved, and hence in that case his wife was not considered a widow and could not remarry.[108]

Finally, the Palestinian Tannaites directed their attention to the question of whether or not fruits and vegetables grown or carried aboard ships coming from foreign lands were liable to tithes, since the rule was that fruits and vegetables grown in foreign parts were not subject to tithes, but those grown in Eretz Israel were. The decision of the Palestinian Tannaites was that the law of tithes became applicable to fruit grown or carried aboard and belonging to Jews as soon as the ship reached the shores of Eretz Israel.[109]

Chapter 11

SIMILES AND PARABLES

IN ADDITION to the technical, historical, and legal aspects of seafaring presented above, ancient Jewish sources supply us with material of quite a different kind: with similes and parables in which references to the sea, ships, and sailors are used to illustrate human thought, wishes, and experiences, as well as events in many different spheres of life. These similes and parables show that seafaring and experiences connected with the sea lived in the imagination of the people, even of those who took no direct part in seafaring but were nevertheless well aware of its attraction, problems, dangers, rewards, and significance in general.

THE SAND AND THE SEA IN BIBLICAL SIMILES

The sand on the shore of the sea which cannot be measured is a picture that recurs frequently in the Bible when reference is being made to something too multitudinous to be counted. God's promise of numerous descendants, given to Abraham and the other fathers of Israel, is repeatedly couched in such terms as "I will multiply thy seed as the stars of the heavens and the sand which is upon the seashore," or, "as the sand of the sea which cannot be numbered for multitude" (Gen. 22:17; 32:13. Cf. also 2 Sam. 17:11; 1 Kings 4:20; Jer. 32:22; Hos. 2:1). Again we read that "Joseph gathered corn as the sand of the sea, very much" (Gen. 41:49). The armies of the kings who opposed Joshua were "even as the sand that is upon the sea shore in multitude" (Josh. 11:4). The camels of the Midianites and Amalekites who fought Gideon were "without number as the sand by the sea for multitude" (Judg. 7:12). In the poetic language of the Psalmist, the quails sent by God to serve as food for the Children of Israel in the desert are described as "feathered fowls like as the sand of the sea" (Ps. 27:27). Of the sad plight of the people of Jerusalem after its destruction Jeremiah says: "Their widows are increased to me above the sand of the seas" (Jer. 15:8).

Even the number of days in a long life is compared to the sand. When Job speaks of his old age, he says, "I shall multiply my days as the sand" (Job 29:18). The simile "like the sand of the sea" was so commonly used that it lost its original picturesque meaning; it acquired a purely metaphorical sense, and was used as a simile not only for something numerous but also for something large. Thus we get a statement such as "God gave Solomon . . . largeness of heart even as the sand that is on the sea shore" (1 Kings 5:9). A somewhat different simile refers not to the large number of the sand grains, but to their weight: Job says that if his "calamity were laid in balances" it would be found "heavier than the sand of the seas" (Job 6:2–3).

The sea itself figures as a symbol of restlessness and of rebellious strength: "The wicked are like the troubled sea, for it cannot rest, and its waters cast up mire and dirt" (Isa. 57:20). Job asks God in despair: "Am I the sea or a dragon that Thou settest a watch over me?" (Job 7:12). The allusion is to the ancient myth of the primeval dragon that symbolized the sea and had to be subdued when God created the world.[1]

The rumbling of the approaching enemy brings to the prophet's mind the sound of the stormy sea: "Their voice is like the roaring sea" (Jer. 6:23). The Psalmist compares the power of God with the might of the sea: "Above the voices of many waters mightier are the breakers of the sea, mightiest is the Lord on high" (Ps. 93:4).

Both disaster and righteousness are compared to the sea: "O, virgin daughter of Zion! Thy breach is great like the sea!" (Lam. 2:13). "O that thou wouldest hearken to my commandments! Then would thy peace be as a river, and thy righteousness as the waves of the sea" (Isa. 48:18). Also "the earth shall be full of the knowledge of the Lord as the waters cover the sea" (Isa. 11:9); and again, "The earth shall be filled with the knowledge of the glory of the Lord, as the waters cover the sea" (Hab. 2:14).

SAND AND SEA IN THE TALMUD

Similes drawn from the sea and its waves punctuate Talmudic literature. The shellfish from which the Tyrian purple dye was produced is stated to be "similar to the sea, and the sea is similar to the firmament, and the firmament is similar to the sapphire stone, and the sapphire stone is similar to the Seat of Glory."[2]

The teachings of the Torah are compared to the waves of the sea: "Just as in this sea, between one great wave and the other there are small waves, so between one teaching and the other there are subtleties and details of the Torah."[3]

Rabbi Eliezer said at the time of his illness: "Much Torah did I learn, and yet I did not subtract from [the learning of] my masters even as much as a dog licking from the sea."[4]

The beauty of the waves was deemed of a higher order than that of golden decorations:

Whosoever has not seen the Temple while it stood, never saw a beautiful building. Which Temple? Abbaye, and according to others, Rabh Ḥisda, said: "The building of Herod." Of what material did he build it? Rabba said: "Of marble and polished stone." Others said: "Of marble, blue marble, and polished stone." One row of stones was set in deeply, and one row was protruding, so that it might hold the lime. He wanted to plate the walls with gold, but the sages said to him: "Let it be, for this way it is more beautiful, for it looks like the waves of the sea."[5]

SHIPS IN BIBLICAL SIMILES

In addition to Ezekiel's ship metaphor for Tyre (see above, Chapter 2), the Bible contains a number of similes in which various things are explicitly compared to ships. Isaiah compares the vanquished enemy to a damaged ship: "Thy tacklings are loosened, they do not hold the stand of their mast, they do not spread the sail" (Isa. 33:23). The drunkard is addressed in the Book of Proverbs thus: "Yea, thou shalt be as he that lieth down in the midst of the sea, or as he that lieth upon the top of a mast" (Prov. 23:34). The virtuous housewife is described in the same book: "She is like the merchant-ships, she bringeth her food from afar" (Prov. 31:14). Job complains that his days "are passed away like papyrus boats" (Job. 9:26), that is, they are gone rapidly and are no more.

The verse that is traditionally translated as "We bring our years to an end as a sigh" or "as a tale that is told" or "as a passing thought" (Ps. 90:9; the Hebrew word is *hegeh*), is explained in a Midrash by Rabbi Yehuda son of Rabbi Simon, "We spent our days like unto a rudder," taking the word *hegeh* to mean "rudder," which indeed is one of its meanings.[6] The apocryphal Wisdom of Solomon likewise compares the swift passing of life to that of a ship: "As a ship passing through the billowing water, whereof, when it is gone by, there is no trace to be found, neither pathway of its keel in the billows . . . So we also, as soon as we were born, ceased to be."[7]

In another apocryphal book, the Testament of Naphtali, the misfortunes that befell the People of Israel as a result of the disagreements between the tribes of Judah and Joseph (that is, the kingdoms of Judah and Israel), are spoken of as the distress of a ship on the stormy sea.[8]

SHIP SIMILES IN TALMUDIC LITERATURE

A fuller version of the last-mentioned parable, which speaks of the disagreement between Judah and Israel as a shipwreck, has come down to us in a medieval Midrash, given here in a literal translation:

And again I saw in my dream that we, all the twelve tribes, stood with our father Jacob by the shore of the sea. And behold, a great ship was sailing in the heart of the sea with nobody on it. And our father said to us: "See you anything?" And we said to him: "A sort of a ship do we see which sails in the sea without captain and without pilot." And Jacob took off his garments and waded into the sea and all of us followed, and ahead went Levi and Yehuda, who jumped into the ship, and our father Jacob with them. And in the ship were all the riches of the world, and all of us boarded it.

And Jacob their father said to them: "Look upon the mast and see what is written thereon, for there exists no ship in the world on which they do not inscribe the name of its master." And Levi and Yehuda looked, and saw, and behold, it was written on the mast, "This ship belongs to Ben Berakhel with all the riches in it." [Berakhel is the Aggadic name of Isaac; Ben Berakhel, "the son of Berakhel," is Jacob.] When Jacob heard this, he was exceedingly happy, and gave praise and thanks to God. And he said: "As though it were not enough that God blessed me on land, He has added to me in the sea!" And our father said to us: "My sons, let each one now be strong, and each one take his share in navigating the ship!"

Immediately Levi climbed up the big mast, and Yehuda climbed up the second mast, and they sat thereon. And the other brothers grasped the oars, and Jacob took hold of the rudder to steer the ship.

And Joseph alone remained, and he did not take hold of anything. Jacob said to him: "Grasp one oar!" But he would not listen to his father. Thereupon Jacob said to him: "My son, approach, and take hold of the rudder and steer the ship, and your brothers will row with the oars until we reach the shore. And steer the ship slowly, and fear not, and be not alarmed by the waves of the sea and the stormy wind."

And it happened that when Jacob finished instructing his sons, he disappeared from them. And Joseph took hold of the two rudders, one from the right and one from the left, and his brothers grasped the oars, and they steered the ship, and it sailed on the water. And Levi and Yehuda sat on the masts to see that it followed a straight course.

As long as Joseph was agreed with Yehuda, he steered the ship on the right course and directed it without hindrance. But as time went on, a quarrel broke out between Joseph and Yehuda, and they did not take care of the ship as their father had instructed them, and they led it on a tortuous path, and the waves of the sea smote it against the rocks, and the ship was about to break up.

And Levi and Yehuda descended from the masts to save themselves, as also did the other brothers: each of them saved himself and they came to the shore. And also our father came there, and he found us driven hither and thither. He said to us: "Perhaps you did not steer the ship well as I instructed you?" And we said to him: "Upon thy life, we did not depart from your orders, except Joseph, who sinned against your commands, and he was wroth with Levi and Yehuda in his jealousy of them. And it is for this reason that the ship went on a tortuous path and sank."

Our father said to us: "Show me the place!" They said to him: "It is where the waves foam." And Jacob looked, and behold, the heads of the masts were visible. And he gathered us around him, and threw himself first into the sea, and took the ship, and healed it [repaired it]. And he and his sons entered it, and he reprimanded Joseph, and said to him: "My son, do not continue to anger your brothers, for they almost perished through you." And Joseph said: "I will not do it again."

This lengthy and detailed parable is an indictment of Joseph, that is, of the tribes of Efrayim and Menasheh, the two sons of Joseph, who, after the death of Solomon, broke away from his son and their King Rehoboam, and set themselves up as an independent kingdom, often in enmity with the Kingdom of Judah.

The comparison of the drunkard to one who lies on the top of a mast is elaborated in a Midrash: "Like unto this ship that sleeps in the heart of the sea . . . Like unto this captain, who sits upon the top of the mast, swaying back and forth, back and forth. . . ."[10]

A pious gentile who dies uncircumcised is compared to a ship: "Our masters said: It is a pity if a ship sets sail without having paid the customs."[11] Setting sail is here a metaphor for dying. A ship that sails without having paid the customs dues is about to encounter troubles; likewise a gentile, even if he was pious, if he dies without having been circumcised, can expect trouble in afterlife. The same saying was known also to Jewish women of the Talmudic age in the Aramaic vernacular.[12]

The well-known proverb, "All Israel are responsible for one another" is illustrated by Rabbi Shim'on ben Yohai in a parable: "An example [mashal]. Like unto people who were sitting in a boat. One of them took a drill, and began to drill beneath himself. His companions said to him: 'What are you sitting and doing?' He replied: 'What business is it of yours? Am I not drilling beneath myself?' They said to him: 'But the water will rise and flood the ship upon all of us.'"[13] The lesson contained in the parable is not explained, but it did not have to be: all the listeners understood that it spoke of the wrongful behavior of a single Jew that can cause a calamity for the entire people.

According to Rabbi Yohanan it is incumbent upon a man to seek diligently the way in which he may fulfill a commandment, like the captain of a ship who seeks the right way for his ship on the sea.[14]

The leader of a generation was called "the captain of the ship." The Talmud, in telling of Abraham's death, exclaims, "Woe to the ship that has lost its captain!" When the sages wished to reproach Rabban Gamliel, they said to him: "Woe to the ship that has you for its captain!"[15]

A Midrashic comment compares the fate of the People of Israel "to one who has fallen into the water. The captain has flung a rope to him, and said: 'Grasp this rope in your hands, and do not let it go, for if you let it go you have no life!' Even so said the Holy One, blessed be He, unto Israel: 'Keep the commandments. Ye that did cleave unto the Lord your God are alive every one of you this day' (Deut. 4:2, 4). And so it is said, 'Take fast hold of the instruction [*musar*], let her not go, keep her, for she is thy life'" (Prov. 4:13).[16]

What God did and does for Israel is compared to the acts of a king in charge of warships:

> Like unto a king who sailed with his sons on the sea, and pirates' ships surrounded them. He said unto them: "Behold, prepared are my warships [*liburnae*] in which I cross the waves and with which I fight." Even so the Holy One, blessed be He, said to them: "O ye wicked ones, do you plot against my children? Prepared are my warships [*liburnae*]." As it is written, "He saved them for His name's sake" (Ps. 106:8).[17]

So long as the people of Israel study the Torah, they need not fear any attack. The ship parable of Rabh Huna illustrating this thesis was presented above. We have heard the parable of the ships tied together in the harbor, upon which the royal palace can safely stand. The parable illustrates the idea that the very security of Israel depends on their doing the will of God (Chapter 3).

The dependence of Abraham upon his wife Sarah is made explicit by comparing it to the dependence of the captain upon his ship:

> An example [*mashal*]. It is like unto a brave captain who had a ship and conquered the waters and the winds. Pirates attacked him, but he stood up to them and killed all of them. After a time he came to the entrance of a harbor, and a strong wind rose against him, and his ship was wrecked. Thereupon he began to ask for mercy from the people: "I entreat you, save me!" They said to him: "Only yesterday you were a conqueror of the waters, you killed the pirates, and now you beg others that they should save you?" He said to them: "So long as my ship was whole, I was strong and needed no help; but now that my ship is broken, my strength is broken." Even so Abraham the hero: pirates came against him, but he stood up to them and killed them all, as it is written "And he divided himself against them by night, he and his servants, and smote them" (Gen. 14:15). They said to him, "Only yesterday you ruled the whole world, as it is written, "Blessed be Abram of God Most High" (Gen. 14:19), and now you say, "I am a stranger and a sojourner" (Gen. 23:4)? He said to them: "What can I do, for my wife died, as it is written, "That I may bury my dead" (ibid.). Immediately "Abraham became old" (Gen. 24:1).[18]

No greater accolade than this to the importance of a wife in a man's life can be imagined, or, indeed, can be found in ancient Jewish literature.

The roles Noah and Moses played in the history of their people are compared to the acts of two ships' captains:

> What are they like unto? Two ships which sailed on the sea, and there were in them two captains. One of them saved himself, but did not save his ship; and one of them saved both himself and his ship. Whom will people praise? Surely the one who saved both himself and his ship. Even so Noah saved only himself, but Moses saved both himself and his generation.[19]

We have seen above that in a Midrashic parable birth was compared to a ship leaving port, and death to the ship reaching its port of destination. The voyage of a ship as a metaphor for human life occurs elsewhere, too, in the Midrash. Acording to the skeptical view of the preacher, it is better not to be born than to be born, for "he that hath not seen the sun nor known it, hath more rest than the other" (Eccl. 6:5). The Midrash illustrates this with a parable taken from the life and experiences of the seafarers who, when going ashore in a seaside city, see there many precious things that they are unable to acquire, and return to their ship unhappy.

> An example. Like unto two men who were sailing in a ship. When they reached a harbor, one of them went ashore and entered the town, and saw there all sorts of food and drink, and contentment. When he returned to the ship he said to his friend: "Why did you not visit the town?" His friend responded: "And you, who did go ashore and enter the town, what did you see there?" He said to him: "I saw all sorts of food and drink, and contentment." The other said to him: "And did you enjoy it?" He said, "No." His friend said: "I, who did not visit the town, am better off than you, for I did not go ashore and did not see." This is the meaning of what is written "This hath more rest than the other."[20]

The Book of Esther tells of King Ahasuerus that he ordered his officers "that they should do according to every man's pleasure" (Esther 1:8). The Midrash asserts that this was an order impossible to fulfill, and illustrates this view with a parable of two ships seeking opposite winds when trying to leave the harbor, which we have quoted above (see Chapter 7). We have also seen the parables illustrating the difference between the acts of a mortal king and the creative work of God, and the similarity between the work of a shipbuilder and the nation of Edom inviting kings from different places (Chapter 3).

More down to earth are those similes in which objects or shapes are compared to ships: the letter *waw* in the name Wayzatha (one of the sons of Haman, Esther 9:9) should be given, according to the Talmud, an elongated form, so as to resemble the rudder of a *liburna*.[21] The loaves of bread offered in the Jerusalem Temple had the form of a "dancing ship."[22] The ladle used to draw wine from the jug is stated to have had the shape of a ship floating in the sea.[23] The red and purple stuffs in the palace of King Ahasuerus were folded around silver rods "like unto this sail of a ship."[24]

The transitory nature of riches in the world is made vivid by comparing them to the pails used in emptying the bilge water of a ship: the empty one becomes full, the full one empty.[25]

The setting of the sun and the days of the year are compared to parts contained in a ship:

> Rabbi Shemuel bar Naḥmani said: "The sun goes like unto the sail of a ship." Rabbi Berekhya said: "Like unto a ship that comes from Carmania, and has 365 ropes corresponding to the number of days in the solar year. [Or] like a ship that comes from Alexandria and has 354 ropes corresponding to the number of the days in the lunar year."[26]

The earth itself is stretched over the abysses (*tehomoth*) like unto a ship that sails in the heart of the seas.[27] This world is like unto the land, and the world to come is like unto the sea, "and if one does not prepare for himself on land, what will one eat on the sea?"[28]

Emotional and mental states, too, are compared to ships' parts. The power of the evil inclination in a man's heart is apt to grow: in the begininning it is like a spider's thread, but in the end it is like a ship's rope.[29] The insatiability of man is like the loop through which the rope is led, and which never becomes filled up. The rope and the loop serve also as the simile for death: the departure of the soul from the body is as difficult as the passing of the rope through the loop.[30]

The abundance of such comparisons to ships and parts of ships, touching not only on people's external but on their internal lives as well, shows that in the mental world of the Jews, as in their economic activities and legal relations, ships played a significant role. By the Talmudic age, certainly, they had become prominent figures in the Jewish imagination.

Chapter 12

SEA LEGENDS AND
SAILORS' TALES

IN COMING NOW to present the myths and legends that circulated among the ancient Hebrews and Jews about the sea and seafaring, we have to go back to our biblical sources. Although the references to sea legends contained in the Bible are fragmentary, they enable us to form some idea of the mythical mirror in which the ancient Hebrews saw the sea and which both influenced and expressed their attitude to that most formidable and elemental part of nature.

It has been noted by several biblical scholars that in the sober, matter-of-fact account of the creation of the world given in Genesis 1 it is not stated that God created the sea, but that the abyss (Hebrew *t'hom*) and water (Hebrew *mayim*) are mentioned as preexisting entities. Other biblical books are less reticent, and in them we find brief statements that read as references to well-known myths. From them we learn that among the biblical Hebrews there existed a mythical tradition according to which the sea resisted God's creative work, so that He had to use force against it. Job 26:12 states:

> With His power He stilled the sea,
> And by His understanding He smote Rahab,
> By His wind the heavens were made fair,
> His hand pierced the twisting serpent.

Rahab is the name of a mythical sea monster, or rather of the mythical embodiment of the sea; evidently a lost ancient Hebrew myth knew that it dared to oppose God at the time of creation.

As for, "the twisting serpent," it is an epithet of Leviathan, another sea monster of which Job knew (Job 40:25), and whose enormous size and power he describes in some detail: Leviathan "laugheth at the rattling of the javelin" (41:21), and "maketh the deep to boil like a pot, he maketh the sea like a seething mixture" (v. 23). Yet, despite the awesome power of the sea, God set limits to it:

> Who shut up the sea with doors,
> When it broke forth and issued from the womb?
> When I [God] made the cloud its garment,
> And thick darkness its swaddling band,

And prescribed for it My decree,
And set bars and doors and said,
Thus far shalt thou come, no further,
And here shall thy proud waves be stayed.

(Job 38:8–11)

To make sure that the sea, or the dragon (Hebrew *tannin*) who likewise personified it, did not transgress the boundaries drawn for it by God, He set a watch over it (Job 7:12). However, in Job's mythical imagination there existed masters of enchantment, who knew how to "curse the day, who were skilled in rousing up Leviathan" (Job 3:8), and thereby endangered the world order as established by God.

The discovery of the Ugaritic texts in the northeastern corner of the Mediterranean, dating from about the fourteenth century BCE, has thrown much light on the enigmatic figure of Leviathan. In one passage, Mot (the god of death) addresses Baal (the chief god of vegetative life): "You smote Litan [Leviathan] the twisting serpent [and] made an end of the crooked serpent, the tyrant with the seven heads." This is almost exactly duplicated by Isaiah (27:1), who, however, transposes the event from the mythical past into the eschatological future: "In that day Yahweh, with His sore and great and strong sword, will punish Leviathan the twisting serpent, and Leviathan the crooked serpent, and He will slay the dragon that is in the sea." Evidently, the imagery of two mythical monsters called Leviathan (Litan), opposing the deity and slain by him, was a common *Kulturgut* of Ugarit and biblical Israel.

That Leviathan and the other sea monsters are personifications of the sea is confirmed by several other biblical references. Thus there is an evocative passage in Psalms 74:13–14, in which there is also an allusion to the many (seven?) heads of Leviathan: "Thou [God] didst break the sea in pieces by Thy strength, Thou didst shatter the heads of the sea monsters in the waters, Thou didst crush the heads of Leviathan, Thou gavest him to be food to the sharks of the sea." In another Psalm (89:10–11), the crushing of the heads of Rahab is associated with God's rule of the sea:

Thou rulest the proud swelling of the sea,
When its waves arise, Thou stillest them,
Thou didst crush Rahab as one that is slain,
With the arm of Thy power Thou didst scatter Thy enemies.

Next to these references to a primeval combat, in which Yahweh crushed Leviathan and thus tamed the sea, there survived in Hebrew folklore an image of Leviathan as the plaything of God, which illustrated better than any other image the infinite superiority of God even in relation to such a gigantic monster. Psalm 104:25–26 speaks of the wonders of the sea:

> Yonder sea, great and wide,
> There are creeping things innumerable,
> Living creatures both small and great,
> There go ships, [and] this Leviathan
> Whom Thou hast formed to play with.

The same idea is expressed in a passage in Job (40:29) in which Yahweh describes the frightening size and strength of Leviathan that make it impossible for an ordinary human to catch him with a fish hook, and asks

> Canst thou play with him as with a bird?
> Or canst thou bind him for thy maidens?

The unstated but evident answer is: no, you cannot; this is something only Yahweh can do.

Deutero-Isaiah, in holding out the promise of the redemption of Israel, combines the great myth of the primeval combat that preceded the creation of the world with the Hebrew national myth of the passage through the Red Sea. In doing so, he speaks of both Rahab and an unnamed dragon slain by God:

> Awake, awake, put on strength,
> O arm of Yahweh,
> Awake as in the days of old,
> The generations of ancient times.
> Art thou not it that hewed Rahab into pieces,
> Who pierced the dragon?
> Art thou not it that dried up the sea,
> The waters of the great deep,
> That made the depths of the sea a way
> For the redeemed to pass over?
>
> (Isa. 51:9–10)

But to return from sea monsters to the sea itself, of all the created things it was the sea alone that resisted God's verbal creative fiat, so that He had to rebuke it and even use force against it. Alluding to a lost myth that must have told about the sea's reluctance to obey God, the Prophet Habakkuk says,

> Is it, O Yahweh, against the rivers,
> Is Thy wrath kindled against the sea?
> That Thou dost ride upon Thy horses,
> Upon Thy chariots of victory!
> . . .

Thou hast trodden the sea with Thy horses,
The foaming of mighty waters . . .

(Hab. 3:8, 15)

The association of a divine power with horses riding upon the billowing sea reminds us of the Greek myths about the horses of Poseidon, god of the sea.

God's acts in relation to the sea often take the form of rebuking it. Isaiah (50:2) hears Yahweh say, "Behold, with My rebuke [Hebrew *b'ga'arati*, literally "with My angry shout"] I dry up the sea, I make the rivers a wilderness." The same verb and the same mythical image is used by Nahum (1:4): "He rebuketh the sea, and maketh it dry, and drieth up all the rivers." Likewise in Psalms (106:9), which speaks of Yahweh having "rebuked the Red Sea, and it was dried up" to allow the Children of Israel to pass through it. Apparently, even when speaking of this historical miracle the Psalmist was influenced by the ancient myth according to which the sea obeyed God only when He intimidated it with an angry shout.

The biblical books contain additional references to acts God performed with the sea, and all of them involve more than the superior, purely verbal fiats that were sufficient for creating everything else in the world. There can be little doubt that the power of the sea was so impressive for the ancient Hebrews (and for the other peoples whose myths influenced them) that they could not but imagine a primeval battle, or at least a confrontation, that had to take place between God and the sea before He could proceed with his work of creation.

We come now to post-biblical Rabbinical sources in which the sea is usually called "the great Oqyanos sea," the term "Oqyanos" being, of course, derived from the Greek *Okeanos*.[1] In Talmudic cosmology the ocean, or rather Tohu (Gen. 1:2), which was taken to refer to the ocean, was described as "a green line (*qaw* in Hebrew) that surrounds the whole earth."[2]

In Talmudic literature we find two distinct types of legendary material about the sea: one consists of accounts told by various sages, the other of tales quoted as having originated among sailors. As can be expected, the latter type is characterized by much wilder flights of fantasy than the former. Typical of the sea legends told by the sages is the tendency to cite miraculous events on the sea as illustrating the rewards one reaps from performing *mitzvoth*, religious-moral good deeds. In accordance with their moralistic worldview, the sages held that true piety was a safeguard in case of shipwreck. This is the basis of the following story told by Rabbi Akiba:

Once as I was sailing upon the sea I saw a ship going down, and my heart became filled with grief over a young scholar who I knew was among the passengers of that ship and must have drowned when it sank. But when I reached Cappadocia, lo and behold, I saw him approach, sit down before me, and ask questions. I said to him, "My son, how did you rise from the sea?" He said to me, "Rabbi, thanks to your prayers one wave carried me to another, and the other to yet another, until they brought me to the shore." I said to him: "My son, what good deed had you done?" He said, "As I was embarking on the ship, a poor man met me and said to me, 'Gain merit through me!' And I gave him a piece of bread. He said, 'Just as you restored my soul through your gift, even so may your soul be restored to you.'"[3]

Such miraculous friendliness of the waves toward the pious is attested in an even more marked manner in the following tale:

It happened to a pious man who was wont to give ample alms that once he went and embarked on a ship. The wind came, and his ship sank in the sea. Rabbi Akiba [sailing on another ship] saw this, and went to the Law Court to give evidence so that the wife of the drowned pious man might remarry. But before the time came for him to rise and give witness, the man appeared and approached him. Akiba said to him, "Are you he who was shipwrecked in the sea?" "Yes," answered the man. "And who raised you up from the sea?" "The alms I was wont to give," said the man, "they raised me up from the sea." "How do you know this?" asked Akiba. The man's answer was: "When I sank into the depths of the abyss, I heard a great tumult among the waves of the sea, and I heard the waves saying to another, 'Hurry up and let us raise up this man, for he has given alms all his life.'"[4]

Other legends have it that at times it is not only a single person who is saved through his good deeds, but the ship as a whole:

It happened to a big ship that sailed upon the Great Sea that the wind took her and carried her to a place where there was no moving water [a most dangerous place, according to Jewish sea lore, from which the ships are unable to extricate themselves]. When the passengers saw that their lives were as good as forfeit, they said, "Come, let us divide our food equally. If we die, let us all die, and if we live, let us all live." Thereupon God inspired them to take a lamb, roast it, and hang it over the west side of the ship. A huge [sea]animal, attracted by its smell, came and began to pull at it, until he dragged the ship into moving water, so that she could sail on. When they arrived at Rome and entered the city, they told Rabbi Eliezer and Rabbi Joshua what had happened to them, and the two sages applied to them the verse, "Cast thy bread upon the waters, for thou shalt find it after many days" (Eccl. 11:1).[5]

THE "PLACE OF SWALLOWING"

Acording to Rabbinic legend there is a place in the sea called *bē b'li'ē* ("the place of swallowing").[6] Of this place, which is reminiscent of Charybdis in the ancient Greek story, the following legend is told in Midrashic sources:

> It happened to Rabbi Eliezer and Rabbi Joshua that when they were sailing in the Great Sea, the wind took them and carried them to the place where the waters do not move. They said, "Surely, it is only for the sake of a test that we are driven here." What did they do? They took some water [in a vessel] from that place, and carried it along with them. When they came to Rome, Caesar Hadrian asked them, "The waters of the ocean, what is their nature?" They answered, "Water which swallows water." He said to them, "Is it possible that 'all the rivers run into the sea, yet the sea becomes not full' (Eccl. 1:7)?" They answered him, "The waters of the ocean swallow them." Hadrian said, "I do not believe you." Thereupon they took a cup, filled it with the water they had brought along from that place, and poured into it great quantities of water. And, behold, it swallowed them all.[7]

This legend seeks to explain the seemingly puzzling fact that, although many great rivers flow into the sea, the latter's level does not rise ("the sea becomes not full"). It was therefore supposed that there must be a place somewhere in the middle of the sea which possesses the miraculous power of being able to swallow all the waters poured by the rivers into the sea. That place is the *bē bl'i'ē*, "the house of swallowing."

VICTIMS OF SHIPWRECK

It was considered a very meritorious act, in addition to being a moral obligation, to help the victims of a shipwreck. The Midrash repeatedly dwells on the rewards of those who fulfill this *mitzvah*:

> Once as Bar Kappara was walking along the seashore of Caesarea he saw a ship sinking in the Great Sea, and saw the proconsul of Caesarea coming naked out of the water. Bar Kappara approached him, inquired after his health, and gave him two *sela*'s [coins]. What else did he do? He took him home, gave him to eat and to drink, and gave him another three *sela*'s, saying, "A great man like you will surely spend another three *sela*'s." A long time thereafter some Jews were arrested and put in prison by the adviser of the king. They considered, "Who could go and speak for us?" They said to each other, "Bar Kappara, for he is influential with the government [of the Romans]." When they asked him to do so, he said to them, "Don't you know that this government does nothing without payment!" They said to

him, "Here are five hundred denari, take them and speak for us." He took the money, and went to the government. When the proconsul saw him, he rose to his feet, inquired after his health, and said to him, "Why have you, Rabbi, troubled to come here?" He answered, "It is our request that you have compassion for these Jews." He said to him, "Don't you know that this government does nothing without payment?" Bar Kappara replied, "I have five hundred denari with me, take them and speak for them." The proconsul said to him, "Let these five hundred denari be retained by you for the five *sela*'s you gave me, and let your people obtain their liberty for the food and drink which you gave me in your house, and you yourself go in peace and in great honor." And all applied to him the verse, "Cast thy bread upon the waters . . ."[8]

A similar story is told about Rabbi Eleazar ben Shamu'a. He, too, was once walking along the shore of the Great Sea, and

saw a ship being tossed about in the sea. Within a short time the ship sank and down with it went everything that was in it. Then he saw a man sitting on a plank of the ship and riding from wave to wave until he reached the shore. The man was naked and hid himself on the shore. This happened at a time when the Israelites were making the pilgrimage to Jerusalem, and the man said to them, "I am from the sons of Esau your brother, give me some clothes that I may cover myself, for the sea stripped me of my clothing, and I have nothing left." They answered him, "Even so let all the sons of your people be stripped."[9]

The man lifted up his eyes and saw Rabbi Eleazar ben Shamu'a walking amongst them. He said to him, "I see that you are an old man and honored by your people. You surely have regard for the dignity of human beings. If so, gain merit through me and give me a garment that I may cover myself with it, for the sea has stripped me naked." Rabbi Eleazar, who was wearing seven garments, took off one and gave it to him. Then he took the Edomite to his house and gave him to eat and to drink, and gave him two hundred denari. He then rode with him for a distance of fourteen parasangs, and gave him great honor, until he brought him home.

After many days the wicked Caesar died, and the Edomite was elected king in his stead. He issued a decree against the Israelites: Every man to be executed and every woman to be made spoil of! The Israelites begged Rabbi Eleazar, "Go and speak for us!" He said to them, "Do you not know that this government does nothing without payment?" They said to him, "Here you have four thousand denari, take them and go and speak for us." He took the money and went.

He came to the gate of the king, and said [to the servants], "Go and tell the king, a man, a Jew, stands at the gate and wishes to inquire after the well-being of the king." The king said, "Let him come up!" When the king saw Rabbi Eleazar, he rose from his throne, fell on his face, and said to him, "What business has the Master here, and why did he trouble himself to come here?" He answered, "That you may have compassion for this country and annul that decree." The king said to him "Your Torah, is there any lie written in it?" Rabbi Eleazar said, "No." The king said, "Is it not written in the Torah, 'An Ammonite or Moabite shall not enter into the congregation of the Lord' [Deut. 23:4]? Why? Is it not because they 'met you not with bread and with water' [v. 5]? And is it not written, 'Thou shalt not abhor an Edomite for he is thy brother' [Deut. 23:8]? And I, am I not a son of your brother Esau? But they showed no charity to me. And whosoever transgresses the commandments of the Torah is bound to suffer the death penalty."

Rabbi Eleazar replied, "Even though they be guilty before you, leave them alone and have compassion for them." The king said, "But do you not know that this government does nothing without payment?" Rabbi Eleazar said, "I have here with me four thousand denarii, take them and have compassion for my people!" The king said "Let those four thousand denarii be yours for the two hundred you gave me, and let the whole country be saved for your sake, for the food and drink you gave me. And you go to my treasury and take for yourself seventy garments for the garment you gave me. And go in peace to your people. I shall spare them for your sake." And they applied to Rabbi Eleazar the verse, "Cast thy bread upon the waters. . . ."[10]

The Sea Gives Amply and Takes Amply

That "the sea gives amply and takes amply" was a popular saying summarizing the experiences of those who went down to the sea in ships or who entrusted their fortune to the treacherous waves. In a Midrash we read: "There are two who take amply and give amply: the sea and the government."[11] According to Rabbinic legend the seashore at Jaffa was the place where the gifts of the sea could be found in the greatest abundance: "All the ships that are lost in the Great Sea, and bundles of silver and of gold, and precious stones and pearls, and all the desirable vessels are spewed out by the sea of Jaffa, and hidden for the pious for the future."[12] One of the sages who, according to pious legend, was rewarded by the bounty of the sea was Rabbi Akiba, the great second-century CE Palestinian master: "On every ship there is a kind of ram; once such a ram was left on a cliff in the sea, and Rabbi Akiba came and found it. . . . Once he gave four *zuzim* [coins] to seafarers and commissioned them to bring him something [from overseas]. But they found nothing but a box on a cliff in the sea, and brought it to him, saying, 'Use it to keep things in it.' Then it turned out that it was full of denarii. For a ship sank, and all the goods were in that box it carried aboard."[13] We have seen above (Chapter 3) that a ram's head was used as a decoration of the ship's prow; in the legend it is evidently considered a kind of receptacle, similar to the box spoken of in the sequel.

Another story tells of "a man who was wont to throw a piece of bread into the Great Sea every day. One day he went and bought a fish, and when he opened it he found a treasure in it. They said of him, 'This is the man whose piece of bread brought him a reward.'"[14] What is interesting in this legend is the unusual view expressed in it, that to feed the fishes of the sea is an act of such great charity that it is rewarded by a gift of riches by the sea.

Cyrus, the great Persian king who permitted the Judeans to rebuild the Temple of Jerusalem, was rewarded by treasures hidden in the Euphrates River: "Nebuchadnezzar decreed and made big copper ships, filled them with money, dug and hid them in the Euphrates, and then let the river cover them. And on the very day on which Cyrus rose and decreed that the Sanctuary should be rebuilt, the Holy One, blessed be He, revealed them to him."[15]

JONAH, JESUS, AND NIKANOR

That the sea "takes amply" was not merely legend but the experience of many a seaman. We have seen that attempts to save the ship in a storm included casting the cargo overboard. Although this was a practical measure intended to lighten the ship, it may have had a magical aspect as well. Ancient peoples believed that in order to appease the wrath of the stormy sea it was necessary to mollify it by offering presents and sacrifices. Traces of this magical idea can still be seen in the story of Jonah. Even though both Jonah and the pagan seamen ostensibly believe that the storm is the expression of divine wrath, they also believe that by casting Jonah into the sea they will calm the sea, and indeed the casting of Jonah into the sea is represented as having the direct effect of making the sea "cease from its raging" (Jon. 1:15).

Rabbinic imagination supplied a profusion of details about what happened between Jonah, the mariners, and the raging sea:

Jonah went down to Jaffa but found no ship to embark upon. The ship on which he finally sailed was then at a distance of two days' sailing from Jaffa. In order to test Jonah, what did the Holy One, blessed be He, do? He brought upon the ship a stormy wind in the sea and brought it back to Jaffa. When Jonah saw it, he felt glad in his heart, and said, "Now I know that my voyage is straight open before me." He said [to the sailors], "I wish to sail with you." They said to him, "But we are about to sail to the islands of the sea and to Tarshish." He replied, "I shall sail with you." Now it is the way of all ships that a passenger pays his fare when he disembarks; but Jonah, in the joy of his heart, paid for the voyage in advance. . . .

When they were one day out of port, a great storm arose. Right and left of them all the other ships made their way in peace in a quiet sea, but the ship in which Jonah sailed was in great danger. . . . People from each of the seventy tongues of the earth were among the passengers of the ship, and they took their idols into their hands, and said, "Let each one of us call upon his god, and the god who will answer and save us from this danger, let him be god." And each one of them called upon his god, but they did not help.

And as to Jonah, his soul was troubled, but he fell asleep. He slept until the captain approached him and said to him, "We stand between life and death, and you sleep? To what people do you belong?" Jonah said to him, "I am a Hebrew." Then the captain said, "And have we not heard that the god of the Hebrews is great? Get up and call upon your god, perchance he will have mercy upon us and perform for us miracles as he did for you in the Red Sea."

Jonah said to them, "I shall not deny before you that it is because of me that this peril has overtaken you. Now take me and cast me into the sea, and then the sea will cease troubling you and quiet down. . . ."

The sailors, however, did not want to throw Jonah into the sea, so they cast lots, and the lot fell upon Jonah. . . . What did they thereupon do? They took the vessels that were on board and threw them into the sea in order to lighten the ship, but it availed naught. Then they tried to row and reach the shore, but could not. What did they then do? They took Jonah and stood with him at the side of the ship and said, "God of the World, Lord, do not make us shed innocent blood, for we do not know what is the nature of this man." But Jonah said to them, "It is because of me that this peril has come upon you, take me therefore and cast me into the sea." They took him and dipped him into the sea as far as his ankles, and immediately the sea ceased raging. They lifted him back into the ship, and the sea began again assailing them in storm. So they dipped Jonah into the water up to his navel, and the sea ceased raging. They lifted him back into the ship, and the sea went on storming against them. They dipped him into the water up to his neck, and the sea again ceased from wrath. They again lifted him up and back into the ship, and the sea went on storming against them. Thereupon they cast him bodily into the sea, and the sea ceased immediately from its wrath.

The fish which swallowed Jonah was ordained for this purpose from the six days of creation. Jonah entered its mouth as a man who enters a great synagogue, and he stood upright in it. The two eyes of the fish were like open windows and gave light for Jonah. A pearl was hung in the belly of the fish and it gave light for Jonah like unto the sun which shines at noon. And the fish showed Jonah everything that is in the sea and in the abysses. It said to Jonah, "Know you that my day has come to be eaten by Leviathan." Jonah said to the fish, "Take me to him." Jonah said to Leviathan, "It is for you that I came here, in order to see the place in which you dwell, for I shall put a rope through your tongue and draw you up and slaughter you for the great feast of the righteous." And Jonah showed him the seal of Abraham [that is, the sign of circumcision], and said to him, "See you the sign of the covenant!" When Leviathan saw it, it fled before Jonah to a distance of two days' journey.

Thereupon Jonah said to the fish, "Now that I have saved you from the mouth of Leviathan, show me everything there is in the sea and in the abysses." The fish showed him the great river of the waters of Okeanos, and it showed him the Red Sea through which the Children of Israel had passed, and it showed him the place of the breakers of the sea and all the waters issuing forth from it, and it showed him the pillars of the earth and its foundations, and it showed him the Valley of Hinnom, and it showed him the deepest Sheol [underworld], and it showed him the palace of God . . . and it showed him the Shetiyyah Stone [the Foundation Stone of the earth] fixed in the abyss underneath the palace of God, and the Sons of Korah standing and praying upon it.

Then the fish spoke to Jonah, "Jonah, you are now beneath the palace of God, pray and you will be hearkened to." Jonah said to the fish, "Stay here, for I do wish to pray." The fish stayed there, and Jonah began to pray before the Holy One, blessed be He:

"Lord of the World! You have been called the one who casts down and the one who lifts up. I have been cast down, now lift me up! You have been called the one who causes death and who resurrects. Behold, my soul has reached death, now resurrect me!"

But he was not answered until these words left his mouth, "I will pay that which I have vowed [Jon. 2:9], to bring up Leviathan and to slaughter him before You. I will pay on the day when Israel is helped. . . . "

Immediately the Holy One, blessed be He, gave a sign to the fish, and it spat Jonah out. . . .

When the sailors saw all the great signs and miracles which the Holy One, blessed be He, performed for Jonah, they arose and each one cast his gods into the sea. . . . And they returned to Jaffa, and made the pilgrimage to Jerusalem, and had themselves circumcised. . . . And they vowed and fulfilled the vows that each one would bring his wife and all that was his to serve the God of Jonah.[16]

There are several interesting details in this complex legend about Jonah. One is at its very beginning, where we are told that when Jonah saw that a ship which had recently left port was driven back to Jaffa by a gale so that he could board it, he took this for a good omen, saying "Now I know that my way lies open before me." In fact, this is an example of divination by means of ships, which was practiced by the Jews in Talmudic times. In the Babylonian Talmud we read that when Rabh once traveled to visit his son-in-law, Rabh Ḥanan, he reached a river that he had to cross. Just as he approached the river, he saw the ferry coming toward him, and he took this to be a good omen. In general, it was the habit of Rabh to make a journey dependent on the presence or absence of a ferry: if he found a ferry waiting for him, he set out on the journey; if not—if he found a ferry only after many exertions—he did not go.[17] Likewise, a Midrashic explanation includes the floating of ships among the methods of divination used by the king of Babylon in deciding which city to attack (Ezek. 21:26–27): Nebuchadnezzar "set ships afloat in the Euphrates River on the name of Rome—and they did not float; on the name of Alexandria—and they did not float; on the name of Jerusalem— and they did float." This made him decide to attack Jerusalem.[18]

But to return to the Jonah legend: according to Talmudic lore, Leviathan, the gigantic monster that dwelt in the sea, was destined to be killed and eaten by the righteous at a great eschatological banquet expected to take place at the end of days. Shetiyyah Stone was the designation of the rock that formed the foundation of the Holy of Holies in the Solomonic Temple, and it can still be seen in the Muslim Dome of the Rock on the Temple Mount in Jerusalem. According to ancient Jewish legend, this rock was sunk by God into the abyss as the first act of creation, and the earth was built up around it, as the body of a child is built up around its navel.[19] That the Shetiyyah Stone is at the same time also "fixed in the abyss" under the Temple ("the palace of God"), so that the sons of Korah, who were swallowed by the earth (Num. 16:32), could stand and pray on it, requires a certain effort of the imagination: the rock, whose surface was visible in the Temple, is imagined as simultaneously lying on the bottom of the abyss. The same illogical imagery places the Valley of Hinnom, an actual valley to the east of Jerusalem, in the depth of the abyss.

Other Jewish legends, which largely follow the story of Jonah, stress the difference between God and the idols, between the Almighty Ruler over the elements and the helpless wooden or stone images.

Echoes of the Jonah story are found in the Gospel according to Mark, in which we are told that when Jesus finished teaching his disciples on the shores of the Sea of Gennesareth toward evening, he said to them: "Let us pass over unto the other side" of the lake. "They took him, even as he was, in the boat. . . . And there arose a great storm of wind, and the waves beat into the boat, insomuch that the boat was now filling [with water]. And he himself was in the stern, asleep on a cushion. And they awake him and say unto him, 'Master, carest thou not that we perish?' And he awoke and rebuked the wind, and said unto the sea, 'Peace, be still!' And the wind ceased, and there was a great calm. And he said unto them, 'Why are ye fearful? Have ye not yet faith?' And they feared exceedingly, and said one to another, 'Who then is this that even the wind and the sea obey him?'" (Mark 4:35–41).

This story has several details that repeat what is told about Jonah: both Jonah and Jesus set out on a ship, a storm arises and creates great fear among the mariners, but both Jonah and Jesus remain unaffected by it and fall peacefully asleep. Both are awakened by the mariners, who are astonished and rather taken aback by the apparent unconcern of the sleeper with the danger threatening the ship. Thereupon both Jonah and Jesus bring about the calming of the storm. There seems to be little doubt that the passage in Mark was written under the influence of the Jonah story, but at the same time it appears that Mark intends to show that Jesus was greater than Jonah: Jonah could only offer his life to save the ship; Jesus was able to do it by simply commanding the wind and the sea to be still.

Another Talmudic legend relates the effort of the sailors to calm the stormy sea by casting into it the most valuable object aboard: the elaborately decorated Temple gates that Nikanor was bringing on the ship from Alexandria to Jaffa:

> It happened as they were sailing in a ship that a great storm arose against them in the sea, whereupon they took one of the gates and cast it into the sea, but still the wrath of the sea did not abate. They wanted to cast also the second gate into the sea, but Nikanor arose, and embraced the gate, and said to them, "If you throw it overboard, throw me with it." And he wept and mourned, until they reached the port of Jaffa. When they reached that haven, the first gate came bobbing up from underneath the ship.[20]

According to another version of this legend, "a creature in the sea swallowed the gate, and vomited it out on to the shore."[21] The miracle was evidently due to divine providence: the gates prepared for the Temple of Jerusalem were too sacred to be lost at sea. The gates about which these miracles were told were those of the eastern entrance to the Temple of Jerusalem. According to Rabbi Eliezer ben Jacob, they were of "Corinthian copper which shone like gold,"[22] and they still formed part of the Temple structure in the days of Josephus.[23]

THE STORM CONVERTS THE IDOLATORS

The story of a storm at sea gives the narrator a welcome opportunity to point to the difference between the idols of the pagans and the God of Israel. For instance, one legend of Palestinian Tannaitic provenance tells of a Jewish child who sailed in a ship, of a storm that arose, and of the

crew who cried to their gods in vain. The child said to them: "How long
will you continue in your foolishness? Cry to Him who created the sea."[24]
The reaction of the gentile sailors to the admonition of the wise child is
related in the Jerusalem Talmud:

> Rabbi Tanḥuma said: "It happened to a ship of the gentiles that was sailing
> on the Great Sea, and on which there was a Jewish child, that a great storm
> arose against them in the sea, and each one of them got up and began to
> take his idol in his hands and to cry to it. But it availed naught. When they
> saw that they received no help, they spoke to that Jewish child, 'My son, get
> up, call unto your God, for we have heard that he answers you when you call
> unto him, and that he is mighty.' Instantly the child arose and with all his
> heart called upon the Holy One, blessed be He, who accepted from him his
> prayer—and the sea became silent. When they reached land, each one of the
> crew went ashore to buy what he needed. They said to the child, 'Do you
> not need to buy anything?' He said to them, 'What do you want of this
> miserable stranger?' [A common self-deprecating expression.] They said to
> him, 'You a miserable stranger? We are miserable strangers. We are here and
> our idols are in Babylonia, we are here and our idols are in Rome, we are
> here and our idols are with us, but they do not help us in the least. But you,
> wherever you go your God is with you.' "[25]

In this story, just as in the story of Jonah, the gentile sailors appear as
misguided but pious men, who are ready to recognize the supremacy of
the God of Israel. According to another Midrashic story, this recognition
comes even without their being imperiled by a storm:

> It happened to a ship that was wholly gentile, and there was in it one Jew.
> They came to an island and said to that Jew, "Take money and go ashore on
> this island and buy us something there." He said to them, "Am I not a
> stranger, do I know where to go?" They said, "Is there a Jew who is a
> stranger? Wherever you go, your God is with you. Here is one whose gods
> are near to him."[26]

In another legend the point made is the greater value of being learned
in Jewish lore as against the value of merchandise:

> Our sages said: "It happened with a ship in which there were merchants, and
> there was also a scholar. The merchants said to the scholar, 'What is your
> merchandise?' He replied, 'It is hidden away.' They said to him, 'Why should
> you not show it to us?' He answered, 'When I reach port, I shall show it to
> you.' The merchants thereupon began to search the ship, and when they did
> not find it, they mocked him.
>
> When they arrived in port, the customs collector arose and took away
> everything the merchants had with them, so that they had nothing to eat and

nothing to wear. That scholar, however, went to the synagogue, sat down, and began to teach the congregation, which honored him and provided for his needs.

The merchants who had been with him on the ship then came to him, entreated him, and said, 'Pray, plead in our favor, since you know us!'

What caused the scholar to be saved? The Torah [Law], which he had in his heart."[27]

Experiences such as this are reflected in the various Talmudic sayings that extol the value of Torah above that of any merchandise.

THE SEA THREATENS AND PUNISHES

In Talmudic lore the sea is a force of justice, and, as in the case of Jonah, expresses God's wrath at wrongful human behavior. Those who deserve it are punished by God through the sea. "It happened to a man who vowed to offer a burnt offering and delayed its fulfillment that his ship sank in the sea."[28] The sea helped Alexander the Great punish the Jews who sinned by settling in Egypt despite the express divine prohibition (cf. Deut. 17:16). Alexander set out in his ships against them, planning to reach Alexandria in ten days, but a favorable wind brought his ships there within five days. He then fell upon the Jews of Egypt, and killed them all.[29]

Of Rabban Gamliel it is related that on the very day on which he put Rabbi Eliezer ben Hyrcanos under a ban, he boarded a ship. "Soon a storm arose, threatening to wreck his ship. Rabban Gamliel said in his heart, 'It would seem to me that this has come because of Rabbi Eliezer.' He rose to his feet and said, 'Lord of the World! It is revealed and known to Thee that I did not do it for my honor, nor for the honor of my father's house, but for the sake of Thy honor, so that dissensions may not increase in Israel!' Thereupon the sea ceased from anger."[30]

Talmudic legend ascribes even to Titus, the quintessence of evil in Jewish lore, a knowledge of God's might at sea:

What did he [Titus] do? He took the Veil of the Sanctuary, made a sort of a bag out of it, collected all the vessels of the Sanctuary and put them into it, and took them with him on a ship in order to triumph with them in his city. . . . Then, when a storm arose in the sea to sink him, he said, "It seems that the power of their God is only upon water: when Pharaoh came, he drowned him in water, when Sisera came, he drowned him in water, and also against me he arises to drown me in water. If he is mighty, let him come up to land and make battle with me!" Thereupon a celestial voice issued forth and spoke to him, "O you wicked one, the son of a wicked one, grandson of the wicked Esau! I have a tiny creature in my world and mosquito is its name. . . . Go ashore and it will fight against you!" When he landed, a mosquito came and entered his nose, and pecked at his brain for seven years.[31]

SUICIDE AT SEA

A rather different legend tells about four hundred Jewish youths and maidens who voluntarily sought death in the sea rather than become male and female prostitutes, for which purpose the Romans were taking them to Rome:

> Once four hundred youths and maidens were captured and destined for shame. When they understood what they were being held for, they said, "If we throw ourselves into the sea, will we have a share in the World to Come?" The oldest among them quoted to them, "The Lord said, I will bring back from Bashan, I will bring back from the depths of the sea" (Ps. 68:23). "I will bring back from Bashan [*mibashan*]—even from between the teeth [*mibashen*] of a lion; I will bring back from the depth of the sea—those who are drowned in the sea." When the maidens heard this, at once they all jumped up and threw themselves into the sea. Thereupon the youths drew a conclusion, and said, "If these, for whom it [sexual relations with men] is the natural thing, did it, all the more must we, for whom it is unnatural, do it. And they too threw themselves into the sea."[32]

SAILORS' TALES

All the sea stories quoted thus far reflect the moralistic-religious worldview of the Talmudic sages. Of a totally different character are the sailors' yarns that found their way into Rabbinic sources, and have thus been preserved. These stories, typically, are full of fantastic exaggerations, and tell about the immense size of the sea, of its depths, its mighty waves, and the wondrous creatures living in it. Some of these tales are explicitly stated to come from the mouth of sailors, whereas others are attributed to sages who, in turn, probably heard them from sailors. We have already mentioned the friendly relations between sages and sailors, which enabled the sages to learn the lore of the sea from the mouth of those whose "home was the ocean," as the British poet put it. A great part of these tall tales recorded in Rabbinic literature is attributed to Rabba bar Bar-Ḥana, a third-century CE sage who was born in Babylonia, but spent many years of his life in Palestine before returning to Babylonia, where he disseminated much of the teachings of the great Palestinian master Rabbi Yoḥanan. The lasting renown of Rabba bar Bar-Ḥana, however, was based on his wondrous tales full of hyperbole and impossibly exaggerated details, to which the reaction of some of his colleagues was outspokenly negative. Some of them even condemned him to his face, saying, "Every Abba is an ass, and every Bar-Ḥana is a fool."[33] (They called him Abba, since the name Rabba is a contraction of R[abbi] Abba.)

Rabba bar Bar-Ḥana's tall tales fall into two categories: some of them, which he purportedly heard from Arabs, tell about marvels encountered in the desert; others, attributed by him to the "descenders of the sea," speak about miraculous things they experienced in the sea. We shall confine our presentation to the latter.

> Rabba [bar Bar-Ḥana] said: "The descenders of the sea told me: This wave which sinks the ship appears as if it had a pale fiery fringe at its head. But we beat it with a stick on which is inscribed 'I am that I am (Ex. 3:14), Yah, the Lord of Hosts, Amen, Amen, Sela,' whereupon it becomes subdued."
>
> Rabba [further] said: "The descenders of the sea told me: Between one wave and the other there is a distance of three hundred parasangs [or Persian miles, each of which equals three and a half miles], and the height of the waves is likewise three hundred [parasangs]. Once we sailed in the sea, and a wave lifted us up to such a height that we were able to see the resting place of a small star, and it was of the size of a field needed for the sowing of forty measures of mustard seed. And had it lifted us up still higher, we would have been burned by its breath. And one wave called to the other, 'My friend! Have you left anything in the world without inundating it? I shall go and destroy it.' But the other replied, 'Go and see the might of your Master: I cannot pass the sand of the shore even as far as the breadth of a thread, as it is written, "Fear ye not me, saith the Lord, will ye not tremble at My presence? Who have placed the sand for the bound of the sea, an everlasting ordinance which it cannot pass"' (Jer. 5:22)."[34]

Some of his tall tales Rabba bar Bar-Ḥana told not in the name of seamen, but as his very own experiences in the sea:

> Rabba bar Bar-Ḥana said: "Once we sailed in a ship, and saw a fish in whose nostrils a devouring worm settled [causing it to perish], and the water lifted the fish and threw it on to the shore. Through it sixty cities were destroyed, sixty cities ate its meat, and sixty cities salted its meat, and out of one of its eyeballs they made three hundred barrels of oil. And when we returned there after a year of twelve months, we saw that out of its bones they had sawed beams in order to rebuild those cities."
>
> Rabba bar Bar-Ḥana said: "Once we sailed in a ship and saw a fish on whose back sand settled and grass grew. Since we thought that was dry land, we went up on it and baked and cooked on its back. But when it felt the heat, it turned over, and were it not for the ship that lay nearby, we would all have perished."[35]

Let us interrupt the flow of Rabba's tall tales and remark that his story of the giant fish taken by the sailors to be an island parallels the tale told as one of the marvelous adventures of St. Brendan while he and his monks sailed the Atlantic in a hide-covered coracle: they landed upon what they took to be an island, but the island turned out to be a big fish.[36]

Rabba was especially fond of telling of the enormous size of the fish he encountered on the high seas:

> Rabba bar Bar-Ḥana said: "Once we sailed in a ship, and the ship sailed between one fin of a fish and the other for three days and three nights, while the fish swam upward and we sailed downward [that is, in the opposite direction]. And lest you think that the ship did not sail fast enough, when Rabh Dimi came he said that in the time required for the heating up of a kettle of water it sailed sixty parasangs. When a hunter shot an arrow, the ship overtook it."

This yarn was too much for Rabh Ashi, who remarked, when he heard it, with caustic sarcasm: "And that was but a small fish, which had only two fins."[37] The depth of the sea also attracted Rabba's imagination:

> Rabba bar Bar-Ḥana said: "Once we sailed in a ship and saw a bird standing in the water up to its ankles, and its head reached to the sky. We thought that the water was not deep [since it reached only to the bird's ankles], and wanted to get down into it in order to cool ourselves. But a celestial voice was heard saying to us, 'Do not get out here! Seven years ago the axe of a carpenter fell into the water at this spot, and it has not yet reached the bottom, and not only because the water is deep, but also because it has a tearing current.'"

Rabh Ashi had a caustic comment on this tale too: "That bird," he said, "was the *ziz saday* [the *ziz* of the fields], as it is written, 'and the *ziz* of the fields is with Me.' (Ps. 50:11)."[38] The Talmudic sages took the word *ziz* to mean a fabulous bird.[39]

Rabba bar Bar-Ḥana was not the only Talmudic sage to tell tall tales about the sea. The great depth of the sea is also referred to in a story told by other sages:

> It happened that the Emperor Hadrian wished to measure the end [that is, the depth] of the sea. He took ropes and unrolled them for three years. Then he heard a celestial voice saying "Hadrian is finished!" He also wished to know what praise of the Holy One, blessed be He, the waters sing. He made glass boxes and had men seated in them, and let them down into the ocean. When they came back up, they said, "Thus we heard Okeanos praising, 'Mighty is the Lord on high (Ps. 93:4).'"[40]

Rabbi Yoḥanan, who was the master of Rabba bar Bar-Ḥana, was himself a teller of tall sea tales. He lived in the third century CE, was a man of exceptional beauty, became the head of the Talmudic academy of Tiberias, and even though he was an outstanding halakhist whose teachings compose a major portion of the Jerusalem Talmud, fantastic sea tales are also attributed to him and recorded in the Babylonian Talmud together with the tales of Rabba bar Bar-Ḥana:

> Rabbi Yoḥanan said: "Once we sailed in a ship and we saw a fish that lifted up its head from the sea, and his eyes were like unto two moons, and it blew up water from its two nostrils like unto the two rivers of Sura."
>
> Rabbi Yoḥanan said: "Once we sailed in a ship and saw a box studded with precious stones and pearls, and a sort of fish called *karesha* was guarding it. A diver went out to bring in the box, but the fish noticed him and tried to bite his hip. The diver threw upon the fish a hide full of vinegar, whereupon the fish fled. Then a celestial voice was heard: 'What do you want of this box which belongs to the wife of Rabbi Ḥanina ben Dosa and into which she will in the future put purple-blue threads for [the garments of] the righteous?' "[41]

Several details in this story require comment. The precise meaning of *karesha* is unclear; among the suggested meanings are: shark, sunfish (*mola*), stingray. But since we are dealing here with a fish of fantasy, its zoological identification is of minor importance. Rabbi Ḥanina ben Dosa was a first-century CE Palestinian Tanna, famous for his exceeding piety, which was shared by his wife; both are said to have been "accustomed to miracles."[42] The purple-blue threads, dyed with the *ḥilazon*, the purple-fish or purple snail, were used for making the ritual fringes on the *tallith*, the prayer shawl.[43]

The passage in Isaiah (54:12) in which the prophet has God say to Jerusalem, "I will make . . . thy gates of carbuncles," occasioned Rabbi Yoḥanan to deliver himself of a fantastic tale:

> Once Rabbi Yoḥanan sat and taught: "In the Future the Holy One, blessed be He, will bring precious stones and pearls the size of thirty cubits by thirty cubits, and will cut openings in them the size of ten by twenty cubits, and set them up in the gates of Jerusalem." A student derided him and said, "If they do not exist even as big as the eggs of a dove, how could there be some of that size?" Many days later that student sailed in a ship in the sea, and saw ministering angels sitting and sawing precious stones and pearls. He asked them for whom they were, and they said to him, "The Holy One, blessed be He, will in the Future set them up in the gates of Jerusalem." Thereupon he returned to Rabbi Yoḥanan and said to him, "Teach, O Master, it is fitting that you should teach, as you said so did I see it." Rabbi Yoḥanan answered, "You good-for-nothing! Had you not seen it, you would not have believed!

You mock the words of the sages!" And he fixed him with his eyes, and the student turned into a heap of bones.[44]

In the same collection of tall tales that found its way into the Babylonian Talmud, several stories are recorded in the names of various sages who heard them from the mouth of Rabbi Yohanan.[45] Most prominent among those sages is Rabba bar Bar-Hana, who seems to have absorbed more Aggada than Halakha from his master. Among the other Talmudic masters who transmitted tall tales of the sea are Rabh Safra, Rabh Yehuda the Indian, and Rabh Dimi.

Rabh Safra said: "Once we sailed in a ship and saw a fish that lifted up its head out of the water; it had two horns, and upon them was engraved: 'I am a small creature of the sea and I measure three hundred parasangs. I am now going into the mouth of Leviathan.'" Rabh Ashi said, "That was a sea-goat that has horns with which it searches for food."[46]

Rabh Yehuda the Indian said: "Once we sailed in a ship and saw a precious stone and a dragon was coiled around it. A diver went down to fetch it, but the dragon came and wanted to swallow the ship. A raven came and bit off the head of the dragon, and the water turned into blood. A second dragon came, and placed the stone on the first dragon, whereupon it came to life. It again approached and wanted to swallow the ship, and another bird came and bit off its head. Thereupon the diver took the precious stone and threw it into the ship. We had with us salted fowl aboard, and when we placed the stone upon them, they [came to life, and] took it and flew away with it."[47]

A rather peculiar fantastic legend, recorded in a large number of sources, the earliest of which are Tannaitic, finds it possible to connect the desert wanderings of the Children of Israel with the supposed treasures hidden in the sea. While sojourning in the desert, the Children of Israel were supplied with water by the so-called "Miriam's Well," which was a miraculous source:

The well that was with the Children of Israel in the desert was like a rock full of sieves, from which water rose and gushed forth, like from the mouth of a ewer. It went up with them to the mountains, and went down with them to the valleys, wherever Israel halted, it halted opposite them, in front of the door of the Tabernacle. The princes of Israel would surround it with their staffs in hand, and would chant to it the song, "Spring up, O well, sing ye unto it" (Num. 21:17), whereupon the water would gush forth and rise like a column, and each one of them would draw it with his staff to his tribe and his family, as it is written, "The well which the princes digged, which the nobles of the people delved, with the scepter, and with their staves. And from the wilderness to Mattanah, and from Mattanah to Nahaliel, and from Nahaliel to Bamoth, and from Bamoth to the valley . . . " (ibid. vv. 18–20).

And it surrounded the whole camp of God, and watered the face of the wilderness, and became great rivers, as it is written "and streams overflowed" (Ps. 78:20). And they were sitting in light boats [Hebrew *isq̇faoth*], and went one to the other, as it is written, "they ran, a river in the dry places" (Ps. 105:41). . . . And they turned into a big river, and flowed into the Great Sea, and brought from there all the treasures of the world.[48]

This legend makes the "Well of Miriam" supply water to great navigable rivers flowing into the sea, and envisages the Children of Israel enjoying the hidden treasures of the sea while still wandering in the desert!

LEVIATHAN

Many of the Talmudic sea tales concentrate on Leviathan, the gigantic sea dragon that, according to biblical myths, was slain by God in the days of creation.[49] Of Jonah's encounter with Leviathan we have heard above.

The Rabbis taught: "Once Rabbi Eliezer and Rabbi Joshua were sailing in a ship. Rabbi Eliezer slept, while Rabbi Joshua stayed awake. Suddenly Rabbi Joshua trembled, and Rabbi Eliezer awoke, and said to him, 'Joshua, why did you tremble?' He answered, 'I saw a great light in the sea.' Rabbi Eliezer said, 'You probably saw the eyes of Leviathan, of which it is written, "His eyes are like the eyelids of the morning" (Job. 41:18).'"[50]

According to Rabbi Yoḥanan, God created "Leviathan the slant serpent and Leviathan the tortuous serpent" (cf. Isa. 27:1) in the six days of creation.[51] Other sages knew many more details about these sea monsters:

R. Yehuda [the Indian] in the name of Rabh: "Everything that the Holy One, blessed be He, created in His world, He created male and female. Also Leviathan the slant serpent and Leviathan the tortuous serpent He created male and female. Had they copulated, they would have destroyed the world. What therefore did the Holy One, blessed be He, do? He castrated the male and killed the female and salted it away for the pious in the world to come."

When Rabh Dimi came he said in the name of Rabbi Yoḥanan: "When Leviathan is hungry, it exhales from its mouth a heat that boils up all the waters in the abyss . . . and would it not stick its head into the Garden of Eden, no creature could stand its evil smell. . . . When it is thirsty, it makes furrows upon furrows in the sea."

When Rabh Dimi came he said in the name of Rabbi Yoḥanan: "In the Future [the archangel] Gabriel will arrange a hunt for Leviathan . . . and would the Holy One, blessed be He, not help him, he would not be able to catch it."[52]

The phrase "When Rabh Dimi came . . ." refers to the fact that Rabh Dimi, a Babylonian, spent many years in Palestine, where he was a student of Rabbi Yoḥanan, and then arrived in Babylonia bringing with him much Palestinian Rabbinic lore.

Rabba [Bar-Ḥana] in the name of Rabbi Yoḥanan: "In the Future the Holy One, blessed be He, will prepare out of the meat of Leviathan a banquet for the pious. . . . Whatever will be left over will be distributed among them, in order to sell it in the market of Jerusalem."

Rabba further said in the name of Rabbi Yoḥanan: "In the Future the Holy One, blessed be He, will make out of the skin of Leviathan a booth for the pious."[53]

Fanciful details about the encounter between Jonah, the fish, and Leviathan, are supplied in a medieval Midrash entitled "Midrash Jonah."

Jonah was three days in the innards of the fish and did not pray. The Holy One, blessed be He, said, "I gave him ample space in the belly of the fish so that he should suffer no discomfort, and he does not pray before Me. I shall order for him a female fish, pregnant with 365,000 small fishes, so that he should suffer and pray before Me. For I desire the prayer of the pious." In that hour the Holy One, blessed be He, ordered there a female fish, and she went and approached the male fish. She said to him, "A prophet-man is in your belly, and the Holy One, blessed be He, sent me to swallow him. If you spit him out, fine, and if not, I shall swallow you together with him." The male fish said to the female fish, "Who knows whether what you say is true?" She said, "Leviathan knows." They both went to Leviathan. The female fish said to Leviathan, "King of all the fishes of the sea, don't you know that the Holy One, blessed be He, sent me to this fish to swallow the prophet who is in his belly?" He said to her, "Yes." The fish asked Leviathan, "When?" He said to him, "In the last three hours [of the day], when the Holy One, blessed be He, came down to play with me, that is when I heard it." And he said to the female fish, "Go and swallow the prophet who is in the belly of the fish!" The male fish spewed him out, and the female fish swallowed him.

As soon as Jonah entered the belly of the female fish he began to suffer greatly from the dirt and the refuse that were in the female fish. Instantly he directed his heart toward the Holy One, blessed be He, and prayed. . . .[54]

Only one comment: the idea that God is playing with Leviathan is biblical. In Psalm 104:25–26 we read:

> Yonder sea, great and wide,
> Therein are creeping things innumerable,
> Living creatures, both small and great.

There go the ships;
There is Leviathan, whom Thou hast formed to sport therein.

RAHAB, PRINCE OF THE SEA

Another mythological figure connected with the sea is the Prince of the
Sea, Rahab by name, a figure akin to the rebellious angels, who repre-
sents the sea and plays a role especially in the days of Creation.

When the Holy One, blessed be He, created His world, He said to the
Prince of the Sea, "Open your mouth and swallow all the waters that are in
the world!" He said before Him, "Master of the World! It is sufficient for me
to stand as I am." And he began to cry. Instantly the Holy One, blessed be
He, [threatened to] slay him. . . . What did the Holy One, blessed be He,
do? He subdued the waters, and the sea accepted them . . . and he set for
them the sand as a bolt and doors. . . . The sea said to him, "Master of the
World! If so, my salty waters will be mixed with the sweet water!" God said
to him, "Each one of them will have a treasure house of its own. . . . " In
the hour when the Holy One, blessed be He, wanted to tear apart the sea
before Israel, so that the Egyptians should drown, Rahab, the Prince of the
Sea, pleaded for the welfare of Egypt and said before the Holy One, blessed
be He: "Master of the World! Why do you want to drown the Egyptians? It
is sufficient for Israel that you save them from the hands of Egypt!" In that
hour the Holy One, blessed be He, lifted up His hand and gave a blow to
Rahab, the Prince of the Sea, and to all his cohorts, and killed them and cast
them into the depths of the sea, and from there its stench rises. When Israel
saw this, they said, "The deeps cover them" (Ex. 15:5).[55]

Chapter 13

PORTS AND PORT CITIES

THE EARLIEST biblical references to places where ships could anchor or tie up along the coast of Eretz Israel are found in two poetical passages. One is in the so-called "Blessing of Jacob" in which it is said of Zebulun that he "shall dwell at the shore of the sea and he shall be a shore for ships, and his flank shall be upon Zidon" (Gen. 49:13); the other is in the Song of Deborah, in which Dan is referred to as "sojourning by the ships," and Asher as "dwelling at the shore of the sea and abiding by its ways" (Judg. 5:17). However, these vague poetical references tell us of nothing more than the existence of some knowledge of ships that plied the waters of the Mediterranean.

RED SEA PORTS

The first concrete reference to port cities in Israel is that to the Red Sea ports of Ezion-Gebher and Elath. It has been contended that the military expedition of Chedorlaomer, king of Elam (Gen. 14:1–6) was organized mainly with the purpose of subjugating Elath.[1] From the biblical references to the Children of Israel passing by Ezion-Gebher and Elath in the course of their desert wanderings (Num. 33:35–36; Deut. 2:8) it appears that Israelite tradition assumed the existence of those localities in Mosaic times. Again, from the references in 1 Kings 9:26, it seems that in the days of Solomon both places had already existed for some time as two different townships near each other. There we read: "And King Solomon made a navy of ships in Ezion-Gebher, which is beside Eloth [Elath] on the shore of the Red Sea, in the Land of Edom." That this verse refers to two different localities is confirmed by the wording of the parallel passage in 2 Chron. 8:17: "Then went Solomon to Ezion-Gebher and to Eloth [Elath] on the seashore in the land of Edom." The naval expedition launched from Ezion-Gebher–Elath is described in 1 Kings 9:27–28: "And Hiram sent with the navy his servants, shipmen that had knowledge of the sea, together with the servants of Solomon. And they came to Ophir, and fetched from thence gold, four hundred and twenty talents, and brought it to King Solomon." This is reinterpreted by the Chronicler, according to whom the ships themselves were not built in Ezion-Gebher–Elath but in another, unnamed place. The sequel of the passage just quoted reads: "And Huram [Hiram] sent him by the hands of his servants ships, and servants that had knowledge of the sea. And they came with the servants of Solomon to Ophir, and fetched from thence four hundred and fifty talents of gold, and brought them to King Solomon" (2 Chron. 8:18).

Also according to 1 Kings 10:11, it was "the navy of Hiram that brought gold from Ophir" and not a joint navy of Hiram and Solomon. This statement is again changed by the Chronicler, who speaks of "the servants of Huram and the servants of Solomon that brought gold from Ophir." In addition to gold, that expedition brought sandalwood and precious stones from Ophir (1 Kings 10:11; 2 Chron. 9:10).

The geographical location of Ophir has been the subject of much speculation, but no definite conclusion has been reached. The Arabian Peninsula, East Africa, South Africa, and India have been suggested, and some have considered "Ophir" to be not a place name but a description of the fine quality of the gold.[2]

Toward the end of Solomon's reign Edom seems to have regained its independence (1 Kings 11:14–25), which meant that the Red Sea ports were no longer accessible to Solomon and his successors. However, King Jehoshaphat (ruled ca. 873–849 BCE) reconquered Edom, including the port of Ezion-Gebher, and tried to duplicate Solomon's feat in sending ships to Ophir. But as the biblical text laconically reports, his ships "went not, for the ships were broken at Ezion-Gebher" (1 Kings 22:49). What seems to have happened is that Jehoshaphat's ships, lacking the expert assistance of Phoenician shipwrights, proved unseaworthy, and were wrecked, probably by a storm, while still in harbor at Ezion-Gebher. When Ahaziah, king of Israel, later suggested to Jehoshaphat that they organize a joint expedition to Ophir, Jehoshaphat, disheartened by this fiasco, refused (1 Kings 22:50).

In the parallel account of the Chronicles a moralizing twist is given to the story, and the facts marshaled are contrary to the account in Kings:

> And after this did Jehoshaphat king of Judah join himself with Ahaziah king of Israel, who did very wickedly. And he joined himself with him to make ships to go to Tarshish, and they made ships in Ezion-Gebher. Then Eliezer the son of Dodavahu of Mareshah prophesied against Jehoshaphat saying, "Because thou hast joined thyself with Ahaziah, the Lord hath made a breach in thy works." And the ships were broken that they were not able to go to Tarshish (2 Chron. 20:35–37).

The Chronicler not only contradicts the account in Kings but also misunderstands the expression "Tarshish ships" which appears in 1 Kings 22:49. "Tarshish ships" was the designation of large seagoing vessels (cf. Isa. 23:1, 14; 60:9). The location of Tarshish has not been definitely established, but most scholars consider it a land bordering on the Mediterranean. The Prophet Jonah embarked in Jaffa with the intention of sailing to Tarshish (Jon. 1:3). Hence to say that ships built in the Red Sea port of Ezion-Gebher were intended to sail to Tarshish is absurd, unless we assume that Tarshish was the name given to several places.

Under Jehoram son of Jehoshaphat (851–843 BCE), Edom again "revolted from under the hand of Judah and made a king over themselves" (2 Kings 8:20, 22). As a consequence, Judah was again debarred from the use of the port of Ezion-Gebher. Amaziah king of Judah (798–769 BCE) again reconquered part of Edom (2 Kings 14:7, 10), and his son Azariah-Uzziyah (785–733 BCE), who became coregent with his father at the age of sixteen, "rebuilt Elath [Eloth] and restored it to Judah" (2 Kings 14:21–22; 2 Chron. 26:1–3). Following this reannexation, the Judeans must have settled in Elath in considerable numbers, for it is recorded that when "Rezin king of Aram recovered Elath to Aram" he "drove the Jews from Elath [Eloth], and the Edomites came to Elath and dwelt there unto this day" (2 Kings 16:6).

Ezion-Gebher has been identified with Tell el-Kheleyfeh, where the excavations of Nelson Glueck revealed no fewer than five layers of settlement, dating from Solomonic times to the fifth century BCE. The mound lies at about the center of the northern coast of the Gulf of Elath (Aqaba). More recent research has instead identified Ezion-Gebher with the small island of Jezirat Far'on in the Gulf of Elath. This would correspond to similar constructions of harbors on islands near the seashore at Tyre and Leptis Magna.

Even if the harbor of a town was not located on an offshore island, many port cities of ancient Palestine consisted of a double or twin arrangement: a port city situated on the seashore, and a second city, probably of larger size, located not far from it farther inland. We shall be dealing below in more detail with these twin seaside towns. This was probably the case with Ezion-Gebher and Elath: Ezion-Gebher was the harbor, and Elath the nearby inland town. From 1 Kings 9:26 it would seem that Elath was the larger of the two and the better known, for Ezion-Gebher is described there as "Ezion-Gebher which is beside Eloth." Josephus too refers to Ezion-Gebher as "a place . . . not far from the city of Eloth."[3]

The meaning of the name Ezion-Gebher (Hebrew 'esyon gebher) is uncertain, but according to one tradition, preserved in the Jerusalem Targum, it meant K'rakh Tarn'gola, that is "Fort of the Cock."[4] Although the word tarn'gola appears repeatedly in Rabbinic literature in the sense of "fort," it seems unlikely that K'rakh Tarn'gola would mean "fort of the fort." It seems more probable that the author of the Jerusalem Targum took the work gebher to mean "cock," as it does frequently in Rabbinic literature, and thus translated it into Aramaic as "fort of the cock." The naming of localities after animals was nothing unusual in Palestine in antiquity (cf. Migdal Nunaya—"Tower of the Fish"; Susita-Hippos—"Horse").

In Hellenistic times Ezion-Gebher served as a Ptolemaic port and was called Berenike. Both Strabo and Pliny refer to Elath as a Nabatean port, named Aila, from which an important road led to Gaza.[5]

Eusebius of Caesarea (ca. 260–339 CE), the Christian historian, biblical scholar, and theologian, states in his *Onomasticon*, an extremely important work on biblical geography, that Ezion-Gebher and Elath were two distinct towns, and that the biblical Ezion-Gebher is identical with the place called in his day Essia or Asia, situated near the Red Sea and Elath.[6] The name 'Asia or 'Asia also appears in Talmudic sources, from which we learn that it was situated on the seashore and that its inhabitants were Jews, who formed an important community and whose members occupied themselves, among other things, with fishing and related trades. Of one of the Jewish inhabitants of 'Asia it is related that his trade was the cutting of sponges under water, for which purpose he was let down by a rope into the sea. We know, moreover, that the Jews of 'Asia had close connections with the other Jewish centers of Palestine, which they often visited, whereas, on the other hand, sages and teachers from the central seats of learning came to visit the town in order to perform various religious functions. 'Asia also had a system of water supply of its own, and even warm-water thermae.[7]

From Koranic references it can be concluded that Ayla-'Asia had a Jewish population in the days of Muhammad. Two passages refer to a legend according to which the Jewish inhabitants of a city that stood by the sea transgressed the Sabbath by fishing on that day of rest, whereupon they were transformed into apes.[8] According to later Muslim tradition this reference is to Elath. The tenth-century Muslim geographer al-Istakhri writes that Ayla (Elath) "is a city of the Jews whom Allah forbade to fish on the Sabbath, and he turned some of them into apes and swine. And in it is found in the hands of the Jews a treaty of peace with the apostle of God." The treaty referred to is that entered into by Muhammad with Yuḥanna ibn Ru'ba, the bishop of Ayla, who made peaceful submission to Muhammad.

In the second half of the tenth century, the famous Arab geographer al-Muqaddasi describes Ayla as "the port of Palestine," a great and beautiful city, rich in inhabitants, palm trees, and fishes. It was a center of trade with the Hijaz, and its harbor was the greatest in Palestine. Then he continues: "The common people call the city Ayla, but the real Ayla is situated next to Wilah (or: Waylah) near the mountain, and is a ruin now."[9] In 1116 Baldwin I conquered Ayla (Helim), and this was the end of the Jewish population of the town. Subsequently an Arab settlement developed in the place, called 'Aqabat Ayla ("Pass of Ayla"), which name later came to be abridged as 'Aqaba.[10]

MEDITERRANEAN PORTS

As mentioned above, all along the Mediterranean coast of Palestine we find coastal settlements that took the form of twin cities, one at the waterfront, the other one to three miles inland. The reason for this dual form of settlement is not far to seek. The seashore of Palestine is in general covered with sand dunes several hundred yards wide or even more, unsuitable for any cultivation. The inhabitants of the ancient settlements were agriculturists who would have had to live near their fields. Hence it seems probable that the original settlements were founded along the borderline between the sand and the fertile land. When, in the course of time, occupations connected with the sea—shipping and fishing—gained in importance, some of them settled on the seashore opposite the original town, and so a "daughter settlement" would come into being.

This procedure of founding "daughter settlements" (in Hebrew called *banoth*, "daughters") in the vicinity of the ancestral town or village was and is well known in Palestine from both biblical and modern times. In the Bible several cities are mentioned as having had such "daughters." We hear of "Ekron and her daughters," "Ashdod and her daughters," and "Gaza and her daughters" (Josh. 15:45–47)—three of the five Philistine cities on the seashore—and likewise, farther inland, "Megiddo and her daughters" (Judg. 1:27) and "Beth Shean and her daughters" (Josh. 17:16), and so on.

In modern Palestine the same process went on in the Arab villages. If the inhabitants of a village possessed land at such a distance from the village as to make it difficult to return to it after work, it would often happen that some of them would build first temporary, then permanent, lodgings amid the faraway fields, and in this manner a new village would soon come into being. This new village would then be regarded as a branch ("daughter") of the original village, though in the course of time it might become socially and economically independent, and be called by a different name.

It is in some such way that we must picture the origin of twin cities on the Mediterranean coast of Palestine. This assumption is strengthened by a consideration of those coastal towns that lack this double character. They are of two kinds: either ancient towns situated at a spot where natural conditions prevented the encroachment of sand dunes, and thus where one settlement could satisfy the need of the inhabitants for the proximity of both fertile land and the sea; or more recent towns, founded in Greek and Roman times, with the express purpose of serving as harbor towns. The outstanding example of the first kind is Jaffa (Joppe), whereas such ports as Anthedon are of the second kind.

Let us now present a brief outline of the Mediterranean ports of Palestine-Eretz Israel, proceeding from the south to the north (see Map 1).

Rhinokorura

Very little is known of this southernmost coastal town of ancient Palestine. Josephus lists it among the coastal towns that belonged to the Jews, and mentions that Titus prepared his march on Palestine there.[11] It was situated at the mouth of the present Wadi el-'Arish, the biblical Naḥal Mizrayim, which, according to the Bible, was the border between the land of Canaan and Egypt.

Raphia (Hebrew Rafiaḥ)

The first references to Raphia, located to the northeast of Rhinokorura, are found in Egyptian documents dating from the thirteenth century BCE. It is mentioned again in a geographical list from the time of Pharaoh Shishak (945–924 BCE), whose incursion into Judea took place, according to 1 Kings 14:25, in the fifth year of the reign of Rehoboam, son of Solomon. Some two centuries later a neo-Assyrian annal of King Sargon claims that he defeated Hanno king of Gaza and Sib'e, the Turtan of Egypt, who had set out against him from Rapihu (Raphia). Sargon burned and destroyed Raphia and took captive nine thousand of its inhabitants together with their numerous possessions. Again, in an inscription of Esarhaddon (680–669 BCE) it is mentioned that he marched as far as the town of Rapihu in "the region adjacent to the Brook of Egypt."

In 307 BCE, during the war of Antigonus against Egypt, his fleet, led by his son Demetrius, was driven by a storm to Raphia, and was wrecked there. Polybius and Strabo report that in 217 BCE Ptolemy IV Philopator won there a decisive victory over Antiochus the Great, the consequence of which was the loss of Palestine for the latter. In 193 BCE the wedding of Ptolemy V Epiphanes with Cleopatra, daughter of Antiochus, was celebrated in Raphia. Josephus reports that early in the first century BCE Alexander Jannaeus "made an expedition upon the maritime parts of the country, Raphia and Anthedon . . . and took even that by force." Following this conquest, Raphia, with a number of other cities on the seashore, remained in the possession of the Jews until Pompey detached it from Judea, although its name does not figure in the list given by Josephus of cities "restored to their own inhabitants" by Pompey.

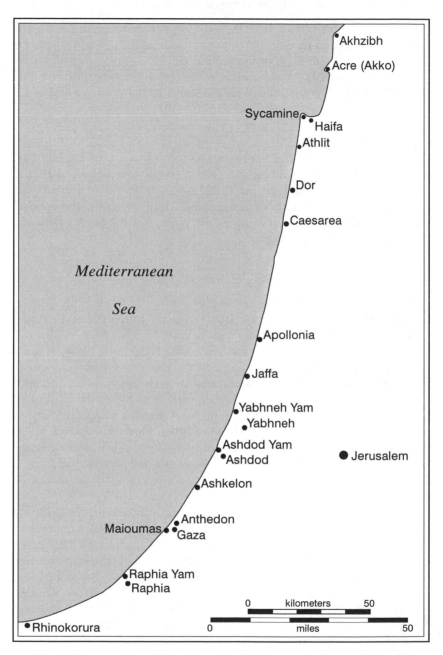

Map 1. Ports and Port Cities along the Mediterranean Shore of Palestine in Ancient Times.

Subsequently the city was rebuilt by the Roman general Gabinius, and for this reason the coins of Raphia from the days of the Roman emperors (from Commodus to Philippus Arabus) show an era reckoned from the date of the rebuilding of Raphia by Gabinius, that is, about 57 BCE. When Titus marched from Egypt to Palestine, he took the road along the seashore, the famous Via Maris, and the fourth station on his way was Raphia, "the beginning of Syria."[12]

In Rabbinical sources Raphia (Rafiaḥ) appears among the frontier towns of Eretz Israel. Talmudic sources identify Raphia with the biblical Hazerot (Num. 11:35) and call it also by the name Hazor.[13] It lay at some distance from the sea, and for this reason was regarded by both Pliny and Ptolemy as an inland town.[14] The remains of this Raphia are to be sought in the mound called today Tel Rafaḥ or Khirbet Bir Rafaḥ, on the Israel-Egyptian border, near the Arab village of Rafah, some two miles from the sea. To the northwest of this mound, on the very seashore itself, there is another, smaller mound, also called Tel Rafah, and it would seem that this seaside Tel Rafah was the port "daughter" of inland Rafah in ancient times. When Josephus mentions Raphia among "the maritime parts of the country," and when Diodorus says that the ships of Demetrius were driven by the storm to the town of Raphia, where the shore is "hard to land on and formed a shoal of water," they doubtless refer to the harbor town of Raphia (Raphia Yam).[15]

The coins of the town permit us to form some idea of the Hellenistic cults that prevailed in Raphia in Roman times. The coins show the figures of Apollo and Artemis, and are purely Greek in conception; the patron deity of Anthedon was Astarte, the Phoenician goddess. According to the geographical lexicon of Stephanus Byzantinus, Raphia was called by this name because its foundation was connected with the story of Dionysus, who was also called by the epithet *eriphios* ("of a kid"). The Greek or Hellenized inhabitants of Raphia did, no doubt, see in the name of their town an allusion to Dionysos Eriphios. A late survival of the Dionysian cult may be seen in the annual sacrifice to the sea of a kid by the Arab inhabitants of Rafah in modern times.[16]

By the beginning of the fifth century CE Raphia was the seat of a bishop, and bishops of Raphia are also known from the early sixth century. After the conquest of Palestine by the Arabs the town of Rafah is often mentioned by Arab geographers as a frontier town on the southern borders of Palestine. The town had a market, a mosque, and caravanserais, and was surrounded by gardens watered by good wells. After the Arab conquest Jews again settled in Rafah, and from a document it is known that as late as in 1015 there was a Jewish community there with a judge and elders at its head. A Hebrew letter from about 1080 mentions "the holy community which lives in the fortress of Ḥazor," that is,

Raphia. The famous Hebrew poet and traveler Yehuda Alḥarizi (ca. 1190–1235 CE), mentions in his *Taḥkemoni* that he traveled *miZor v'ad Hazor*, that is, from Tyre to Raphia.[17]

From Samaritan sources we learn that in the Middle Ages there was also a Samaritan community in Raphia. The Samaritans called the town by its biblical name, Ḥazerim. In consequence of the Crusaders' conquests, Raphia became desolate, but it was settled again in the days of the Mameluks. The Turkish regime again brought about a desolation of Raphia.[18]

Gaza (Hebrew 'Azzah)

The data pertaining to the history of Gaza are very rich, and several books have been written about it. In the following we confine ourselves to a brief presentation of the main points in the 3,500-year history of this important south Palestinian port city.

The city of Gaza lies at a distance of about eighteen miles to the northeast of Raphia, and some two and a half miles inland from the sea. This distance is about the same as that between inland Raphia and the sea. And just as Raphia had its port section, so had Gaza.

The name of Gaza appears for the first time in the annals of Thutmose III in 1469 BCE, at which time Gaza had already been the capital of the Canaan province of Egypt for about a century. Egyptian rule over Gaza lasted until about 1150 BCE. In the course of the twelfth century BCE the Sea Peoples, coming partly in ships from Cyprus and partly by the land route from Anatolia, conquered the territory around Gaza and founded the five Philistine cities that formed a confederation, with Gaza the leading power among them. The Israelites, who at about the same time conquered the inland parts ("the hill country") of the land of Canaan, were unable to dislodge "the five lords of the Philistines: the Gazite, and the Ashdodite, and Ashkelonite, the Gittite, and the Ekronite" (Josh. 13:3), because "they had chariots of iron" (Judg. 1:19). Gaza figures prominently in the story of Samson as a city inimical to the Israelites (Judg. 13–16). The city was surrounded by a wall whose gates were closed for the night (Judg. 16:1–3), a prison house (v. 21), and a large, colonnaded temple of the Philistine god Dagon, which could accommodate no fewer than three thousand people (vv. 23–26). That Gaza was a luxurious city surrounded by a wall and boasting of palaces was referred to some four centuries later (ca. 760 BCE) by Amos, who also knew that the Philistines had come from Caphtor (Amos 1:7; 9:7).

Soon after the days of Amos, Gaza became a tributory of Assyria, and in the Assyrian tribute list of 738 BCE the name of Hanno king of Gaza appears.[19] Zechariah's prophecy that "the king shall perish from Gaza" (Zech. 9:5) may have something to do with Hanno's capture and the huge tribute imposed by Tiglath-pileser upon Gaza in 734 BCE. Gaza became a vassal city of Assyria and remained in that status until King Hezekiah of Judah (ruled ca. 715–687 BCE) "smote the Philistines unto Gaza and the borders thereof from the tower of the watchmen to the fortified city" (2 Kings 18:8). After Sennacherib crushed Hezekiah's rebellion, he allocated coastal territories to the Philistine kings who had remained loyal to him; among the recipients of Assyrian favor was Sil-Bel (or: Sillibel) king of Gaza, under whose long rule Gaza again became the leading city among the Philistine city states.[20] The downfall of Gaza (as well as of three other Philistine cities and the entire "seacoast" inhabited by "the nation of the Cherethites") is predicted in a prophecy of Zephaniah (2:4–5); and Jeremiah (47:5), "Baldness is come upon Gaza, Ashkelon is brought to nought," seems to refer to the conquest and destruction of Gaza and Ashkelon by Nebuchadnezzar in 604 BCE.

With the conquest of Egypt in 525 BCE by Cambyses, Gaza came under Persian rule and became a strong fortress town. Herodotus passed through Gaza in about 450 BCE, and recorded that the town was almost as large as Sardis.[21] Coins found on the site of Gaza show that there must have been lively commercial connections between it and Greece. Alexander the Great, after having conquered Tyre in 332 BCE, besieged Gaza with his fleet and army, and it took him two months to conquer the strongly fortified city. In the fighting all the men of Gaza were killed, and after its conquest the women and children were sold into slavery, and the city was repopulated by neighboring tribesmen.

After the death of Alexander, Gaza was under Ptolemaic rule for more than a century (301–198 BCE) and was a prosperous economic center for trade with Egypt. Most sought after among the many types of merchandise traded at Gaza were the spices and perfumes coming from Arabia Felix. Under Seleucid rule the Hellenization of Gaza proceeded, and the city, renamed Seleucia, attained more autonomy as a *polis*. In 145/44 BCE Jonathan the Hasmonean attacked Gaza; the city sued for peace and entered into a treaty of friendship with him.[22]

After the death of Queen Cleopatra III (101 BCE), the Hasmonean king Alexander Jannaeus attacked Gaza, which had been taken by Ptolemy IX Lathyrus, and "utterly overthrew" the city, slaying the five hundred city senators who had fled into the temple of Apollo. In that campaign Alexander Jannaeus also took Raphia and Anthedon, the two neighboring cities of Gaza. Despite this destruction, Gaza continued to exist as a populated city, and Antipas, the governor Alexander Jannaeus appointed over Idumaea and Gaza, "made a league of friendship with the Arabs and the Gazaeans."[23]

When Pompey conquered Palestine (63 BCE), he restored independence to what still existed of Gaza, and under Gabinius the city was rebuilt somewhat to the south of the old city. Both old and new Gaza lay at a distance of some two miles from the sea. In 30 BCE Gaza came under the rule of Herod the Great, after whose death it was again attached to the province of Syria. As such it became a target of the Jews who rebelled in 66 CE against the Romans, and it was partially destroyed by them.[24]

The port of Gaza, as distinct from the city, is called *Gazaion limen* by Strabo and Ptolemy. It was situated opposite the inland city. Under Constantine the Great this port settlement received the status of a city and was called Konstanteia. The emperor Julian, however, deprived it of both status and name, so that it was thereafter referred to simply as Maioumas ("harbor place").[25]

From Rabbinical sources and archaeological finds we know that Gaza had, from the first or second century CE on, a Jewish community. The Palestinian Talmud discusses the question of whether it was permitted for a Jew to take part in the annual fair that was held in Gaza in honor of a Greek deity. The early sixth century CE synagogue discovered at Maioumas shows that a sizable and prosperous Jewish community lived there at the time. In the Middle Ages (tenth-eleventh centuries), too, there was a considerable Jewish community in Gaza.[26]

Anthedon

As its name indicates, this port city was founded in Hellenistic times. It is first mentioned by Josephus, who states that Alexander Jannaeus "made an expedition upon the maritime parts of the country, Raphia and Anthedon," and ""took Raphia and Gaza, with Anthedon also." As for the location of Anthedon, Josephus gives contradictory indications. Once, when he enumerates the seaside towns in the possession of the Jews, he lists Anthedon between Gaza and Raphia, that is, as lying to the south of Gaza; but in most of his references to Anthedon he places it between Gaza and Jaffa, that is, to the north of Gaza.[27] Gabinius, the governor of Syria, rebuilt Anthedon, and Augustus presented it to Herod, who embellished it with many beautiful buildings, and renamed it Agrippias or Agrippeion in honor of M. Agrippa, friend and son-in-law of Augustus. In the days of the procurator Gessius Florus (64–66 CE), when the Greek inhabitants of Caesarea massacred all the Jews of the city, the Jews retaliated by "entirely demolishing Anthedon and Gaza." Soon, however, Anthedon was rebuilt, and in Byzantine times it became the seat of a bishopric.

The site has been identified with Tel Iblakhiyye, on the seashore some one and a half miles north of the port of Gaza. The old name Anthedon was preserved in the vicinity in the name of a hill farther north called Teda, the name applied by the twelfth-century Arab geographer al-Idrisi to the harbor of Gaza.[28]

Ashkelon (Greek Askalon, Hebrew Ashq'lon)

Ashkelon, situated twelve miles north of Gaza, was again a twin city. The main settlement lay inland, while the port city, called in Byzantine times Maiouma Ascalonis, lay on the coast itself. As late as in the sixth century CE, sources mention a bishop of Ascalon and a bishop of Maiouma Ascalonis. The remains of the former must be sought at the usual distance of some two to two-and-a-half miles from the seashore, at modern Mejdel; the latter, hard on the seashore, was excavated by John Garstang.[29]

Ashkelon is mentioned in Egyptian texts and inscriptions beginning with the eighteenth century BCE. In the fourteenth century BCE Ashkelon succeeded in shaking off the Egyptian yoke, but Merneptah reconquered it in 1207 BCE, and the so-called Israel Stele of Merneptah mentions that he "carried off Ashkelon."

The role of Ashkelon in the history of the period of the Hebrew judges (twelfth and eleventh centuries BCE) is well known. In that period Ashkelon was one of the five cities that formed the Philistine Pentapolis (Josh. 13:3; 1 Sam. 6:7), whose linkage continued throughout the biblical period and into Hellenistic-Roman times.[30] The Assyrian rulers Tiglath-pilesar III, Sennacherib, and Esarhaddon conquered Ashkelon, and later it was laid waste by the Scythian invasion (630 BCE). Under the Pharaohs Psammetich I and Necho II, Ashkelon was subject to Egypt, and after the victory of Nebuchadnezzar it became a tributary of Babylonia. In Persian times Ashkelon belonged to Tyre. Alexander the Great had coins struck in Ashkelon; afterwards it was ruled by the Ptolemies, and later by the Seleucids. The Greek authors Herodotus, Diodorus, and Pausanias report that there were in Ashkelon temples of Derecto (Atargatis), the Syrian goddess, who had the form of half woman, half fish, and in whose honor sacred fish were kept in pools.[31] Ashkelon was the only harbor town not conquered by the Hasmonean rulers, who were satisfied with a formal submission of the city. In 104 BCE Ashkelon became independent, and remained so in the days of Herod the Great, who nevertheless presented the city with public buildings, including baths, fountains, and large courts with cloisters.[32]

In the second and first centuries BCE there was in Ashkelon a sizable Jewish community, which was under the jurisdiction of the Jewish High Court of Jerusalem. Talmudic sources mention "the gardens of Ashkelon." In 66 CE the Jews attacked and plundered Ashkelon, whereupon the non-Jewish Ashkelonites massacred the 2,500 Jews who lived in their midst. The Jews tried to attack Ashkelon again, but were beaten off by the city's defenders, resulting in heavy losses.[33] It may have been partly due to the unsettled conditions in Ashkelon that from the third century

BCE on there was an emigration from the city to Greek and Roman cities, as attested by the presence in Athens, Delos, Rhodes, and Puteoli of Ashkelonite merchants and bankers.[34]

In the fourth century CE Ashkelon became a Roman colony. It was a flourishing Hellenistic center, with cults and festive games. The city produced several philosophers, grammarians, historians, and actors, who were famous in their time.[35]

Talmudic literature contains a number of references to the religious duties of Jews who lived in this city of gentiles. In Hellenistic times the Jews had a synagogue in Ashkelon. In the sixth-century CE Madeba mosaic map the Byzantine city of Ashkelon is shown surrounded by walls. Some of the Jewish inhabitants of Ashkelon must have been engaged in fishing, for the light boats of Ashkelon (*n'didaya diAshq'lon*) are referred to in the Talmud. The Jewish community of Ashkelon survived the Arab conquest, and was destroyed during the Crusades.[36]

Ashdod (Greek Azotus)

Ashdod, another twin seaside town, located about ten miles to the northeast of Ashkelon and identified with modern Tel Ashdod, is first mentioned in the Ugaritic tablets dating from the fourteenth to thirteenth centuries BCE in connection with its maritime trade. Ashdod figures prominently in the Bible as one of the five cities of the Philistines, housing the temple of the god Dagon (1 Sam. 5). According to Joshua (11:22), after the conquest of Canaan by the Hebrew tribes, some of the Anakim (giants?) remained living in Gaza, Gath, and Ashdod. King Uzziyah "broke down the wall of Gath, and the wall of Jabneh, and the wall of Ashdod, and he built cities in [the country] of Ashdod and among the Philistines" (2 Chron. 26:6). In 712 BCE Tartan, the general of Sargon, took both Ashdod (Isa. 20:1), and Ashdod-immu (Ashdod Yam), that is "Ashdod of the Sea," the port city located on the seashore. The cities were rebuilt and repeopled with captives from other quarters. Ashdod was subject also to Sennacherib, Esarhaddon, and Ashurbanipal, and was conquered, after a siege lasting several years, by Psamtik (Psammetich) of Egypt. After Nebuchadnezzar's conquest of Judea, a king of Ashdod is mentioned as a captive at the Babylonian court.[37]

In Maccabean times Ashdod was ravaged by Judas Maccabeus. His brother Jonathan defeated Apollonius at Ashdod and burned the whole city, including the temple of Dagon. Under Alexander Jannaeus, Ashdod belonged to Judea, until it was separated from it by Pompey. Rebuilt by Gabinius in 55 BCE, Ashdod seems to have fallen to Herod (in 30 BCE), after whose death it passed to his sister Salome.[38]

It must have been owing to the numerous Jewish inhabitants of the

town that Vespasian found it necessary to put a garrison into it. The
Romans called Ashdod by the name Hippinos. In Greek it was called
Azotus, by which name it was known to Herodotus. Ptolemy refers to
Azotus as a seaside town, while Josephus mentions both an inland and a
seaside Azotus. In Roman and Christian times the former was called
Azotus mesogaios ("inland Azotus"), the latter Azotus paralios ("Azotus-
on-the-Sea"). The two Ashdods are also depicted on the mosaic map of
Madeba, dating from the sixth century CE. Today, seaside Ashdod is
Minat Asdud ("Port of Asdud") or Minat al-Qal'a, whereas inland Ash-
dod is the village Isdud at a distance of some three miles from the shore.[39]

The existence of a Jewish community in Ashdod in Hellenistic times is
also proven by the ruins of a synagogue with Greek and Hebrew inscriptions.[40] Medieval Arab geographers called the surroundings of the city
Mahuz Isdud ("District of Ashdod").[41]

Yabhneh (Greek Jamnia)

Nine miles northward of Ashdod (and thirteen miles south of Jaffa), at a
distance of four miles from the seashore, lies the city of Yabhneh (Greek
Jamnia). Like Raphia, Gaza, Ashkelon, and Ashdod, Yabhneh too was a
twin city, and had the greatest distance between the inland town and its
seaport, Yabhneh Yam. The inland town, corresponding to the modern
Arab village of Yibna, was originally a Philistine settlement, and was occupied by King Uzziah (2 Chron. 26:6). Both Pliny and Ptolemy distinguish between the town Jamnia and its port, whereas Josephus refers to
Jamnia alternately as an inland town and a port.[42]

Special reference to the harbor of Yabhneh is made in the second book
of the Maccabees, where it is recounted that Judas Maccabeus attacked
the city, which was inhabited by gentiles, and burned its harbor together
with its fleet. (This burning of the harbor seems to indicate that the
harbor consisted of not much more than a wooden jetty, similar to the
one that was in use in modern Gaza.) After Alexander Jannaeus, Yabhneh
had a large Jewish population and belonged to Judea, until Pompey detached it. Gabinius rebuilt Yabhneh, which later belonged to Herod,
from whom it passed to his sister Salome, then to Livia and Tiberius.
Still, the majority of the city's population was Jewish, and to keep control
over it Vespasian had to garrison it twice.[43]

After the destruction of Jerusalem (70 CE) Yabhneh became the main
seat of Jewish learning, where, under the leadership of Rabban Yohanan
ben Zakkai, the foundations were laid for the Mishna and the Talmud,
and a Judaism without a Temple.[44]

The Syriac translation of the Life of Petrus of Iberia (ca. 453–488)
mentions "Mahuza diYabhnin," that is, the port of Yabhneh, as well as

"the village and the town of Jamnia." In this same source it is also related that Petrus healed in Yabhneh a sick Jewish fisherman[45]—evidently Yabhneh had a Jewish population in the fifth century. The Jewish traveler Benjamin of Tudela (1166–1171) refers to Yabhneh by the name Ibelin, given to it by the Crusaders, and states that no Jews lived there.[46]

Jaffa (Hebrew Yafo, Greek Joppē)

Jaffa is the only port along the entire Mediterranean coast of Palestine-Israel that possesses anything like a natural harbor, in the form of a long line of low and partly submerged rocks, which run out into the sea in a rough semicircle toward the northwest from the southern end of the town. Moreover, it occupies a natural defensive position provided by a rocky eminence some 130 feet high, projecting seaward and forming a bold cape. Behind the hill there stretches a tract of fertile soil, rich in water at a moderate depth, protected by the hill from the sand dunes that everywhere else along the Mediterranean coast of that land generally form a barrier between the sea and the fertile maritime plain.

It was on this hill that the city of Jaffa was built in prehistoric times. The great antiquity of the site may have influenced the ancient tradition according to which Jaffa was founded prior to the deluge.[47] The name of the city is derived from the Phoenician word meaning "the beautiful." Thutmose III conquered Jaffa in the fifteenth century BCE, and thereafter contingents of the Egyptian army were regularly transported by the fleet to Jaffa to assume garrison duty in Palestine and Syria. From the Amarna letters we know that under Amenhotep IV (Ekhnaton) Egyptian officers guarded "the gate of Azati [Gaza] and the gate of Yapu [Jaffa]," and that Jaffa was an Egyptian stronghold containing royal granaries. In the Papyrus Anastasi I (thirteenth century BCE) an Egyptian royal official gives account of his experience in Jaffa and describes it as abounding in blooming gardens, and as inhabited not only by workmen skilled in repairing chariots and in the working of wood, metal, and leather but also by impudent thieves. The fleet and the land forces of Rameses III (1198–1167 BCE), in the eighth year of his reign, defeated the invading Peoples of the North on the coast of the Nile delta, and settled their remnants in the maritime plain, which probably accounts for the beginning of the Philistine settlements along the southern coast of Palestine.[48]

Biblical tradition places the western boundary of the inheritance of the tribe of Dan immediately opposite Jaffa (Josh. 19:46); that is, Jaffa itself was not included in it. A few miles north of Jaffa, at the mouth of the Yarkon River, on Tell el-Kudadah, the remains of a tower were discovered in the course of excavations conducted by the Hebrew University, at a site that was continuously occupied from the days of the Hebrew Judges down to Second Temple days (ca. 1200 BCE–70 CE).

In the days of Solomon, Jaffa served as his harbor for sea traffic with Syria: it was to Jaffa that the timber brought for the construction of the Temple was floated down from Lebanon (2 Chron. 2:15). From the story of Jonah we may conclude that Jaffa was also the main port of embarkation for the non-Jewish inhabitants of Palestine when sailing overseas (Jon. 1:3).

In 700 BCE Sennacherib of Assyria, on the way to fight King Hezekiah, plundered Jaffa (Iappu), which at the time belonged to Zidka, king of Ashkelon.[49] When the Jews returned from the Babylonian captivity and began building the Second Temple, Jaffa again played the role it had in the days of Solomon: "They gave money also unto the hewers, and to the carpenters; and food and drink and oil unto them of Zidon, and to them of Tyre, to bring cedar trees from Lebanon to the sea, unto Jaffa, according to the grant they had of Cyrus king of Persia" (Ezra 3:7). In the sixth century BCE the Persians gave Dor (Tantura) and Jaffa and the whole plain lying between them to Eshmunazar king of Sidon.[50] At this time a temple was built in Jaffa in honor of Eshmun, the Phoenician deity. However, in 350 BCE Jaffa again became independent of the northern cities, and a few decades later, offering no resistance, it was occupied by the fleet of Alexander the Great commanded by Hephaestion. Therewith the Hellenistic period of Jaffa began, and its name was given the Greek form of Joppe or Jope. Greek myths began to circulate about the origin of Joppe: according to one it was named after Jope, the daughter of Aeolus, the god of the winds; according to another, it was founded by Kepheus, the father of Andromeda.[51]

After Alexander's death the possession of Jaffa became one of the main bones of contention between his generals and successors until, in 301 BCE, it was definitely incorporated into the domains of the Ptolemies. A hundred years later, with the annexation of Palestine to the Seleucid kingdom by Antiochus III the Great, Jaffa too became subject to his rule.

During the entire Hellenistic period Jaffa had a considerable Jewish community. When the Maccabean revolt began, the Jews of Jaffa fell victim to the vengeance of the city's Greek inhabitants. On the occasion of a popular festival, "the men of Jaffa prayed the Jews that dwelt among them to go, with their wives and children, into the boats which they had prepared, as though they had meant no hurt; but when they were gone forth into the deep, they drowned no less than two hundred of them." Judas Maccabeus thereupon raided the harbor of Jaffa, which was outside the city walls, and "burned the haven by night, and set the boats on fire, and those that flew thither he slew" (2 Macc. 12:3–6). After Judas's death, his brothers Jonathan and Simon, challenged by Apollonius Daos, the general of Demetrius I Soter, marched against Jaffa (in 148 BCE), but "when Jonathan was preparing to besiege them, they were afraid he would take them by force, and so they opened the gates to him."[52] In 143 BCE Simon occupied Jaffa, and in the following year annexed it definitively as part of the Jewish state. He expelled the Greek inhabitants, rebuilt the town, strengthened its fortifications, and carried out extensive improvements in the harbor. The Book of Maccabees records: "In addition to his [other] glory, Simon took Jaffa for a haven, and made it an entrance to the isles of the sea."[53] During the following two centuries, that is, until its destruction by the Romans, Jaffa remained a purely Jewish city, and served as the port of Judea.

The importance to the Jewish state of the possession of a port of its own, which was, moreover, until the development of Caesarea by Herod, the best port on the entire coast from the Egyptian border to Tyre, cannot be overestimated. It not only meant a direct gateway to the lands around the Mediterranean but it had great significance as an asset in the state budget. The import and export duties introduced by the Syrian kings could henceforth be levied for the benefit of the Jewish treasury.

In 113 BCE Antiochus IX Kyzenikos, king of Syria, seized Jaffa and Gezer, whereupon John Hyrcanus lodged a complaint against him with the Roman Senate. In response the Senate issued a decree which, incidentally, shows that maritime trade was a most valuable asset to the Jewish state. The decree ordered that Antiochus "should do no injury to the Jews, the confederates of the Romans; and that the fortresses and the havens and the country, and whatsoever else he had taken from them, should be restored to them; and that it may be lawful to them to export their own goods out of their own havens; and that no king nor people may have leave to export any goods, either out of the country of Judea, or out of their havens, without paying customs, but only Ptolemy, the king of Alexandria, because he is our confederate and friend."[54]

The successor of John Hyrcanus, Alexander Jannaeus (103–76 BCE), continued to enjoy possession of Jaffa; certain of the coins struck by him bear the image of a ship's anchor, a symbol of Judea's maritime power (Figure 14). Such coins were also struck by his wife and successor, Alexandra, indicating the continued possession of Jaffa by the Hasmonean ruling family.

Pompey, in 63 BCE, declared Jaffa as well as other cities of the coastal region "free towns." In 47 BCE, however, Julius Caesar restored Jaffa to the Jews. Josephus reports that Caesar decreed,

> It is our pleasure that the city Joppa, which the Jews had originally, when they made a league of friendship with the Romans, shall belong to them as it

formerly did, and that Hyrcanus, the son of Alexander, and his sons, have as tribute of that city from those that occupy the land, for the country, and for what they export every year to Sidon, twenty thousand six hundred and seventy-five modii every year, the seventh year, which they call the sabbatic year, excepted, whereon they neither plough nor receive the product of their trees.[55]

Jaffa remained a predominantly Jewish city down to the days of the Jewish revolt, when Cestius Gallus took it by surprise (66 CE), slaying 8,400 of its inhabitants. Immediately, however, Jaffa was again settled by Jews, so that two years later (68 CE) Vespasian had again to take it by force. The course of that battle has been related in Chapter 9. Josephus, before telling about it, describes the harbor of Jaffa:

Now Jaffa is not naturally a haven, for it ends in a rough shore, where all the rest of it is straight, but the two ends bend toward each other, where there are deep precipices, and great stones that jut out into the sea, and where the chains wherewith Andromeda was bound have left their footsteps [impressions], which attest to the antiquity of that fable. But the north wind opposes and beats upon the shore, and dashes mighty waves against the rocks which receive them, and renders the haven more dangerous [namely, for the Jews who fled thither before the Romans] than the country they had deserted.[56]

As early as the first century CE some of the Jewish inhabitants of Jaffa became adherents of Christianity. Jaffa was the scene of the resurrection of the woman Tabitha (Dorcas) by Peter, which caused many "to believe in the Lord" (Acts 9:36–42; cf. 10:1–23). After the destruction of Jerusalem, and especially after the revolt of Bar Kokhba (132–135 CE), when the Jews were forbidden by the victorious Romans on pain of death to enter Jerusalem, Jaffa received a steady influx of Jewish settlers, mainly merchants from all parts of the Roman empire, drawn there by the reviving commercial activity of the city and its port.

The predominantly Jewish character of Jaffa in the second to fourth centuries is well attested both by the numerous inscriptions found in the Jewish cemetery of the city and by Talmudic sources. The sepulchral inscriptions are either in Hebrew or Aramaic, or are bilingual, Hebrew and Greek. The inscriptions often mention the place of origin of the deceased, and thus we know that during the centuries in question many Jews came from other parts of Palestine or from abroad, and settled in Jaffa. The places of origin mentioned in the tomb inscriptions include Alexandria (several times), Emmaus, Babylonia, Diospolis (Lydda), Tarsos, Neapolis (?), Ptolemais (Acre), Pentapolis (in Corynna?), and Chios. From one of the inscriptions we learn that there was in Jaffa a community of Cappadocian Jews with an elder at its head. Another of the inscriptions mentions a family of fishermen from Jaffa. Other trades mentioned are: washerman, cumin seller, baker, messenger, ironmonger, and cloth merchant.[57]

Jaffa was also a seat of Jewish learning. Talmudic sources mention quite a number of Jewish sages from Jaffa, as well as rulings in religious matters connected with buying merchandise from ships anchored in Jaffa harbor.[58]

In the first half of the fifth century, St. Cyril of Alexandria describes Jaffa as an important commercial center and the place of embarkation for those who travel from Judea to other countries of the Levant. At about the same time Jaffa became the seat of a bishopric. The Arabs conquered Jaffa in 636 CE, and thereafter the city, known as Yafa (an Arabicized form of the Hebrew Yafo), continued to play its role as chief port of Palestine. During the Crusades it was taken and retaken by the Franks and by the Saracens, and fell into a state of ruin.[59]

Apollonia (Arabic Arsuf)

About ten miles north of Jaffa was located Apollonia, yet another of the twin-type harbor towns. The inland town was located about one mile east-northeast of the harbor itself. It seems to have been built on or near the site of the Canaanite city Rishpon, so called after the Canaanite deity Reshef, whose name is preserved as one of the sons of Ephraim in 1 Chron. 7:25. Rishpon was a frontier town of the kingdom of Israel, and served it as a harbor until it was overrun by Tiglath-pileser III (in 732 BCE) and made subject to Assyria.[60]

Apollonia was founded on the site of or next to Rishpon by Seleucus IV (186–174 BCE) and named after the Greek god Apollo, with whom Reshef was presumably identified. It was captured by Alexander Jannaeus and attached to his own domain, and remained in Jewish possession until Pompey gave it independence. It was subsequently rebuilt by Gabinius.[61]

In the Byzantine period, Apollonia reached its largest expansion, covering some 130 acres and serving as a main commercial, industrial, and maritime center. After the Arab conquest the town was again called by its old Semitic name in the Arabicized form Arsuf. In the centuries both preceding and following the Arab conquest, the town was also inhabited by Samaritans, who called it Ra'shpan. King Baldwin captured the city in 1101, and under Crusader rule it was called Arsur, a corruption of Arsuf, and served as a commercial center, especially for the Genoese.[62]

Caesarea (Hebrew Qisrin)

Forty miles north of Jaffa was located the Hellenistic castle Stratonos Pyrgos (Straton's Tower), so named after a fourth-century BCE Sidonian

king named Strato, who established a trading post at the site. Toward the
end of the Persian period the coastal strip both to the north and south of
Straton's Tower belonged to the Sidonians. Alexander Jannaeus subjected Straton's Tower to his rule, and it remained part of the Hasmonean kingdom until given independence by Pompey. Later it was presented by Augustus to Herod. The name is preserved in the Talmudic
sources in the form of Migdal Sharshan (Sharshan's Tower).[63]

Herod, who rebuilt the whole site, called it Caesarea, in honor of Augustus Caesar. This name appears in the Talmud as Qesarin (popularly
pronounced Qisrin). The port of Caesarea is called in the Talmud Lime-
nah shel Qesarin, that is, "Port of Caesarea," whereas in Greek sources it
is referred to as Sebastos. The city and the port were at some distance
from each other, for on coins of Nero, for example, we read *Kaisaria he
pros Sebasto limeni* (Caesarea which is near the port of Sebastos).[64]

In Caesarea Herod built a great port, pagan temples, a theater, a hippodrome, and an amphitheater, and made it the center of Hellenistic
culture in his kingdom. Josephus describes the city and the port in considerable detail:

> Now upon his [Herod's] observation of a place near the sea, which was very
> proper for containing a city, and was before called Strato's Tower, he set
> about getting a plan for a magnificent city there, and erected many edifices
> with great diligence all over it, and this of white stone. He also adorned it
> with most sumptuous palaces and large edifices for containing the people;
> and what was the greatest and most laborious work of all, he adorned it with
> a haven that was always free from the waves of the sea. Its largeness was not
> less than the Pyraeum [at Athens]; and had toward the city a double station
> for the ships. It was of excellent workmanship; and this was the more re-
> markable for its being built in a place that of itself was not suitable to such
> noble structures, but was to be brought to perfection by materials from other
> places, and at very great expenses. This city is situated in Phoenicia, in the
> passage by sea to Egypt, between Joppa [Jaffa] and Dora, which are lesser
> maritime cities, and not fit for havens, on account of the impetuous south
> winds that beat upon them, which rolling the sands that come from the sea
> against the shores, do not admit of ships lying in their station; but the mer-
> chants are generally there forced to ride at their anchors in the sea itself. So
> Herod endeavoured to rectify this inconvenience, and laid out such a com-
> pass towards the land as might be sufficient for a haven, wherein the great
> ships might lie in safety; and this he effected by letting down vast stones of
> above fifty feet in length, not less than eighteen in breadth, and nine in
> depth, into twenty fathoms deep; and as some were lesser, so were others
> bigger, than those dimensions. This mole which he built by the sea-side was
> two hundred feet wide, the half of which was opposed to the current of the

waves, so as to keep off those waves which were to break upon them, and so
was called Procymatia, or the first breaker of the waves; but the other half
had upon it a wall, with several towers, the largest of which was named
Drusus, and was a work of very great excellence, and had its name from
Drusus, the son-in-law of Caesar, who died young. There were also a great
number of arches, where the mariners dwelt; there was also before them a
quay [or landing place], which ran round the entire haven, and was a most
agreeable walk to such as had a mind to that exercise; but the entrance or
mouth of the port was made on the north quarter, on which side was the
stillest of the winds of all in this place: and the basis of the whole circuit on
the left hand, as you enter the port, supported a round turret, which was
made very strong, in order to resist the greatest waves; while, on the right
hand, as you enter, stood two vast stones, and those each of them larger than
the turret, which was over against them; these stood upright, and were
joined together. Now there were edifices all along the circular haven, made
of the most polished stone, with a certain elevation, whereon was erected a
temple, that was seen a great way off by those that were sailing for that
haven, and had in it two statues, the one of Rome, the other of Caesar. The
city itself was called Caesarea, which was also built of fine materials, and was
of a fine structure; nay, the very subterranean vaults and cellars had no less of
architecture bestowed on them than had the buildings above ground. Some
of these vaults carried things at even distances to the haven and to the sea;
but one of them ran obliquely, and bound all the rest together, that both the
rain and the filth of the citizens were together carried off with ease, and the
sea itself, upon the flux of the tide from without, came into the city, and
washed it all clean. Herod also built therein a theatre of stone; and on the
south quarter, behind the port, an amphitheatre also, capable of holding a
vast number of men, and conveniently situated for a prospect to the sea. So
this city was finished in twelve years; during which time the king did not fail
to go on both with the work and to pay the charges that were necessary.[65]

Although some details in this description remain puzzling, and differ
from those given by Josephus in his earlier account of Caesarea contained
in his *Wars of the Jews*, all in all they have proven to be largely correct by
recent underwater excavations carried out at the site. The Outer Basin
was indeed an engineering marvel: it contained such sophisticated features as a siltation control system that used flushing channels, the extensive use of hydraulic concrete (a building material that was poured into
the sea to harden there), and design elements intended to mitigate the
damage caused by the pounding of the waves. The facility actually contained four interconnected harbors, and its size clearly indicates that
Herod intended it to be a major transshipment point and to assume a
premier role in the maritime affairs of the Roman world. Herod also built

a high-level aquaduct that brought water to Caesarea from springs on Mount Carmel, and which was restored by the Roman Second and Tenth Legions during the Bar Kokhba revolt (132–135 CE).

After the death of Herod, Caesarea passed into the possession of Archelaus, his son and heir, and remained united with Judea. However, in 6 CE Archelaus was removed by Augustus and banished to Gaul, and his kingdom, including Caesarea, was absorbed into the Roman Empire. Caesarea became the seat of the Roman procurators of Judea, as well as the main station of the Roman garrison. The population was in the main gentile, but there was a considerable Jewish minority as well. The situation between these two population elements was always a strained one, and when the Jewish revolt began (66 CE), the Greeks arose against the Jews, and in a single hour massacred all the Jewish inhabitants of the city, twenty thousand persons.[66]

For the Jews of the Mishnaic and Talmudic periods (first to fourth centuries CE), Caesarea was a symbol of Roman rule, of Roman culture, and of all that Rome stood for, in opposition to Jerusalem, emblem of Judaism. According to a Talmudic opinion, Caesarea and Jerusalem cannot both exist at the same time. This is expressed as follows: "If somebody tells you, 'Caesarea and Jerusalem are both destroyed,' do not believe it; [if somebody tells you] 'both are inhabited,' do not believe it; 'Caesarea is destroyed and Jerusalem inhabited,' or, 'Jerusalem is destroyed and Caesarea inhabited,' believe it. It is written, 'I shall be filled with her that is laid waste' (Ezek. 26:2)—if this one is filled, the other is laid waste, if this one is laid waste, the other is filled."[67]

Despite being the symbol, in the eyes of some of the sages, of the very opposite of everything Judaism represented, Caesarea had, by the second century CE, not only a large Jewish community but also an important Talmudic academy. The *Rabbanan diQesari* ("Masters of Caesarea") are often referred to in Talmudic literature. One of the several outstanding Talmudic sages who lived in Caesarea was Rabbi Abbahu, head of the Talmudic school, who represented the Jewish community before the Roman governor. At the same time, however, the great bulk of the Jewish population of Caesarea was Hellenized to such an extent that in its synagogue even the most basic of all Jewish prayers, the Sh'ma' Yisrael ("Hear, O Israel") was said in Greek.[68]

Talmudic literature contains a number of religious enactments, the necessity for which arose in Caesarea in the course of everyday life in a big coastal town inhabited by both Jews and gentiles. Rabbi Abbahu decreed that fish entrails and fish roes might be purchased from anybody in Caesarea, that is to say, there are no ritual injunctions against their purchase, for it may be supposed that they were brought to Caesarea from Pelusium and Hispania, whose waters contain only ritually clean fishes. This statement, incidentally, shows that processed fish parts were imported to Caesarea from overseas countries, and that Jewish customers bought such products from gentile importers. Also in Caesarea it was customary to eat batter cakes that had been placed on top of pots of pickle, so that the cakes had a flavor of pickle, and this too was permittted.[69]

In 235 CE the scholar Origen came to Caesarea and turned the city into a center of Christian learning. Later Eusebius served as archbishop of Caesarea. The city reached its greatest extent in Byzantine times, when the semicircular city wall encompassed an area of some two square kilometers. Caesarea was also inhabited by a large number of Samaritans, some of whom served as city guards. In 556 the Samaritans, suffering under the oppression of Justinian, rose against the Christians of the city, in which uprising they were helped by the Jews. Caesarea was the last Palestinian city to be conquered by the Arabs (in 640). After the Crusades, in the course of which the control of Caesarea often changed hands, the city was several times destroyed and restored. After its final destruction by the Mameluk Baybars in 1265, the site remained in ruins until the late nineteenth century.[70]

Dor (Greek Dora)

The town of Dor, nine miles to the north of Caesarea and eighteen miles south of Haifa, has been identified with modern Khirbet el-Burj near Tantura. Dor is mentioned in Egyptian and cuneiform inscriptions, and archaeological discoveries indicate that it was first settled in the fifteenth to fourteenth centuries BCE.[71] According to Joshua 12:23, the king of Dor was one of the thirty-one kings vanquished by Joshua, but the Book of Judges informs us that "Manasseh did not drive out the inhabitants of Dor and its towns."[72] Under King Solomon, however, "all the region of Dor" appears as one of the districts into which the country was divided for administrative purposes (1 Kings 4:11). Tiglath-pileser III captured Dor in 732 BCE, and made it the capital of the Assyrian province of Duru extending from the Carmel to Jaffa. The Phoenician inscription of Eshmunazar king of Sidon mentions that "the lord of kings [probably Ptolemy I] gave Eshmunazar the lands of Dor and Jaffa."[73]

Alexander Jannaeus took Dor together with several other coastal towns, and it remained under Hasmonean rule until 63 BCE, when Pompey severed it from Judea. According to Josephus, there was a Jewish community in Dora with a synagogue of its own. The relations between the Jews and the Greeks in Dor were tense, as illustrated by an incident that took place under King Agrippa, when "the young [gentile] men of Dor . . . carried a statue of Caesar into a synagogue of the Jews and erected it there." This was not only a desecration of a synagogue but a transgression against public order, and Agrippa lodged a complaint with Publius Petronius, the Roman president of Syria, who sent an angry reprimand to the people of Dor, and ordered them to remove the statue and refrain from interfering with the rights of the Jews.[74]

Dor was deserted as early as the third century CE, but still had Christian bishops until the seventh century.[75]

Athlit

Athlit, about seven miles south of Haifa, has been identified with Kartah, a city of Zebulun, mentioned in Joshua 21:34. Excavations have shown that the site was inhabited in the Iron Age, probably by Phoenicians, and yielded walls, as well as Canaanite, Jewish, and Roman graves, cisterns, wells, canals, altars, and so on. Somewhat south of Athlit there is a small ruin called Khirbet Mallaḥa, which has been identified by Yitzḥak ben-Zvi with the Migdal Mallaḥa ("Tower of Saltmakers") referred to in the Palestinian Talmud.[76]

The anonymous traveler from Bordeaux who visited Palestine in 333 CE mentions a *statio mutationis Certha*, which was located at the same site, and in whose name that of the ancient Kartah may have survived.

The ruins near the seashore, to be seen today at Athlit, are those of the Castrum Peregrinorum (Château des Pèlerins) erected by Crusader pilgrims in 1217. It is built on a promontory jutting out into a bay, which served as its harbor. It was surrounded on three sides by the sea, and on the fourth (the eastern) side it was closed off against the land by a double wall with three massive towers.

Athlit, too, seems to have been one of the twin-type towns typical of the Palestinian seacoast. This is indicated by ruins of a second Crusaders' castle east of the first, called Districtum (Le Détroit), today Khirbet Dustri. It may be supposed that both of these Crusaders' castles were built on the site of more ancient buildings or settlements.[77]

Sycamine (Hebrew Shikmonah)

This ancient Palestinian port was situated near the western tip of the cape formed by the seaward end of Mount Carmel, protruding northward into the sea. The site is occupied today by Tell el-Samak. Under Hasmonean rule it was an important port, and in Mishnaic times it was a Jewish town. Eusebius identifies it with Haifa.

One of the earliest Christian travelers, Antoninus Placentius, who visited Palestine in about 570 CE, calls Sycamine *civitas Sycamine Judeorum*, that is, "Sycamine City of the Jews." Greek sources from about the same period also contain information as to the Jews of Sycamine. The Jewish community there had a head or elder, a priest (*kohen*), and a scribe.[78]

Haifa (Hebrew Ḥēfa)

Haifa is first mentioned in Jewish literature in the first to second century CE as the home town of Jewish scholars. The Palestinian Talmud states that it was a fishing village whose inhabitants could not distinguish between the pronunciation of the Hebrew and Aramaic gutturals *ḥet* and *'ayin*. The Babylonian Talmud states that the murex, the shellfish yielding the purple dye used for the *tallith* (prayer shawl), was caught along the coast between Haifa and the Ladder of Tyre. One passage in the Midrash describes a sage as taking a walk along the seashore of Haifa.[79]

The passage contained in the Benediction of Moses, "They shall suck of the abundance of the seas and of the treasures hid in the sand" (Deut. 33:19), has been taken by the Talmudic sages as alluding to Haifa, where, according to the legend, all the treasures sunk in the depths of the sea are kept for the righteous in the world to come. In this connection it is also mentioned that between Haifa and Acre there were in the sea veritable underwater mountains formed by the accumulation of great quantities of the murex, the purple snail.[80]

The legend about the angels shaping the gates of the Temple of a future Jerusalem out of enormous precious stones (see Chapter 12) is connected in one of the sources recording it with the coast of Haifa. A pious man, this source tells, once saw on the seashore of Haifa the waters open, and in their depths he saw the angels busy sawing and chiseling huge precious stones.[81]

Toward the end of the Talmudic period (fourth century CE), Haifa still had its Jewish community, watched over by the Romans from a neighboring fortress called Castra.[82] When the Byzantines reconquered the country from the Persians (in 628 CE), the Jewish community of Haifa was destroyed, but subsequently, after the Arab conquest, it was reestablished. In 1046 the Persian traveler Nasir-i Khusrau relates that large sailing ships were being built in Haifa. In 1084 there was a Jewish community in Haifa with a religious head and a Talmudic school. In 1100 Haifa was conquered by the Crusaders with the help of the Venetian navy, and all its Jewish defenders—who composed the majority of the population— were slaughtered. In 1156 the Carmelite Order was founded on Mount Carmel, but its monastery was destroyed by the Muslims in 1291.[83]

Acre (Hebrew Akko, Greek Ptolemais)

Acre, situated on a promontory at the northern end of Haifa Bay, fourteen miles north of Haifa, was a very ancient Phoenician coastal town, mentioned in the Egyptian Execration Texts (ca. 1800 BCE), in the Amarna letters, and in other Egyptian documents. It is also mentioned in the Ugaritic tablets, in Assyrian royal inscriptions ("Akku"), and on Phoenician coins ("'Akka" or "'Akk").[84] In the Bible Akko is mentioned only once (Judg. 1:31) as one of the towns that the tribe of Asher did not succeed in conquering. To the Greeks Akko was known as early as pre-Hellenistic times, and they derived its name from the Greek *ake*, healing. Ptolemy II Philadelphus (285–247 BCE) settled Greek colonists in the town, which was thereafter called Ptolemais. From the middle of the third century BCE Ptolemais is referred to several times in Egyptian papyri as a commercial center. Of the Jewish inhabitants of Akko we hear only from the time of the Hasmonean rulers onward.[85]

When the Jewish revolt against Roman rule began (66 CE), the Greek inhabitants of Akko "rose up against the Jews that were among them" and slew "two thousand, and put not a few into bonds." After the destruction of Jerusalem, the daughters of the rich Jerusalemites were brought by force to Akko.[86]

Toward the end of the first and the beginning of the second century CE there was a considerable Jewish community in Akko. The harbor of Akko served as port of embarkation for Jewish sages traveling to Rome, and as home port for their commercial fleet. There also existed a coastal service between Akko and Haifa.[87] Akko was often visited by the spiritual leaders of Palestinian Jewry, including Rabban Gamliel II, Rabbi Shim'on ben Gamliel, and Rabbi Yehuda. The Patriarch Gamliel II did not disdain to bathe in the *thermae* of Aphrodite, which were in Akko.[88] Akko was an important commercial center with a famous fair (*y'rid* in Hebrew) held in honor of the local god.[89] To the port of Akko came ships from Italy, Spain, and Cilicia, bringing fish brine. Of Rabbi Akiba of Akko it is told that he had a watchman placed on board a ship that had brought fish brine to Akko, lest the brine be ritually defiled.[90]

Akko itself was also a great fishing center, and "to bring fishes to Akko" was a popular saying to describe a superfluous proceeding, much like the English "coals to Newcastle." The Jewish fishermen of Akko were pious people who took it upon themselves not to go fishing on the half-holidays,[91] even though religious laws did not prohibit work on those days. It was known that the fish caught at Akko had a special taste, easily distinguishable from that of fish caught elsewhere. One of the sages tells of a fish caught at Akko that weighed two hundred pounds. This fish, it is reported, was caught before the early rains fell. After the early rains had fallen, they caught a fish weighing three hundred pounds.[92]

Near Akko there was a place from which sand was extracted for the manufacture of glass. Josephus describes the wonderful qualities of this place:

The very small river Belus runs by it, at the distance of two furlongs [one quarter of a mile]; near which there is Memnon's monument, and hath near it a place no larger than a hundred cubits, which deserves admiration; for the place is round and hollow, and affords such sand as glass is made of; which place when it hath been emptied by the many ships there loaded, it is filled again by the winds, which bring into it, as it were on purpose, that sand which lay remote, and was no more than bare common sand, while this mine presently turns it into glassy sand. And what is to me still more wonderful, that glassy sand which is superfluous, and is once removed out of the place, becomes bare common sand again. And this is the nature of the place we are speaking of.[93]

What Josephus tries to do in this passage is to give a rational explanation of what seems to have been a popular local wonder tale. In the Middle Ages a very similar tale was told in connection with a field (called by one authority "Field of Damascus") at Hebron, in southern Palestine. The earth of that field was red, it is said, and the people ate of it as a charm against misfortune. The fame of that earth was so great that large quantities of it were removed and exported to faraway countries. However, at the end of each year the big hole dug by the people was miraculously filled up. This is independently reported by a number of Jewish and Christian travelers in the Middle Ages.[94]

In the sixth and seventh centuries CE there were in Akko Jewish, Samaritan, and Christian communities, the last named headed by a bishop. Next to the port was a customs house and a workshop for the repair of ships, where the ships were hauled ashore.[95]

It would seem that in Byzantine days Akko was destroyed, and in 636 it fell to the Arabs. It is only from the tenth century on that we again hear of a Jewish community there. In 1104 Akko fell into the hands of the Crusaders, who called it "St. Jean d'Acre." In the twelfth century it was "the great port for all Christian pilgrims making the pilgrimage to Jerusalem."[96]

Akhzibh (Arabic Al-Zib)

Nine miles north of Akko, near the cliff called "The Ladder of Tyre," is situated the port of Akhzibh, referred to in cuneiform inscriptions by the name Akzibi, and in Egyptian documents as Akhsap. It was included in the ideal inheritance of the tribe of Asher (Joshua 19:29), but was not occupied by them (Judg. 1:31). In the inscription of Sennacherib Akhzibh appears among the towns taken by him from the king of Tyre in 701 BCE. According to the Mishna, Akhzibh was the northernmost point on the seashore of the territory occupied by the Jews after their return from the Babylonian captivity. In Talmudic times we often hear of sages who walked from Akko to Akhzibh, or from Akhzibh to the north, to Tyre. The coastal strip between the Akko-to-Akhzibh road and the seashore was regarded as not being part of Jewish Palestine.[97]

In Akhzibh itself there was a synagogue and a community headed by an elder. South of Akhzibh ran a rivulet (its modern Arabic name is Mafshuh), mentioned in Talmudic sources as the border of Palestine proper, beyond which the fields were free from the ritual duties.[98]

The Greeks called the town Ekdippa, whereas Josephus refers to it as Ecdippon. The Crusaders named it Casal Imbert. In modern times the site was occupied by the Arab village called az-Zib. About two thirds of a mile to the south of this village are the ruins of Minet az-Zib, the Port of Akhzibh.[99]

We have discussed above sixteen seaside towns or localities (many of them twin towns), which dotted the Mediterranean coast of Palestine in ancient times. In addition to them there were several smaller localities we know of from literary references or from the testimony of ruins.

A brief concluding remark may be made to this geographical-historical survey of those townships in ancient Palestine which were located on or near the waterfront, and served as the basis for shipping, fishing, and related trades. Considering the small size of the country and its coast's unfavorable straightness and lack of protective bays, it is surprising that such a relatively large number of localities existed on the seashore, providing livelihood to what must have been a considerable proportion of the population, and that the largest of these settlements also served as points of embarkation for sailing to other Mediterranean countries and for trading with them. Although seafaring was never a major occupational specialization in the country, it did have its economic significance and, beyond that, it supplied an important dimension to the worldview of the biblical Hebrews and their successors, the Jews in Talmudic times in both the land of Israel and Babylonia.

Chapter 14

LAKE KINNERET

LAKE KINNERET, Palestine-Israel's only major fresh-water lake, was in ancient times the scene of much waterborne traffic and an intensive fishing industry.

In the Bible the lake is called Yam Kinneret, "Sea of Kinneret" (Num. 34:11; Josh. 12:3, 13:27), the name being derived from the Hebrew *kinnor*, lyre, referring to its shape. In early post-biblical times it was referred to as "Waters of Gennesaret" (1 Macc. 11:67), or "Lake of Gennesareth."[1] In the Gospels it is called "Sea of Gennesareth," "Sea of Galilee," "Sea of Tiberias," or simply "the Sea" (Matt. 4:18, 17:27; Luke 5:1; John 6:1, 21:1). In Talmudic sources it is usually called "Sea of Tiberias."[2]

According to the biblical scheme for dividing the land of Israel among the tribes, the western shores of the lake, including the "fortified cities of Hammath and Rakkath and Kinnereth," were within the possession of Naphtali (Josh. 19:35) whereas the territory of Gad extended to its southern end (Josh. 12:3, 12:27).

An important feature of the lakeshore was the hot springs whose beneficial effects are mentioned in the Papyrus Anastasi I, and which gave its name to Hammath, the first of the three fortified cities on its shore mentioned in Joshua.

FISHING ON THE LAKE

Lake Kinneret is described by the Jewish historian Flavius Josephus, who served as commander of the Jewish forces on the shore of the lake in the early phases of the Jewish-Roman war (66–70 CE). Josephus praises the lake's sweet waters, its purity, and its richness in fishes of several kinds, "different both to the taste and the sight from those elsewhere."[3] Fishing was one of the major sources of livelihood for the inhabitants of the townships around the lake, as becomes evident from those passages of the Gospels that refer to the time Jesus spent on the shores of the lake, about a generation prior to Josephus. The favored time for fishing was at night, and if the catch was poor the fishermen had to stay in their boats all night (Luke 5:5; John 21:3). On the other hand, it could also happen that the catch was so rich that the nets were torn by the weight of the fish (Luke 5:6; John 21:6, 11). If that happened, the nets had to be mended, which was best done right there in the boats (Mark 1:19). Fishing seems to have been an occupation passed on from father to son, and occasionally a father and his sons worked together. In addition, the owners of boats also employed hired hands to help them in the work, which required considerable physical effort (Mark 1:19–20; Matt. 4:18, 21–22). Although most of the fishing was done with nets, the fishermen also used line and hook to catch fish (Matt. 17:27). According to a Talmudic passage,[4] when Joshua conquered the Land of Israel he decreed that it was permitted to fish on the Sea of Tiberias with either nets or lines, but it was not allowed to spread out an enclosure in the water, because that would impede the movement of ships. Although the attribution of such a rule to Joshua is certainly pure Aggada, the statement shows what methods of fishing were practiced on Lake Kinneret in Talmudic times. Several Talmudic passages contain regulations concerning the extent to which fishermen have to conform to religious laws.[5]

The prevalence of fishing as the occupation of breadwinners along the shores of the lake explains the otherwise puzzling detail that when Jesus was walking by the Sea of Galilee and called upon men, seemingly at random, to become his followers, all four of those whom he thus addressed—Simon-Peter, Andrew, and two sons of Zebedee, James and John—were fishermen (Matt. 4:18–22; Mark 1:16–20; Luke 5:3–11). Also, no fewer than six of the disciples to whom Jesus manifested himself at the Sea of Tiberias after he was risen from the dead were fishermen who seem to have worked in partnership on one boat (John 21:1–3). All in all, according to the joint testimony of the Gospels, eight of the disciples of Jesus were fishermen on the Sea of Galilee. Eight or even six men are a considerable crew for a fishing boat, which has to be large enough to accommodate all of them. A night's fishing, if successful, yielded a correspondingly large catch: John tells of a haul of 153 fishes (John 21:11). On the other hand, if the night's expedition was unsuccessful the fishermen had nothing to eat next day (Luke 21:3–5; John 21:3). Another hazard the fishermen had to face was the changeability of the winds. If the winds were contrary, the fishing boats were unable to get back to the shore (Matt. 15:24). The fishing boats were also equipped with oars, so that if the winds gave out the vessel would nevertheless be able to move. Also, when people used boats to go from one lakeside town to another, they used oars (John 6:17, 19).

TOWNSHIPS AROUND LAKE KINNERET

Hammath

The first of the three cities mentioned in Joshua is also referred to in the Bible by the variant names Hammoth-Dor and Hammon (Josh. 21:32; 1 Chron. 6:61), and is called by the Hellenic form, Emmaus, by Josephus (see Map 2). The name is derived from the Hebrew *ham*, hot, and means something like "hot spring." In Mishnaic and Talmudic times it was a suburb of Tiberias, one mile to its north. According to the Mishna, the temperature of the water of the springs was hot enough to cause injury.[5] Modern topographical research has identified Hammath with the site called in Arabic Ḥammām Tabariyye (that is, "Bath of Tiberias"), about one mile south of Tiberias, on the shore of the lake. Excavations there have unearthed the foundations of bath houses, synagogues, parts of city walls, and a tower, dating back to the first century CE. By that time the hot springs were renowned for their healing power.[7] Josephus explains the name: "Emmaus, if it is interpreted, may be rendered 'a warm bath,' for therein is a spring of warm water useful for healing."[8] After the destruction of the Second Temple (70 CE) priests settled in Hammath, and many Talmudic sages, among them Rabbi Meir (whose traditional tomb is still venerated on the spot), lived there. The most important remains are those of a synagogue, of which three layers have been discovered: one of the third century CE; the second above it, with an outstanding mosaic pavement, from the early fourth century; and the third, on top of the second, from the sixth century.[9] These remains show that Hammath had a considerable Jewish population until at least the sixth century. The Palestinian Talmud identifies Hammath with Hammtah, and the Babylonian Talmud with Tiberias.[10]

Rakkath

The second city mentioned in Joshua, Rakkath, cannot be as unquestioningly identified with present-day remains as can Hammath. Both the Palestinian and the Babylonian Talmuds identify Rakkath with Tiberias, but another opinion in the Babylonian Talmud identifies it with Sepphoris.[11] Modern archeologists have suggested various other identifications. In view of the general tendency of biblical place names to survive in the Arabic place names, and especially in the names of tels (the typical coffin-shaped mounds of ruins), it would seem likely that Tel Raqqat, less than five miles north of Tiberias on the lakeshore, contains the remains of ancient Rakkat,[12] rather than the Khirbet Qunaytirah, preferred by the *Anchor Bible Dictionary*.[13]

Kinneret

In the English Bible translations this is called Chinnereth; it is the third of the three fortified cities mentioned in Joshua, and has been identified with Tel el-'Oreimeh (Tel Kinrot) on the western shore of the lake, to the north of Tiberias, on the el-Ghuwayyer plain. First mentioned in

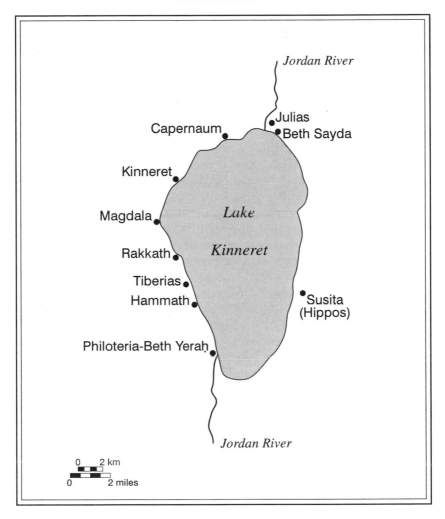

Map 2. Settlements around Lake Kinneret in Ancient Times.

Egyptian papyri, it must have been an important city in the Hebrew monarchic period, since the lake was named after it ("Sea of Kinneret," Num. 34:11; Deut. 3:17; Josh. 12:3, 13:27). Following the Assyrian conquest of Israel, the city was abandoned, but in Roman times it was replaced by a new settlement called Gennesareth (Matt. 14:34; Mark 6:53). The Palestinian Talmud explicitly identifies Kinneret with Ginnesar.[14] In the Midrash a popular etymology of "Ginnesar" is given: it is said to be derived from *Ganne Sarim*, "Gardens of Princes."[15]

Tiberias (Hebrew T'verya)

In modern times this has been the only city on the shores of Lake Kinneret. Located in the south-central part of the western lakefront, it was founded by Herod Antipas, tetrarch of Galilee and Perea (ruled 4 BCE–39 CE), as his new capital city. He named it in honor of the Roman emperor Tiberius in 20 CE. According to Josephus, "he built it in the best part of Galilee, at the lake of Gennesareth. There are warm baths at a little distance from it, in a village named Emmaus." Josephus also reports that Herod (as he called Herod Antipas) populated Tiberias by forcibly bringing people to it from other parts of his domains. To induce them to stay in Tiberias, Herod provided them with "very good houses at his own expenses, and by giving them land also."[16] The city was built at a place where there were ancient Jewish tombs, which Herod had removed.[17] The region was famous for its wine, figs, and wheat, and, according to Rabbinic sources, there were separate markets in it for wheat and barley.[18]

Relatively more is known of the history, buildings, administration, and so on of Tiberias than of the other townships surrounding Lake Kinneret, but this is not the place to present these details. As for its shipping and fishing, the Gospel of John mentions in passing that inhabitants of Tiberias used boats to go to other places along the shores of the lake, including Capernaum (John 6:23–24).

As in many other cities of Palestine in Hellenistic and Roman times, so in Tiberias differences, and even hatred, arose between the Jewish and the Greek inhabitants. Among the Jews there were many fishermen, and Josephus reports that they formed "a party." The head of this "seditious tumult of mariners and poor people" was a certain Jesus ben Sapphias, under whose leadership they rioted and "slew all the Greeks that were inhabitants of Tiberias, and as many others as were their enemies before the war began."[19]

From Mishnaic and Talmudic sources we know that inhabitants of Tiberias engaged in fishing with nets, and hence were called ḥaramē T'verya, "net-fishers of Tiberias."[20] In the second to fifth centuries, Tiberias was one of the most important cities of Palestine, the location of several synagogues, and the seat of the Sanhedrin and the central Talmudic academy, in which was largely composed the Palestinian ("Jerusalem") Talmud in the early fifth century CE. It was also in Tiberias in the seventh century that the Hebrew liturgical poetry (piyyuṭ) emerged, and that the Masoretes developed the standard vocalization of the biblical text.

Beth Sayda and Magdala

That fishing was the main livelihood for people living around Lake Kinneret is attested, among other things, by the fact that two of the lakeshore cities had names associated with the fishing industry: Beth Sayda and Magdala-Taricheae.

Beth Sayda (in the Gospels Bethsaida) was located at the northernmost tip of the lake, east of the influx of the Jordan River. The meaning of the Aramaic name Beth Ṣayda is "House of Fishing." Possibly the reading was Beth Ṣayyada, meaning "House of the Fisherman." A variant form of the name seems to be Ṣayyadtah, which is stated in the Palestinian Talmud to be identical with Adami-nekeb, listed in Joshua 19:33 as a border town of Naphtali.[21] In the early first century CE Beth Sayda was the home of three of Jesus's disciples, the fishermen Philip, Andrew, and Peter.

As was the case with many coastal cities along the Palestinian shore of the Mediterranean, Beth Sayda, too, was a double locality: one, Beth Sayda proper, was on the lake front, identified with el-Araj. The other, located 1.7 miles to the north-northeast of it, about one-eighth of a mile to the east of the Jordan, was Julias, founded by Herod Philip, brother of Herod Antipas. Josephus fortified Julias by having a "bank" raised near the Jordan, and sent armed men by ships from Taricheae to Julias.[22] The acropolis of this township is identified with modern el-Tell. Half a mile to the southeast of Beth Sayda–el-Araj, also on the lakefront, is located another tel, el-Misʻadiyye; archaeologists assume that both el-Araj and Misʻadiyye are remains of the large fishing village Beth Sayda.[23]

It was at Beth Sayda that, according to Luke, Jesus fed a multitude with five loaves of bread and two fishes (Luke 9:10–17). Miracles apart, the fact that the only food available was bread and fish shows that the fish of the lake was the main source of nourishment for the inhabitants of Beth Sayda.

The other township whose name is associated with fishing is Magdala, whose full name in Aramaic was Migdal Nunaya ("Tower of the Fishermen"). This locality is mentioned in the Talmud as being situated one mile north of Tiberias.[24] However, Magdala is generally identified with Taricheae, which, according to Josephus—who in this respect must be considered more reliable—was located thirty furlongs (stadia), that is, about four miles, from Tiberias. Yet another location for Taricheae is given by Pliny, who places it south of Tiberias. Strabo, too, speaks of Taricheae on the shore of the lake, and mentions its salted-fish industry.[25] The Greek name Taricheae means "Fish Salting Place."[26] Taricheae was one of the four cities which, with their toparchies, were given by Nero to King Agrippa. Josephus mentions that ships were plying between Tiberias and Taricheae. According to Josephus, he himself fortified the city with a wall, which had several gates. By the time Josephus came to Taricheae it must have been a considerable city, for it had a hippodrome big enough to enable 100,000 armed men to crowd into it. It also had a sizeable harbor, which was able to accommodate more than 230 ships (or rather fishing boats), each of which could be handled by a crew of four.[27]

Capernaum (Hebrew K'far Naḥum)

The Hebrew name of this locality means "Nahum's Village"; in Josephus and the New Testament, "Kapharnaoum" was a township located on the northern shore of Lake Kinneret.[28] It figures prominently in the four Gospels as a locality where Jesus taught in the synagogue and healed several people (Luke 4:31–39; John 6:22–59; Matt. 8:5; Mark 1:21–28, 2:1–13), and whose inhabitants he eventually condemned for their stubbornness (Matt. 11:23–24). In Capernaum was located the house of Simon Peter, mentioned several times in the Gospels (Matt. 8:14, 17:25; Mark 1:29, 2:1, 3:20, 9:33; Luke 4:38), which was found in excavations in 1968.[29] Beginning in 1905, several synagogues were also unearthed in Capernaum, the oldest being that constructed by the Roman centurion according to Luke 7:5—beneath which, however, there was an older dwelling.

Between Capernaum and other localities along the lakeshore there was waterborne traffic by means of rowboats. It was in such boats that "a multitude" came to listen to the preaching of Jesus in Capernaum (John 6:1–2, 17, 22–24).

Capernaum was also a favorite place for fishing, and Josephus mentions the fine "Coracin fish" that was found in its waters.[30]

Susita (Greek Hippos)

Both the Aramaic and the Greek names of this city near the east shore of Lake Kinneret, opposite Tiberias mean "horse." The two localities were separated, according to the rough approximation given by Josephus, by a distance of thirty stadia (or four miles).[31] The Aramaic name of the town is preserved in the present-day Susiyya, a village east of the lake, and in the name of the site on the hill above the Israeli kibbutz 'Ēn Gev, called in Arabic Qal 'at Ḥuṣn, that is "Castle of Horses," where excavations have unearthed the ruins of what seems to have been Roman Hippos, including walls, a colonnaded street, a theater, a basilica, and an aqueduct. The official name of the township was "Antiochia by Hippos," either because it was founded by the Seleucids or perhaps because it was favored by them. Ancient coins found at the site usually show a horse, which, together with its name, indicates that there was some (mythological?) connection between the town and a horse or horses.

Alexander Jannaeus captured Hippos, but subsequently Pompey restored it to its own inhabitants, and established it as one of the cities of the Decapolis. Augustus gave the city to Herod, after whose death it reverted to Syria.[32] In Talmudic times there were both commercial relations and rivalry between Susita and Tiberias. From Susita they shipped a fruit called *qurd'qiyya* (?) for sale in Tiberias. The hostility of Susita to Tiberias is repeatedly referred to in Talmudic literature. The villages in the territory of Susita were freed from such ritual obligations as tithes and the observance of the Sabbatical year.[33] In Byzantine times Hippos was the seat of a bishop; a cathedral and three churches have been excavated there.[34]

Beth Yeraḥ

This was a city on the southwestern shore of Lake Kinneret. It is not mentioned in the Bible, but is referred to in the Babylonian Talmud, which states that the Jordan "began" at Beth Yeraḥ. In ancient times the outflow of the Jordan from the lake was somewhat to the north of its present location, and Beth Yeraḥ was situated on the narrow tongue between the Jordan to the west and the lakeshore to the east, on the site known to the Arabs as Khirbet el-Kerak ("Ruin of the Fort"). According to the Palestinian Talmud, it was surrounded by a wall.[35]

The name, which means "House of the Moon," points to an ancient Canaanite settlement whose deity was a moon god, and excavations on the site have unearthed remains dating back to the end of the Chalcolithic and the beginning of the Early Bronze Age (ca. 3200 BCE). Under the Ptolemies a Hellenistic city, named Philoteria, was established at the site. It was captured in 198 BCE by Antiochus III, and later by Alexander Jannaeus. After the Bar Kokhba war a Jewish priestly family settled there, and in Talmudic times the city was inhabited by a mixed Jewish-gentile population. It was known to be surrounded by an area that was "entirely irrigated."[36] A fort, a synagogue, a bath complex, and a church found at Beth Yeraḥ are dated to the Roman-Byzantine period.[37]

An Unexpected Find

It is a very fortunate coincidence that a fishing boat from around the beginning of the Christian era has been discovered in relatively good condition in the waters of Lake Kinneret. If one picture is worth a thousand words, one actual archeological find is certainly worth several times that many. For the first time we have a concrete representation of what a boat in those days really looked like (Figure 19).[38]

In January 1986 members of a kibbutz on the shore of Lake Kinneret discovered substantial remains of an ancient craft buried in the mud where the lake's shoreline had receded, and where an area normally under water had been exposed by drought. Excavation by Israel's Department of Antiquities revealed a hull 8.2 meters long and 2.3 meters wide, constructed of cedar planks, joined by mortise and tenon joints, and

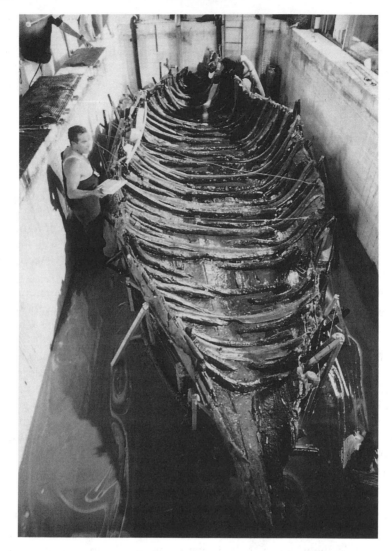

Figure 19. The Lake Kinneret boat in a specially built holding pool
that supported the delicate planks and frames while conservation was
in progress.

nailed to frames made of naturally curved oak branches. These methods
are consistent with boat-building practices extending back to the second
millennium BCE and in use through the Roman period. Other evidence,
including carbon 14 analysis of the wood, dates the vessel to a time just
before or just after the start of the Common era.

Locally built of readily available materials, the boat must have been used for fishing and transport. It had a central mast for carrying a sail and was large enough to accommodate four oarsmen and a helmsman. The fact that the remains show extensive repairs done at various times suggests that the boat, like others of its type, saw long service and was ultimately discarded when worn out.

Today, the preserved remains can be seen at the Yigal Allon Center in Ginosar, Israel, together with a reconstructed model of what it must have looked like in its own time, when many vessels like it plied the waters of Lake Kinneret in pursuit of trade and fishing. To those who see it, it is a vivid reminder of the lively waterborne traffic maintained for centuries by Jewish seafaring in ancient times.

BIBLICAL SEAFARING AND
THE BOOK OF MORMON

John M. Lundquist

MORMONS (members of the Church of Jesus Christ of Latter-Day Saints) view the Book of Mormon as a scripture, along with the Bible and the revelations of Joseph Smith and other Mormon prophets. According to Mormon belief, Joseph Smith (1804–1844), the founding prophet of the Church, received a box containing metal plates, a Urim and Thummim, and a breast plate from the Angel Moroni (the last survivor of Nephite civilization, who buried the plates before he died, around 400 CE), in upstate New York on September 22, 1827. Joseph Smith translated the plates through divine means, and the Book of Mormon was published in 1830, in Palmyra, New York. The plates were returned to Moroni before the book was published. The plates contained (along with sections of the Bible) the histories and downfall of three peoples who migrated from the Middle East to the American continent in antiquity (presumably to parts of Central America and Mexico). The overall chronological framework of the Book of Mormon is from approximately 3000 BCE to approximately 400 CE.

The three main peoples mentioned in the Book of Mormon as having crossed the seas from the Middle East to the Americas are first, the Jaredites (whose history is recounted within the Book of Mormon in the Book of Ether), around 3000 BCE; second, the family of Lehi (contained in the Book of First Nephi), around 600 BCE; and third, the people of Zarahemla, descended from a son of King Zedekiah, named Mulek in the Book of Mormon, who escaped the assassination of Zedekiah's sons reported in the Old Testament, and sailed with members of his family to the Americas following the destruction of Jerusalem in 586 BCE. The Book of Mormon gives no details regarding the journey by sea of this third group. This paper will thus deal with the first two groups mentioned above.

The Book of Mormon Jaredites are placed in the setting of the dispersion of peoples at the time of the great tower of Genesis 11. The family of Jared were saved from the dispersion of peoples that is said to have occurred at that time. They were located, with their flocks and herds, in the "Valley of Nimrod," whence the Lord instructed them to "go forth into the wilderness, yea, into that quarter where there never had man been" (Ether 2:1, 5). They then "did build barges, in which they did cross many waters, being directed continually by the hand of the Lord" (Ether 2:6). In other words, they traveled by water in some inland (inner Middle Eastern) context, before making their great voyage overseas to the promised land. After spending four years "in tents upon the sea-shore" (Ether 2:13), the brother of Jared was told "build, after the manner of barges which ye have hitherto built. And it came to pass that the brother of Jared did go to work, and also his brethren, and built barges after the manner which they had built, according to the instructions of the Lord" (Ether 2:16). They then built eight vessels, which would take them across the seas to a new, promised land.

The barges are described in Ether 2:16–24. They were light, water-tight vessels, dish-shaped, "the length of a tree," with the ends peaked, and without portals. Air was to be supplied through holes drilled in the top and bottom of each barge. They were made in such a way that they would at times be submerged in the sea, submarine-like, but could still remain seaworthy. The barges were constructed to hold both the families of Jared and his brother, and others, along with their animals: "And it came to pass that when they had prepared all manner of food, that thereby thy might subsist upon the water, and also food for their flocks and herds, and whatsoever beast or animal or fowl that they should carry with them—and it came to pass that when they had done all these things they got aboard of their vessels or barges, and set forth into the sea, commending themselves unto the Lord their God" (Ether 6:4). The Book of Ether states that they were at sea for 344 days (Ether 6:11), often "buried in the depths of the sea" (Ether 6:6), before landing some-where on the American continent.[1]

Not long after their arrival they carried out a census, yielding a number of around forty people. It is interesting to note in this regard that the zero date of the Mesoamerican calendar is 3113 BCE, and that it was somewhat later, around 3000 BCE, that the first evidence for village life, along with agriculture and ceramics, appears in Mesoamerica.[2]

Hugh Nibley has gathered together the extensive evidence paralleling these vessels with the Mesopotamian Magur or Makurru boats, the cres-cent-shaped heavenly boats of the moon god Sin, also known as "Deluge Boats" (because of their ability to survive heavy seas for long periods of time), described extensively in the Babylonian Flood accounts, the design of which Utnapishtim (the Babylonian Noah) received in instructions from the deity Anu. There is the same emphasis on "tightness" of the deck or roof in the Magur boats as in the accounts of the Jaredite boats in the Book of Mormon. These were oceangoing houseboats, "floating barnyards," designed to carry humans and animals, and to stay at sea for months at a time. Boats that are thought to have been fashioned after the Magur type have had a long history of use in Asia, and have been documented and illustrated earlier in this century. The Babylonian Flood tablets were discovered and translated after the lifetime of Joseph Smith.[3]

Another remarkable feature of the Jaredite barges was that they were lit by stones "molten out of a rock . . . white and clear, even as transparent glass" (Ether 3:1). These stones were carried by the brother of Jared to the top of a peak called Mount Shelem, where they were touched by the finger of the Lord, "that they may shine forth in darkness" (Ether 3:1, 4–6). Hugh Nibley has compared these stones to the ancient traditions of the *pyrophilus*, the "friend of fire," a transparent crystal formed from certain stones, which gave off light when submitted to intense heat. The purpose of such stones was to guide those who possessed them through the waters' depths. The Magur boat of the moon god Sin is described in the Flood narratives as a brightly lit, crescent-shaped boat traveling through the midst of heaven for twelve months.[4]

The second great seafaring narrative of the Book of Mormon is described in the Book of First Nephi, and revolves around the family of Lehi, a prophet living in Jerusalem at the same time as Jeremiah (during the early years of the reign of King Zedekiah). Lehi was commanded by the Lord to go out into the city to prophesy its destruction, if the people did not repent. Soon thereafter, Lehi was instructed by the Lord to take his family and flee into the wilderness "by the borders near the shore of the Red Sea" (1 Nephi 2:5). Other families were added to this group as they made their way along the edge of the Red Sea, moving in a south-southeast direction, pitching their tents in a place called Shazer (1 Nephi 16:13). They then turned eastward, traveling along the shores of the Indian Ocean, until finally, after eight years, they settled along the seashore in an exceptionally fertile region, watered by a number of streams coming out of a wadi from the mountains to the north (1 Nephi 17). It was in this place that they built the ship that was to take them across the sea.

Two expeditions into this area in 1993 have established a plausible choice for the route taken by the family of Lehi as described in the Book of Mormon. A key to the success of these expeditions was the discovery of a modern place name *NHM*, north of Ṣanaʻa in Yemen, which could correspond to the place mentioned in the Book of First Nephi where one of Lehi's party, a man named Ishmael, was buried. It was from this place, called Nahom in the Book of Mormon (1 Nephi 16:34), that the group turned eastward from the southeasterly direction of travel. The modern place *NHM* (associated today with the Nihm tribe) is at the junction of what in antiquity would have been the normal turning point on the incense road from a southeasterly to an easterly route of travel.

The travelers finally stopped in a place they called "Bountiful," described as being an area of "many waters," with "much fruit and also wild honey," a place "by the seashore," with "mountains" looming overhead, and sources of metal ores in the surrounding area (1 Nephi 17:5, 6, 9). Timber was also said to have been abundant in Bountiful (1 Nephi 18:1–2). The Astons have plausibly identified the Wadi Sayq, which empties into the Indian Ocean at Khor Kharfot ("Port Fort") on the Qamar coast of Oman, as the site of the Bountiful of the Book of 1 Nephi.

Oman was famous in antiquity for its shipbuilding and seafaring traditions, and possessed extensive forests (today virtually all gone) for its shipbuilding activities. The setting of Wadi Sayq as a well-watered, fertile, tree-rich valley, in close proximity to the shore line, fits better than any other site along the coastline the varied descriptions given in the Book of Mormon.[6] Khor Kharfot was a navigable inlet with direct access to the sea until recent times. A recent survey in the region (unpublished) has discovered high-quality, but limited, sources of iron in the region of Wadi Sayq.[7]

It was at this place that Lehi's son, Nephi (the eponymous ancestor of one of the major Book of Mormon peoples—the Nephites), undertook to build the ship. "And it came to pass that they did worship the Lord, and did go forth with me; and we did work timbers of curious workmanship. And the Lord did show me from time to time after what manner I should work the timbers for the ship. Now I, Nephi, did not work the timbers after the manner which was learned by men, neither did I build the ship after the manner of men; but I did build it after the manner which the Lord had shown unto me" (1 Nephi 18:1–2). In due time, the ship was finished; food, seeds, and other provisions were loaded on board; and "we did put forth into the sea and were driven forth before the wind towards the promised land" (1 Nephi 18:8).

Much earlier, during their travels in the wilderness, Lehi had come upon a "round ball of curious workmanship; and it was of fine brass. And within the ball were two spindles; and the one pointed the way whither we should go into the wilderness" (1 Nephi 16:10). This device, which operated according to divine influence, was their navigational instrument on land and aboard ship. It both pointed the way and exhibited written instructions from time to time. At one point during the journey, members of Lehi's family mutinied and tied up Nephi with cords. At this point, the "ball of curious workmanship" ceased to work, and the ship began to founder. This condition persisted for several days. During this time, Nephi, in great anguish and pain as a result of his bonds, prayed continually. Finally, just as the ship was about to go under, Nephi's brothers untied his bonds, he took the navigational instrument in hand, and guided them to their journey's end (1 Nephi 18:8–23).

Hugh Nibley has treated the "ball of curious workmanship" on the analogy of old Semitic belomancy, arrow divination. Based on a 1958 study of T. Fahd, in the journal *Semitica* (vol. 8), it was shown that the "arrows" of arrow divination were actually pointers, without shaft or feathers, that their purpose was to guide travelers in the desert, and that written instructions were inscribed upon them indicating the desired result of the divination.[8]

The Book of Mormon does not give the number of days that the group was at sea, but rather states that "after we had sailed for the space of many days we did arrive at the promised land" (1 Nephi 18:23). Their route presumably took them across the Pacific Ocean, and it is assumed that they landed on the west coast of Central America. According to John Sorenson:

> Lehi and his party launched their vessel into the Indian Ocean from the south coast of the Arabian peninsula. The winds no doubt bore them on the same sea lanes that Arab, Chinese and Portuguese ships used later, touching India and ultimately the Malayan peninsula. From that point Nephi's ship likely threaded through the islands of the western Pacific, then across the open reaches north of the equator to landfall around 14 degrees north latitude. Nephi left us no information in the Book of Mormon about the route, nor did he tell us in modern terms where they landed. But when we analyze the Book of Mormon statements about geography and events, the "land of first inheritance" can lie only on the west (Pacific) coast of Central America.[9]

Apart from the details of seafaring contained within the text of the Book of Mormon, and the study of this subject in the light of our knowledge of seafaring in the ancient Middle East, this study falls under the much broader theme of transoceanic contacts between the Middle East, Asia, and the Americas in pre-Columbian times. On this subject, a vast amount of literature has been published, much of it in recent years. This literature has been brought together in a recent bibliography, and fills two very substantial tomes.[10] It is sufficient to state that there cannot any longer be any doubt regarding the extensive contacts made via the sea routes between Asia and the Americas in pre-Columbian times. We are only now beginning to understand properly and appreciate the extent of these contacts, and their influence upon the inhabitants of the Americas. The pioneering journeys taken by Thor Heyerdahl long ago proved the possibility of sea journeys in antiquity across both the Atlantic and the Pacific oceans. Numerous other scholars, among them such luminaries as Robert von Heine-Geldern (from the Asiatic side) and Cyrus H. Gordon (from the Middle Eastern side), have demonstrated the extent and kinds of cultural influence brought to the Americas from Asia and the Middle East in antiquity.[11]

ABBREVIATIONS
USED IN THE NOTES

'Abhodah Zarah

A tractate of the Babylonian Talmud, the Palestinian Talmud, the Mishna, and the Tosephta. *See* B., Y., M., and T.

Aboth diRabbi Nathan

Aboth de Rabbi Nathan, edited by Solomon Schechter (Vienna, 1887, reprint New York, 1945). This edition contains both versions of the book, which is a midrash of Tannaitic origin with many subsequent additions. Quoted by page.

Aggadath B'reshith

A late Hebrew midrash containing homilies on Genesis, based mainly on the Tanḥuma (*see* Tanḥuma Buber). Edited by Salomon Buber (Krakow, 1903; reprint, New York, 1959).

ANET

James B. Pritchard, *Ancient Near Eastern Texts Relating to the Old Testament* (Princeton, 1955).

'Arakhin

A tractate of the Babylonian Talmud and the Mishna. *See* B. and M.

'Arukh haShalēm

A Talmudic dictionary compiled by Nathan ben Yechiel of Rome ca. 1100, edited by H. Y. Kohut (Vienna, 1926).

B.

The Babylonian Talmud, compiled in Babylonia around 500 CE. Written partly in Hebrew, but mostly in Aramaic. Quoted by tractate (whose title follows the abbreviation B.) and folio.

Baba Bathra

A tractate of the Babylonian Talmud, the Palestinian Talmud, the Mishna, and the Tosephta. *See* B., Y., M., and T.

Baba Metzi'a

A tractate of the Babylonian Talmud, the Palestinian Talmud, and the Tosephta. *See* B., Y., and T.

Baba Qamma

A tractate of the Babylonian Talmud, the Palestinian Talmud, and the Tosephta. *See* B., Y., and T.

Battē Midrashoth

A collection of minor midrashim, compiled and edited by Shelomo Aharon Wertheimer (Jerusalem, 1914). Quoted by volume and page of the second, two-volume edition (Jerusalem, 1953).

Bekhoroth	A tractate of the Babylonian Talmud. *See* B.
Berakhoth	A tractate of the Babylonian Talmud, the Palestinian Talmud, the Mishna, and the Tosephta. *See* B., Y., M., and T.
Bertinoro	Obidiah di Bertinoro (ca. 1450–1509), whose commentary on the Mishna was first published in Venice in 1548/49. Quoted by Mishna tractate.
Bētzah	A tractate of the Mishna. *See* M.
Cant. Rab.	A midrash of the Song of Songs.
Deut. Rab.	Deuteronomy Rabba, a midrash on Deuteronomy, compiled about 900 CE. Quoted by chapter and paragraph of the Vilna, 1884, edition of *Midrash Rabba*.
Demai	A tractate of the Palestinian Talmud and the Tosephta. *See* Y. and T.
Diodorus	Diodorus Siculus, Greek historian, born in Agyrium, Sicily, flourished around 20 BCE. His *Historical Library*, originally forty books, is only partly preserved and published (with translation by C. H. Oldfather et al.) in the Loeb Classical Library (London, 1962–1971).
Eccl. Rab.	Ecclesiastes Rabba, a midrash on Ecclesiastes, compiled in the tenth century. Quoted by chapter and verse of Ecclesiastes, from the Vilna, 1884, edition of *Midrash Rabba*.
'Edyuoth	A tractate of the Mishna. *See* M.
'Erubhin	A tractate of the Babylonian Talmud, the Palestinian Talmud, the Mishna, and the Tosephta. *See* B., Y., M., and T.
Esther Rab.	Esther Rabba, a midrash on the Book of Esther, quoted by chapter and verse of Esther.
Ex. Rab.	Exodus Rabba, a midrash on the Book of Exodus, compiled in Hebrew and Aramaic, in the eleventh century but containing much older material. Quoted by chapter and paragraph of the Vilna, 1884, edition of *Midrash Rabba*.
FLOT	James George Frazer, *Folk-Lore in the Old Testament* (London, 1919).
Gen. Rab.	Genesis Rabba, a midrash on the Book of Genesis, compiled in the fifth century in Palestine. Quoted by page of the critical edition of J. Theodor and Ch. Albeck, 3 vols. (Berlin, 1912–1927).
Ginzberg	Louis Ginzberg, *The Legends of the Jews*, 7 vols. (Philadelphia, 1909–1946). The most important scholarly work on the subject.
Gittin	A tractate of the Babylonian Talmud and the Mishna. *See* B. and M.

Ḥagigah	A tractate of the Babylonian Talmud. *See* B.
Ḥallah	A tractate of the Palestinian Talmud, the Mishna, and the Tosephta. *See* Y., M., and T.
Horayoth	A tractate of the Babylonian Talmud. *See* B.
Ḥullin	A tractate of the Babylonian Talmud, the Mishna, and the Tosephta. *See* B., M., and T.
'Ikkar Tosafoth Yom Tov	Abridged Mishnah commentary of Rabbi Yom Tov Lipmann Heller (1579–1654) of Prague; found in many standard Mishnah editions.
Josephus	Flavius Josephus, Jewish historian of the first century CE. Wrote in Greek. His major works are *The Wars of the Jews* and *The Antiquities of the Jews*. All quotations of and references to Josephus are given in the translation, and according to the book, chapter, and paragraph divisions, of William Whiston, *The Works of Flavius Josephus* (London, 1873).
Kēlim	A tractate of the Mishna and the Tosephta. *See* M. and T.
Kēlim Baba Metzi'a	A tractate of the Tosephta. *See* T.
Kēlim Baba Qamma	A tractate of the Tosephta. *See* T.
Ket.	*See* Kethubhoth.
Kethubhoth	A tractate of the Babylonian Talmud, the Palestinian Talmud, and the Mishna. *See* B., Y., and M.
Kilayim	A tractate of the Palestinian Talmud and the Mishna. *See* Y. and M.
Lam. Rab.	A midrash on the Book of Lamentations.
Lev. Rab.	Leviticus Rabba, a midrash on the Book of Leviticus, probably compiled in the seventh century. Quoted by chapter and section from the Vilna, 1884, edition of *Midrash Rabba*.
M.	Mishna, the first code of Rabbinic law, written in Hebrew and compiled by Rabbi Jehuda Hanasi about 200 CE in Palestine. Quoted by tractate, chapter, and paragraph.
Ma'aser Sheni	A tractate of the Tosephta. *See* T.
Massoreth Ha-ShaS	Talmudic citation index found in the Vilna Talmud edition.
1 Macc.	1 Maccabees, a historical book about the Maccabean period to the death of Simon (135 BCE). Written in Hebrew in Palestine between 104 and 63 BCE. Extant in Greek translation.

IV Macc.	IV Maccabees, a sermon on martyrdom and the rule of reason over the passions, written in Greek but in a strictly Jewish spirit, probably between 56 and 66 CE.
Makhsh.	Makhshirim, a tractate of the Mishna and Tosephta. *See* M. and T.
Megillah	A tractate of the Babylonian Talmud and the Mishna. *See* B. and M.
Menaḥoth	A tractate of the Babylonian Talmud and the Tosephta. *See* B. and T.
MGWJ	*Monatschrift für Geschichte und Wissenschaft des Judentums.* The foremost German Jewish scholarly journal. Appeared from 1852 to 1939 in Dresden and later in Breslau.
Mid.	Midrash, the generic name of a major type of Rabbinic literature, taking the form of exegetic expositions appended to Biblical verses. Midrashim (pl.) were written and compiled from the second to about the twelfth century CE.
Mid. haGadol	Compiled in the twelfth century in Yemen. Quoted by page of Solomon Schechter's edition: *Midrash ha-Gadol al hamishah* (Cambridge, England, 1902).
Mid. Shemuel	A midrash on the Book of Samuel compiled from older writings, in Palestine, during the Gaonic period (seventh to tenth centuries CE). Edited by Salomon Buber, *Midrash Shemuel* (Krakow, 1893). Quoted by chapter.
Mid. Shoḥer Tobh	*See* Mid. Tehillim.
Mid. Tannaim	A midrash on Deuteronomy.
Mid. Tehillim	Also known as Shoḥer Tobh, a midrash on the Book of Psalms, compiled probably during the tenth or eleventh century in Palestine. Sometimes quoted by page of Salomon Buber's edition, *Midrash Tehillim* (Vilna, 1891; reprint New York, 1947).
Miqwaoth	A tractate of the Mishna. *See* M.
Moʻed Qatan	A tractate of the Babylonian Talmud and the Palestinian Talmud. *See* B. and Y.
Nedarim	A tractate of the Babylonian Talmud and the Palestinian Talmud. *See* B. and Y.
Negaʻim	A tractate of the Mishna. *See* M.
Niddah	A tractate of the Babylonian Talmud, the Mishna, and the Tosephta. *See* B., M., and T.

Num. Rab. — Numeri Rabba, a midrash on the Book of Numbers, compiled in the twelfth century. Quoted by chapter and section of the Vilna, 1884, edition of *Midrash Rabba.*

Ohaloth — A tractate of the Mishna and the Tosephta. *See* M. and T.; also a tractate in the Babylonian Talmud (*see* B.). Both tractates deal with ritual impurity.

'Orlah — A tractate of the Tosephta. *See* T.

Otzar Ha-G'onim — Compendium of medieval rabbinic responsa arranged in the order of the Talmud tractates. Edited by Rabbi Benjamin Menasseh Levin (Haifa and Jerusalem, 1928–42).

Pauly-Wissowa — A. F. von Pauly and G. Wissowa, *Paulys Realencyclopädie der Classischen Altertumswissenschaft, Neue Bearbeitung* (Stuttgart, 1893–1978).

Pesaḥim — A tractate of the Babylonian Talmud, the Palestinian Talmud, and the Tosephta. *See* B., Y., and T.

Pesiqta diRabh Kahana — A midrash of some thirty-two homilies which grew out of discourses for festivals and special Sabbaths, compiled not later than 700 CE. Quoted by folio of Salomon Buber's edition (Lyck, 1868; reprint, New York, 1949).

Pesiqta Rabbati — "Great Cycle": a set of homilies on the Torah for festivals and special Sabbaths.

Pirqē Rabbi Eliezer — A midrash on the work of God in His creation, and the oldest history of Israel. Attributed to Rabbi Eliezer ben Hyrcanos, a Palestinian sage ("Tannaite") of ca. 90–130 CE, but actually written during the eighth or early ninth century in Palestine. Quoted by chapter in the edition by G. Friedlander, *Pirhe de Rabbi Eliezer* (London, 1916).

Qid. — Qiddushin. A tractate of the Babylonian Talmud, the Palestinian Talmud, the Mishna, and the Tosephta. *See* B., Y., M., and T.

Qur'an — The Bible of Islam: revealed to the Prophet Muhammad in the early seventh century CE at Mecca and Medina.

Rashi — The commentary of Rabbi Shelomo ben Yitzhak (1040–1105) on the Bible. Quoted by tractate or biblical book, chapter, and verse.

Rosh Hashana — A tractate of the Babylonian Talmud, the Mishna, and the Tosephta. *See* B., M., and T.

Ruth Rab. — A midrash on the Book of Ruth. Quoted by chapter and verse of Ruth.

Samson of Sens, Rabbi — A late twelfth-century commentator on the Mishna.

Sanh.	Sanhedrin, a tractate of the Babylonian Talmud. *See* B.
Shabbath	A tractate of the Babylonian Talmud, the Palestinian Talmud, the Mishna, and the Tosephta. *See* B, Y., M., and T.
Shebhi'ith	A tractate of the Mishna and the Tosephta. *See* M. and T.
Sheqalim	A tractate of the Palestinian Talmud. *See* Y.
Sifrē	A midrash on Numbers and Deuteronomy, of Tannaitic origin (i.e., from second-century CE Palestine). Quoted by folio of M. Friedmann's edition, *Sifrē debē Rab* (Vienna, 1864; reprint, New York, 1948).
Sotah	A tractate of the Babylonian Talmud and Palestinian Talmud. *See* B. and Y.
Sukkah	A tractate of the Babylonian Talmud, the Palestinian Talmud, the Mishna, and the Tosephta. *See* B., Y., M., and T.
T.	Tosephta, a collection of Tannaitic statements and traditions closely related to the Mishna. Probably compiled by Hiyya bar Abba in Palestine, about 200 CE. Usually quoted by tractate, chapter, paragraph, and page of M. S. Zuckermandel's edition, *Tosephta* (Pasewalk, 1880; reprint with additions, Jerusalem, 1937).
Ta'anith	A tractate of the Babylonian Talmud, the Mishna, and the Tosephta. *See* B., M., and T.
Taharoth	A tractate of the Mishna. *See* M.
Tanḥuma	A midrash on the Pentateuch, based on sayings of Rabbi Tanḥuma bar Abba, a Palestinian Amora (Talmudic sage) of the fourth century CE. Quoted by Pentateuchal weekly portion and paragraph to which sometimes the folio number of the Levin-Epstein edition is added (*Midrash Tanhuma al Hamishah humshe Torah* [Warsaw, 1910]). For an older text see next entry.
Tanḥuma Buber	Midrash Tanḥuma, an older version, edited by Salomon Buber, *Midrash Tanhuma: ein agadischer Commentar zum Pentateuch* . . . (Vilna, 1885; reprint, New York, 1946), 2 vols. Quoted by book of the Pentateuch and by page; *see* preceding entry.
Targ.	Targum, the Aramaic translation (or, rather, paraphrase) of the Bible.
Targ. Isa.	The Targum to the Book of Isaiah.
Targ. Onkelos	The Targum to the Pentateuch, completed in Babylonia during the early third century CE.

Targ. Y.	The Jerusalem Targum, a paraphrastic Aramaean translation of the Pentateuch, extant only in fragments. Prepared in Palestine, probably during the first or second centuries CE. Cited from M. Ginsburger, *Das Fragmenten-Thargum . . . zum Pentateuch* (Berlin, 1899).
Targ. Yon.	Targum Yonathan, the Babylonian Targum to the Book of Prophets; it dates from the fourth century CE. Cited from M. Ginsburger, *Das Fragmenten-Thargum . . . zum Pentateuch* (Berlin, 1899).
Tehillim	*See* Mid. Tehillim.
Terumoth	A tractate of the Tosephta. *See* T.
Vulgate	The first Latin translation of the Bible, prepared by the Church Father Jerome, and completed about 405 CE.
Y.	Yerushalmi (Jerusalemite). When followed by the name of a tractate, refers to the Palestinian Talmud, compiled in Palestine in the early fifth century CE and written mostly in Aramaic. Quoted by tractate, folio, and sometimes column.
Yalkut Makhiri	A collection of midrashim from Rabbi Makhir ben Abba Mari.
Yalqut Shim'oni	The most important of several collections of midrashim called Yalqut; it was made in the first half of the early thirteenth century by R. Shimeon Hadarshan of Frankfurt. Quoted by biblical book and paragraph.
Yebhamoth	A tractate of the Babylonian Talmud, the Palestinian Talmud, the Mishna, and the Tosephta. *See* B., Y., M., and T.
Yer.	*See* Y.
Yoma	A tractate of the Babylonian Talmud, the Palestinian Talmud, the Mishna, and the Tosephta. *See* B., Y., M., and T.
ZDMG	*Zeitschrift der deutschen morgenländischen Gesellschaft.*
Zabhim	A tractate of the Mishna and the Tosephta. *See* M. and T.

NOTES

INTRODUCTION

1. Raoul Francé, *Das Buch des Lebens* (Berlin, 1924). p. 146.
2. Lionel Casson, *The Ancient Mariners*, 2nd ed. (Princeton, 1991), p. 6.
3. *Anchor Bible Dictionary* (New York, 1992) s.vv. Philistines, Sea Peoples.
4. Casson, *Ancient Mariners*, pp. 73–74, quoting M. Cary and E. Warmington, *The Ancient Explorers*, 2nd ed. (Harmondsworth, 1963), pp. 45, 61–62.
5. Casson, *Ancient Mariners*, pp. 118–19.
6. Ibid., pp. 121–23.

CHAPTER 1
THE ARK OF NOAH

1. ANET, p. 44.
2. Ibid., p. 93.
3. Ibid., p. 105.
4 Ernst Karl Guhl and Wilhelm Koner, *Das Leben der Griechen und der Römer* (Berlin, 1872), pp. 305ff.
5. Lucian, *Opera*, edited by C. Jacobitz (Leipzig, 1866–1881).
6. James Hornell, *Water Transport: Origins and Early Evolution* (Cambridge, Eng., 1946), pp. 28–87.
7. Pauly-Wissowa, Supplementband 5, col. 920.
8. See full text of Berosus's account of the flood and the ark built by Xisuthrus in FLOT 1:107–10.
9. FLOT 1:109.
10. Gen. Rab. 31:10, Theodor-Albeck 1:282.
11. Gen. Rab. 32:9; 33:7; Theodor-Albeck 1:296, 312.
12. ANET, 25–29.
13. E. A. Speiser, "The Epic of Gilgamesh," ibid., p. 92.
14. Gen. Rab. 31:9, Theodor-Albeck 1:282, and parallel sources there.
15. Gen. Rab. 31:9, Theodor-Albeck 1:281; 31:11, Theodor-Albeck 1:283–84.
16. See sources quoted in Gen. Rab., Theodor-Albeck 1:283–84.
17. Ibid.
18. Gen. Rab., Theodor-Albeck 1:284.
19. Pirqē Rabbi Eliezer, ch. 23.
20. Gen. Rab. 31:11, Theodor-Albeck 1:283.
21. Pirqē Rabbi Eliezer, ch. 23. Cf. also Targ. Yon. ad Gen. 6:16; Yalqut Shim'oni ad Genesis 57: "a precious stone"; B. Sanh. 108b: "Precious stones and pearls."
22. Gen. Rab. 31:11, Theodor-Albeck 1:285, and additional literature, ibid.; B. Sanh. 108b; Pirqē Rabbi Eliezer, ch. 23. Yalqut Shim'oni ad Gen. 54.

23. ANET, 94–95.
24. FLOT.
25. James Hornell, "The Role of Birds in Early Navigation," *Antiquity* 20 (September 1946), pp. 142–49.
26. Pliny, *Historia Naturalis* 6:22.

CHAPTER 2
SHIPS AND SEAFARING IN THE BIBLE

1. See Ginzberg 4:144–45.
2. Ibid., p. 147.
3. Nahman Avigad, "A Hebrew Seal Depicting a Sailing Ship," *Bulletin of the American Schools of Oriental Research* 246 (Spring 1982):59–62.
4. Ibid., p. 61.
5. Ibid., p. 59.
6. Ibid., p. 60.

CHAPTER 3
CONSTRUCTION AND PARTS

1. J. N. Epstein, in MGWJ 69 (July–August 1925), 248.
2. James Hornell, *Water Transport: Origin and Early Evolution* (Cambridge, Eng., 1946), figs. 52, 54, and 55, and Plates XLI and XLIII.
3. A. E. Cowley, *The Aramaic Papyri of the Fifth Century B.C.* (Oxford, 1923), p. 88.
4. Hornell, *Water Transport*.
5. August Köster, *Das antike Seewesen* (Berlin, 1923), pp. 31 and 40; Cowley, *Aramaic Papyri*, p. 88, lines 10, 13, 14, and 17.
6. Odyssey 12:51, 162, 179. Cf. Pauly-Wissowa, Supplementband 5, cols. 910, 912.
7. Köster, *Antike Seewesen*, p. 31 and fig. 6.
8. B. Yebhamoth 121a.
9. B. Shabbath 100b; B. 'Ērubhin 42b.
10. B. Menaḥoth 94b, and Rashi ibid.
11. Num. Rab. 4:14.
12. James Hornell, *The Canoes of Polynesia* (Honolulu, 1936), fig. 245.
13. M. Makhshirim 5:7; T. Kēlim Baba Metzi'a 1:1, p. 578.
14. T. Kēlim Baba Metzi'a 1:1, p. 578; cf. also M. Kēlim 11:2.
15. R. Samson of Sens, Commentary ad M. Kēlim 11:3.
16. M. Makhsh. 5:7; cf. Pauly-Wissowa, Supplementband 5, col. 920; 'Arukh haShalēm 6:247; Bertinoro ad M. Makhsh. 5:7.
17. M. Makhsh. 5:7.
18. T. Makhsh. 3:4.
19. H. G. Liddell and R. Scott, *A Greek-English Lexicon*, new ed., 2 vols. (Oxford, 1925–1940), 1:166, s.v.; cf. Pauly-Wissowa, Supplementband 5, col. 920.
20. Lev. Rab. 34:9; Ruth Rab. ad 2:19.

21. Ludwig Blau, *Papyri and Talmud* (Leipzig, 1913), pp. 18ff.; Samuel Krauss, *Talmudische Archäologie*, 3 vols. (Berlin, 1910–1912), 2:549 note 130.

22. M. Sukkah 2:3; Yer. 'Erubhin 23a; B. Shabbath 101a; B. Sanh. 108a; B. Hagigah 23a; B. Yebhamoth 116b.

23. Cowley, *Aramaic Papyri*, p. 88, lines 11 and 14.

24. T. Shabbath 10:16, p. 124; B. 'Erubhin 55b.

25. M. Ohaloth 8:5; M. Nega'im 12:1; T. Shabbath 10:16, p. 124.

26. B. Bekhoroth 8b.

27. Cf. Pauly-Wissowa, Supplementband 5, col. 933.

28. T. Shabbath 10:16, p. 124.

29. T. Shabbath 10:17, p. 124.

30. B. 'Erubhin 102a.

31. Cf. Köster, *Antike Seewesen*, p. 18.

32. M. Sukkah 2 and 3.

33. Köster, *Antike Seewesen*, p. 74.

34. B. Nedarim 50a.

35. Rashi ad B. Nedarim 50a.

36. Cf. J. Hornell, "The Sailing Ship in Ancient Egypt," *Antiquity* 17 (March 1943).

37. B. Nedarim 50a, where *'ena* and *ēla* are confused.

38. For details see James Hornell, "Boat Oculi Survivals: Additional Records," *Journal of the Royal Anthropological Institute* 68 (July–December 1938), 339–48.

39. Cf. *Folk Lore* 43 (1932):453f.

40. See Hornell, "Boat Oculi Survivals."

41. Targ. Isa. 33:23; M. Baba Bathra 5:1; B. Baba Bathra 73a, 161b; B. Baba Metzi'a 69a.

42. B. Ta'anith 21a; B. Kethubboth 69b–70a; cf. Yer. Qid. 58d mid., where the name is spelled "Hilfay." According to Rashi ad Ket. 69b, "*isqarya dimakhutha* are cedar spars on which are hung the sails of the ship."

43. B. Ta'anith 24a.

44. S. Fraenkel, *Die aramäischen Fremdwörter* (Leipzig, 1886), p. 223.

45. Testament of Naphthali, edited by Shlomo Aharon Wertheimer, *Battē Midrashoth*, 2 vols. (Jerusalem, 1950–1953), 2:10.

46. B. Baba Bathra 161b.

47. *Palestine Exploration Fund Quarterly Statement* (London 1919), pp. 76f; Köster, *Antike Seewesen*, p. 26.

48. M. Zabhim 4:1; T. Zabhim 4:4, p. 585; Cf. also Pesiqta Rabbati, ch. 12, 50b.

49. M. Baba Bathra 5:1, and Bertinoro's comments ibid.; B. Baba Bathra 73a, 77b.

50. B. Shabbath 111b.

51. Cf. Köster, *Antike Seewesen*, p. 28; James Hornell, "The Frameless Boats on the Middle Nile," *Mariner's Mirror* (1940), 25:416–32; 26:125–44.

52. Rashi ad B. Shabbath 111b.

53. Mid. Tehillim, 19:5; Yalqut Shim'oni ad Psalms, par. 673.

54. Cf. Krauss, *Talmudische Archäologie*, 2:682; Marcus Jastrow, *A Dictionary of the Targumim* . . . (New York, Berlin, London, 1926), s.v. *Akharmonia*.

55. Hornell, "Frameless Boats,", 25:428.

56. B. Baba Metzi'a 79b; B. Baba Qamma 116b; cf. B. Bekhoroth 8b.

57. M. Nega'im 2:1; T. Baba Qamma 8:17.

58. T. Kelim Baba Metzi'a 11a, p. 589.

59. Esther Rab. 1:6.

60. Cf. F. Contenau, *La civilisation phénicienne* (Paris, 1926), p. 272; Köster, *Antike Seewesen*, pp. 52f.; Lionel Casson, *The Ancient Mariners* (Princeton, 1991), plates 41, 42, 43, and 45.

61. M. 'Ēduyoth 3:5.

62. Gen. Rab. 22:6, Theodor-Albeck 1:210.

63. B. Baba Metzi'a 87a; B. Megillah 16b.

64. Rashi ad B. Baba Metzi'a 87a. Cf. Arsène Darmesteter and David S. Blondheim, *Les glosses françaises dans les commentaires talmudiques de Raschi*, 2 vols. (Paris, 1929–1937).

65. *Battē Midrashoth* 2:10; cf. Testament of Naphtali 6:10, where only one rudder is mentioned. Cf. also Casson, *Ancient Mariners*, plate 47; George F. Hourani, *Arab Seafaring* (Princeton, 1995), p. 82.

66. M. Zabhim 4:3; M. Makhshi. 5:7.

67. M. Baba Bathra 5:1; B. Baba Bathra 73a.

68. M. Baba Bathra 5:1 (version of the Jerusalem Talmud); Gen. Rab. 83:1, Theodor-Albeck 997; Yer. Shabbath 16a; Yalqut Shim'oni ad Isaiah 314.

69. Sifrē Deut. 346 p. 144a; Yalqut Shim'oni ad Deut. 953, Amos 548.

70. B. Shabbath 100b; Y. Shabbath 13b top.

71. M. Ohaloth 8:1; M. Kēlim 15:1; Y. Baba Bathra 15a top.

72. M. Shabbath 16:8; 'Ikkar Tosafoth Yom Tov commentary ibid.

73. T. Baba Bathra 4:1, p. 402; Y. Baba Bathra 15a top; B. Bekhoroth 8b; cf. B. Baba Bathra 117a, and the comment of Rashi; B. Ta'anith 21b; B. Sanh. 95a; cf. Immanuel Löw in *Festschrift zum 70. Geburtstag David Hoffmanns*, edited by S. Eppenstein (Berlin, 1914), p. 121.

74. T. Baba Bathra 4:1, p. 402; Jacob Levy, *Wörterbuch über die Talmudim und Midrashim*, 2nd ed. (Berlin, 1924), s.v.; and Marcus Jastrow, *A Dictionary of the Targumim, the Talmud Babli, and Yerushalmi* . . . (New York and Berlin, 1926), s.v.

75. Y. Baba Bathra 15a top; cf. also B. Baba Qamma 67a, where *'ubhin* is explained by *mareshoth*, timber.

76. Cf. Pauly-Wissowa, Supplementband 5, col. 946.

77. T. Shabbath 10:17, p. 124; cf. Y. Shabbath 13c top: "planks in the ship"; ibid. 16a: "planks of the ship."

78. G. Busolt, A. Bauer, and I. Müller, *Die griechischen Staats-, Kriegs- und Privataltertümer*, vol. 5 (Nördlingen, 1887), p. 281.

79. B. Sanh. 67a, according to F. Perles, "Beiträge zur rabbinischen Sprach- und Altertumskunde," MGWJ 37 (1893): 6ff.

80. Y. Shabbath 13b top.

81. B. Yebhamoth 121a; cf. at note 8 above.

82. Testament of Naphthali 6:1–9.

83. B. Baba Bathra 77b: "The merchandise which is in it"; see also ibid. 75b.

84. B. Nedarim 50b; in T. Shabbath 14 (15):1 correct: *egoz*. See also Saul Lieberman, *Tosefeth Rishonim*, in *Tarbiz Azkarah* (Jerusalem, 1937), p. 143 (ad Shabbath).

85. M. Kēlim 20:1; M. Baba Bathra 5:1; Y. Shabbath 11d bot.; cf. also M. Miqwaoth 6:5. According to Jastrow, *Dictionary*, s.v., *martzufim*, the Greek *marsipos* (pouch or pocket) and the Latin *marsupium* (bag) are probably of Semitic origin. Cf. also J. N. Epstein, in *Sefer klozner: maasaf le-mada ule-sifrut yafah mugash le-profesor Yosef klozner la-yovel ha-shishim*, edited by Harry Torczyner (Tel Aviv, 1936/37), pp. 87ff.

86. B. Shabbath 156b and Rashi, ibid.; see also Rashi ad B. Shabbath 19b. See also *Otzar haG'onim* ad Shabbath, responsum no. 48.

87. B. 'Ērubhin 43b.

88. Gen. Rab. 12:12, Theodor-Albeck 1:110–11. The word *nawtēhem* is the Greek *nautes*, sailor, with the Hebrew possessive suffix added.

89. Gen. Rab. 83:1, Theodor-Albeck, pp. 996–97. In later rabbinic texts the same simile is quoted with added details; see the notes in Theodor-Albeck's edition of Gen. Rab., ibid.

90. M. Makhsh. 5:7, and Bertinoro's comments.

91. Köster, *Antike Seewesen*, p. 15.

92. Casson, *The Ancient Mariners*, p. 193.

93. Eccl. Rab. 12:7.

94. Cf. Cowley, *Aramaic Papyri*, p. 88.

95. *Battē Midrashoth* 2:10.

96. B. Shabbath 15a and b.

97. B. Shabbath 21b, M. Shabbath 11:5. See Chapter 4.

CHAPTER 4
TYPES OF SHIPS

1. See the Egyptian *teb(t)*; Adolf Erman, "Das Varhältniss des, Aegyptischen zu den semitischen Sprachen," in ZDMG 46 (1892) 123.

2. James Hornell, *Water Transport: Origins and Early Evolution* (Cambridge, Eng., 1946), pp. 51–52.

3. According to Friedrich Delitzsch, *Assyrisches Wörterbuch* (Leipzig, 1896), p. 3; Eduard König, *Hebräisches und Aramäisches Wörterbuch zum Alten Testament* (Leipzig, 1931), p. 1.

4. David Kimhi ad Job 9:26. The reference to "our Master Saadia" is to Saadia Gaon (892–942), author of the important philosophical work *Beliefs and Opinions*.

5. See also James Hornell, *Water Transport*, plate VI.

6. Pliny, *Naturalis historia* 6:24; 7:5; see also Plutarch, *Isis and Osiris* 18; Lucan, *Pharsalia* 4:136; etc.

7. Personal communication by James Hornell to the author.

8. See Hornell, *Water Transport*, Plate IV.

9. T. Sukkah 3:6,7, p. 196; M. Kēlim 15:1.

10. M. Zabhim 3:3.

11. E.g., M. Kēlim 15:1.

12. B. Menahoth 94b; Num. Rab. 4:14.

13. Y. Sheqalim 6, 50a top; T. Sukkah p. 318.

14. Targ. Yer. ad Num. 24:24, where *liburnin* has to be read instead of *liy-*

ionin; B. Sanh. 106a, where *Liburna Aspir* ("Hesperian liburna") has to be read instead of *libun aspir*. Cf. F. Perles, "Beiträge zur rabbinischen Sprach- und Altertumskunde," MGWJ 37 (1893):6f.

15. Y. Sheqalim 50a top; T. Sukkah 3:8; B. Baba Metzi'a 80b.

16. Cf. Perles, "Beiträge," p. 10.

17. B. Baba Metzi'a 80b.

18. Cf. W. Nowack, *Lehrbuch der hebräischen Archäologie* (Freiburg, 1894), 1:204f.; Levi Herzfeld, *Handelsgeschichte der Juden des Altertums* (Braunschweig, 1894), p. 158; Samuel Krauss, *Talmudische Archäologie*, 3 vols. (Berlin, 1910–1912), 2:395.

19. Cf. Pauly-Wissowa, Supplementband 5, col. 922; August Köster, *Das antike Seewesen* (Berlin, 1923), pp. 158f.

20. T. Shabbath 10:14, p. 124.

21. Cf. Pauly-Wissowa, Supplementband 5, col. 921.

22. T. Shabbath 10:14, p. 124.

23. Köster, *Antike Seewesen*, p. 138.

24. B. Shabbath 100b.

25. Ex. Rab. 17:5.

26. Lev. Rab. 25:1.

27. Gen. Rab. 16:4, Theodor-Albeck 149–51; cf. Perles, "Beiträge," pp. 6f.

28. M. Kēlim 2:3; Y. Shabbath 11d bot.; B. Shabbath 83b–84a.

29. Cf. Herzfeld, *Handelsgeschichte der Juden*, p. 157.

30. Hornell, *Water Transport*, pp. 5–6, 34–37, and Plate III.

31. Esther Rab. 2:1; cf. A.E. Cowley, *The Aramaic Papyri of the Fifth Century B.C.* (Oxford, 1923), p. 88.

32. Lev. Rab. 12:1.

33. Lam. Rab. 1:1; Eccl. Rab. 11:1; Y. Mo'ed Qatan 81b top; B. 'Abhodah Zarah 10b; etc.

34. B. Shabbath 83b, 84a; Y. Shabbath 7a mid.

35. Eccl. Rab. 1:15, end.

36. B. Berakhoth 57a.

37. B. Baba Metzi'a 80b; cf. Benedict Zuckermann, *Über talmudische Münzen und Gewichte* (Breslau, 1862), p. 47; Sir William Smith, *Dictionary of Greek and Roman Antiquities*, 2 vols., 3rd ed. (London, 1890–1891) s.v. *ardab* (?).

38. Y. Shabbath 7a mid.

39. Cf. B. Shabbath 67a.

40. B. Baba Metzi'a 34b, 101b.

41. B. Bekhoroth 27a.

42. B. Ta'anith 24b.

43. T. Baba Bathra 4:1, p. 402; Y. Baba Bathra 15a top; B. Baba Bathra 73a, 78b.

44. T. Baba Bathra 4:1, p. 402: Y. Baba Bathra 15a top; B. Baba Bathra 73a, 78b.

45. B. Baba Bathra 73a; B. Shabbath 101a.

46. Targ. Yon. ad Isaiah 33:21.

47. T. Baba Bathra 4:1, p. 402; Y. Baba Bathra 15a top.

48. M. Zabhim 3:1; M. Berakhoth 4:6.

49. Y. Berakhoth 8c top.

50. Cf. H. G. Liddell and R. A. Scott, *A Greek-English Lexicon*, new ed., 2 vols. (Oxford, 1925–1940), s.v.

51. Bertinoro ad M. Nega'im 12:1. See also T. Ohaloth 18:5, and Samuel Krauss, *Die griechischen und lateinischen Lehnwörter im Talmud, Midrash und Targum* (Berlin, 1898–1899) 2:86.

52. B. Shabbath 32a; B. Ḥullin 94a, 95a; B. Kethubboth 105b.

53. M. Kēlim 2:3, and Bertinoro's comments on it.

54. Hornell, *Water Transport*, pp. 1–20.

CHAPTER 5
THE CREW

1. Testament of Naphthali, Hebrew version, in *Batte Midrashoth* 2.10.

2. Ibid.

3. Lev. Rab. 21; Esther Rab. 5.

4. B. Baba Bathra 91b.

5. Massoreth haShaS ad B. Berakhoth 28a.

6. Tanḥuma Buber 31, p. 74; Num. Rab. 17 end.

7. Cf. Num. Rab. 4, where *liburniyoth* has to be read in place of *burniyoth*.

8. B. Shabbath 100b, 125b.

9. August Köster, *Das antike Seewesen* (Berlin, 1923), p. 16, fig. 2; p. 25, fig. 8, and p. 63.

10. Gen. Rab. 12:12, where *notim* is to be read in place of *motin* of the Theodor-Albeck edition (p. 383).

11. B. Pesaḥim 112b.

12. B. Giṭṭin 73a; B. Ta'anith 24b.

13. Y. Baba Metzi'a 4, 9d bot.

14. B. Sotah 48a; B. Baba Metzi'a 107b.

15. B. Ḥullin 94a; Eccl. Rab. 8:1.

16. M. Baba Bathra 5:1.

17. For instance T. Shebhi'ith 6:26, p. 70.

18. T. Baba Metzi'a 9:14, p. 392; cf. B. Mo'ed Qatan 11b; Y. Mo'ed Qatan 82b bot.

19. B. Bekhoroth 8b.

20. B. Rosh Hashanah 21a.

21. This can be deduced from M. Kethubhoth 5:6, which states that the customary frequency of intercourse between a sailor and his wife is once in six months.

22. Gen. Rab. 23:5, Theodor-Albeck 226.

23. M. Kilayim. 9:2; Yer Kilayim 32a top; cf. also Y. Shabbath 4 top.

24. B. Shabbath 20b.

25. See Jacob Levy, *Wörterbuch über die Talmudim und Midrashim*, 2nd ed. (Berlin, 1924); Marcus Jastrow, *A Dictionary of the Targumim, the Talmud Babli, and Yerushalmi . . .* (New York and Berlin, 1926); Lazarus Goldschmidt, tr., *Der babylonische Talmud* (Berlin, 1896).

26. B. Shabbath 21a.

27. Cf. Immanuel Löw, *Aramäische Pflanzennamen* (Leipzig, 1879), p. 353; Ludwig Blau, *Papyri und Talmud* (Leipzig, 1913), pp. 17f.

28. M. Shabbath 9:5; B. Shabbath 90a. A variant reading is *shonana*, to which cf. the Arabic-Persian *ushnan* or *ishnan*, meaning alkali.

29. Cf. Jastrow's *Dictionary* s.v. ashlag.

30. B. Baba Metzi'a 85b.

31. B. Megillah 12a.

32. B. Nedarim 50a.

33. Ibid. 50b.

34. Eccl. Rab. 8:1. The parallel version in Y. Pesaḥim 37c mid. reads *matrona* for *mabbora*.

35. B. Baba Metzi'a 84b, and Rashi's comments ibid.

36. Cf. Zacharias Frankel, *Mevo haYʾrushalmi* (Breslau, 1870), p. 122; F. Perles, "Beiträge zur rabbinischen Sprach- und Altertumskunde," in MGWJ 37 (1893):6f.

37. Cf. Aristophanes, *The Frogs*, 1073; *The Wasps*, 909; as quoted by G. Busolt, A. Bauer, and I. Müller, *Die griechischen Staats-, Kriegs- und Privatalter-tümer*, vol. 4 (Nördlingen 1887), p. 280. For songs and chants of sailors in modern times, see Köster, *Antike Seewesen*, pp. 130ff..

38. B. Sotah 48a.

39. Eccl. Rab. on the verse *ʿEt lʾvaqqesh*.

40. M. Qid. 4:14.

41. Ibid.; cf. also Y. Qiddushin 66b mid.

42. Niddah 14a and Rashi, ibid.; M. Qid. 4:14.

43. B. Berakhoth 50b.

CHAPTER 6

MARITIME TRADE

1. M. 'Abhodah Zarah 5:2; cf. 5:3–4.

2. T. 'Abhodah Zarah 4:12, p. 467.

3. T. Terumoth 2:13, p. 28; B. 'Abhodah Zarah 40b.

4. B. Pesaḥim 40b; B. Kethubhoth 97a; B. Ta'anith 24b; B. Baba Metzi'a 72b.

5. B. Baba Metzi'a 101b.

6. B. Baba Bathra 21a.

7. B. Berakhoth 18a.

8. Y. Demai 22c mid.

9. T. Shebhi'ith 5:2, p. 67; Y. Ḥallah 60b mid.

10. B. 'Abhodah Zarah 34b.

11. Ibid. 39a.

12. Y. 'Abhodah Zarah 42a mid.

13. B. 'Abhodah Zarah 34b.

14. T. Makhsh. 3:4, p. 675.

15. B. 'Abhodah Zarah 39b.

16. B. Ḥagigah 23a; B. Yebhamoth 116b; B. Shabbath 60b.

17. B. 'Abhodah Zarah 40b.

18. M. Kilayim 9:7; Y. Kilayim 32d top.

19. B. Ḥullin 84b.

20. B. Moʻed Qaṭan 213a.

21. B. Shabbath 114a; B. Niddah 20a.

22. B. ʻAbhodah Zarah 40a.

23. B. Giṭṭin 73a.

24. Y. Baba Qamma 4a bot.

25. Cf. Emil Schürer, *Geschichte des jüdischen Volkes im Zeitalter Jesu Christi*, 4th ed., vol. 2 (Leipzig, 1907), p. 221.

26. B. Rosh Hashanah 23a.

27. Cf. Letter of Aristeas to Philocrates, 112–15. The letter is printed in H.B. Swete, *An Introduction to the Old Testament in Greek* (Cambridge, 1900), 519–74. Translation by H. St. J. Thackeray, *The Letter of Aristeas* (London, 1917), pp. 46–47.

28. Strabo, *Geography* 16.2:28; cf. Levi Herzfeld, *Handelsgeschichte der Juden des Altertums*, 2nd ed. (Braunschweig, 1894), p. 77.

29. Philo, *In Flaccum* 8.

30. Josephus, *Contra Apionem* 1:12.

31. Herzfeld, *Handelsgeschichte der Juden*, p. 80; cf. Joseph Klausner, *HaBayith haSheni biG'dulato* (Tel Aviv, 1930), p. 42.

32. Josephus, *Antiquities of the Jews* 15:8:5, idem, *Wars of the Jews* 1:25:5; Pliny, *Naturalis historia* 5:14:69; Klausner, *HaBayith haSheni*, p. 96.

33. B. Pesaḥim 50b.

34. T. ʻArakhin 2:17, p. 545.

35. M. ʻArakhin 4:3.

36. B. ʻArakhin 18a.

37. B. Niddah 31a.

38. B. ʻErubhin 55a.

39. R. H. Charles, *Apocrypha and Pseudepigrapha of the Old Testament in English*, 2 vols. (Oxford, 1913), 2:330.

40. Gen. Rab. 99:9, Theodor-Albeck 1281.

41. Midrash haGadol, and numerous parallel sources listed in Theodor-Aleck's edition of Gen. Rab., pp. 841f. in the notes.

42. Lev. Rab. 25:2; cf. Gen. Rab. 72:5, Theodor-Albeck 843.

43. Aggadath B'reshith, chapter "Wayehi."

44. Sifrē Deut., p. 147a.

45. Rashi ad Gen. 49:13.

46. B. Megillah 6, and Rashi ad Deut. 23:19.

47. B. Pesaḥim 4a.

48. Cf. Louis Ginzberg, *Legends of the Jews* (Philadelphia, 1909–1946) 3:170–71, and sources cited there.

49. Ibid., 3:221.

CHAPTER 7

IN THE HARBOR

1. T. Shabbath 13:11, p. 130; M. Shabbath 16:8.

2. Eccl. Rab. 6:5.

3. To be inferred from T. 'Abhodah Zarah 7:13, p. 472.

4. Shem-Tov Falaquera, *Sefer haM'vaqqesh* (Haag, 1172); published in a free German translation by Micha Joseph Bin Gorion, *Der Born Judas* (Leipzig, n.d.), 4:180–82. Cf. its English version in *Mimekor Yisrael,* translated by I. M. Lask (Bloomington and London, 1976), 3:1334–36. I present Falaquera's parable in a shortened and restyled version.

5. T. Demai 1:11, pp. 45–46.

6. Y. Shabbath 4, 7a.

7. B. Shabbath 100b.

8. M. Ḥallah 2:2; T. Terumoth 2:13, p. 28; Y. Ḥallah 58c top.

9. Rashi ad B. Shabbath 100b.

10. M. Shabbath 11:4; B. 'Ērubhin 43a; cf. R. Patai, *HaMayim* (Tel Aviv, 1936), p. 182.

11. T. Shabbath 10:14, p. 124.

12. Thucydides, *Peloponnesian War* 2:90; Xenophon, *Hellenica* 1:1:6.

13. T. Shabbath 10:13, p. 124; M. Shabbath 11:5.

14. T. Shabbath 10:12, p. 124.

15. Ibid., 10:13, p. 124.

16. B. 'Ērubhin 42b.

17. M. Shabbath 11:5.

18. B. Baba Metzi'a 79b. Cf. below, Chapter 9.

19. B. Baba Metzi'a 79b.

20. B. Nedarim 38a.

21. M. Shebhi'ith 8:5.

22. Y. Mo'ed Qatan 81b top.

23. B. Bekhoroth 8b.

24. B. Kethubhoth 97a.

25. B. 'Abhodah Zarah 34b.

26. T. Baba Qamma 8:17, p. 363; Acts 27:13, 40.

27. T. Baba Qamma 8:17, p. 363.

28. Ex. Rab. 48:1; cf. Eccl. Rab. 7:1.

29. Esther Rab., end of ch. 1, to the words *w'hashtiyyah kadath.*

30. Y. Shabbath 13b top.

31. Esther Rab., ch. 5: "like unto a ship that sleeps in the open sea . . . "; cf. Y. Shabbath 7a: *n'didaya di-Ashq'lon*—"the rocking boats of Ashkelon"; cf. above, Chapter 4.

CHAPTER 8
ON THE HIGH SEAS

1. Lev. Rab. 35:8; Mid. Tehillim 104; Yalqut Makhiri ad Isa. 14:17. Cf. Y. Shabbath 5b.

2. B. Berakhoth 54b.

3. Y. Shabbath 5; cf. also Eccl. Rab., ad *'et laledeth.*

4. Gen. Rab. 6:5, Theodor-Albeck 1:44.

5. Ibid., 44f.; Eccl. Rab. ad *'et laledeth.*

6. Lev. Rab. 35:12.

7. Philo, *Legatio ad Gaium*, 15.
8. Livy, *History of Rome*, 31:47:1.
9. Hesiod, *Opera et Die* (Leipzig, 1913), 663.
10. Varro, *Libri Navales Veget.* (Leipzig, 1912), 4:39.
11. Sophocles, *Antigone*, 355; Philo, *In Flaccum*, 115; Lucian, *Toxaris*, 14, edited by C. Jacobitz (Leipzig, 1832), 2:364; Julius Caesar, *Bellum civile*, edited by A. Klotz (Leipzig, 1926), 3:25; Ovid, *Tristia* 1:11, 3–8; Dio Chrysostom, *Orationes*, edited by Guy de Bude (Leipzig, 1916–1919), 7 beginning.
12. Gen. Rab. 6:5, Theodor-Albeck 1:45; Eccl. Rab., ad *'et laledeth.*
13. M. Giṭṭin 3:4; B. Baba Bathra 153b.
14. B. Baba Bathra 153a.
15. B. Pesaḥim 111b, and Rashi, ibid.
16. Num. Rab. 9.
17. B. Baba Qamma 116b; cf. R. Patai, *HaMayim* (Tel Aviv, 1936), pp. 88f.
18. Cf. James Hornell, "Palm Leaves on Boats' Prows of Gerzian Age," *Man* 45:19 (1945), 25–27; R. Patai, "Palm Leaves on Boats' Prows in Palestine," *Man* 47:46 (1946), 47.
19. M. Baba Bathra 3:20; Cf. Levi Herzfeld, *Handelsgeschichte der Juden des Altertums*, 2nd ed. (Braunschweig, 1984), p. 296.
20. Eccl. Rab. 1:15. Cf. below, Chapter 11.
21. B. Horayoth 10a.
22. August Köster, *Das antike Seewesen* (Berlin, 1923), p. 128, quoting Livy.
23. M. Rosh Hashanah 2:8.
24. B. Berakhoth 28a; cf. Y. Berakhoth 4:1, 7d.
25. B. Horayoth 10a, and Rashi, ibid.; cf. Mid haGadol 1:15, p. 38.
26. B. Berakhoth 58b.
27. Strabo, *Geography* 16:757; Köster, *Antike Seewesen*, pp. 79f.
28. M. Ḥullin 2:9; T. Ḥullin 1:4, p. 500; 2:19, p. 503; 6:6, p. 508.
29. T. Ḥullin 6:6, p. 508.
30. M. Ḥallah 2:2; T. 'Orlah 1:3, p. 44; T. Terumoth 2:13, p. 28.
31. Eccl. Rab. 11:1.
32. Acts 27:38.
33. T. Menaḥoth 11:6, p. 529; B. Menaḥoth 94b. Cf. above, Chapter 4.
34. B. Baba Metzi'a 9b.
35. Gen. Rab. 31:13, Theodor-Albeck 287.
36. Syrtis is the name of two dangerous shallow gulfs off the North African coast. The Greater Syrtis (cf. Strabo, *Geography* 2:5:20) is the modern Gulf of Sirte off the coast of Libya; the Lesser Syrtis is the modern Gulf of Gabes off the coast of Tunisia; cf. *Anchor Bible Dictionary* (New York, 1992), s.v. Syrtis.
37. Eccl. Rab. 11:1; B. Yebhamoth 121a.
38. Below, in Chapter 12, we shall return to this subject.
39. M. Ta'anith 3:7; cf. Patai, *HaMayim*, p. 60.
40. Cf. Patai, *HaMayim*, pp. 59f.
41. T. Ta'anith 2:12, p. 218.
42. T. 'Erubhin 4:8, p. 142.
43. Sifrē Num. 76, fol. 18b.
44. Josephus, *The Life of Flavius Josephus*, 3.

45. M. Yoma 3:6; B. Yoma 85a, etc.

46. Codex Theodosius XIII:5:8 (*De naviculariis*) from the year 390. See Clyde Pharr, *The Theodosian Code: A Translation with Commentary* (Princeton, 1952), p. 394a. Cf. also Semen M. Dubnow, *Weltgeschichte des jüdischen Volkes* (Berlin, 1925–1929), 3:254, 325; Salo W. Baron, *A Social and Religious History of the Jews* 2nd ed. (New York, 1952–1976) 2:249–50.

47. Cf. Jean Juster, *Les Juifs dans l'Empire Romain* (Paris, 1914), 2:324.

48. Cf. Haim Schwarzbaum, *The Mishle Shu'alim (Fox Fables) of Rabbi Berechiah ha-Nakdan* (Kiron [near Tel Aviv], 1979), pp. xxv–xxvi.

49. Ibid., pp. 484–85.

CHAPTER 9

NAVAL WARFARE

1. Gen. 10:13, 22; 1 Chron. 1:11, 17; Jer. 46:9; Ezek. 30:5; Josephus, *Antiquities of the Jews* 1:6:4. Cf. *Anchor Bible Dictionary* (New York, 1992), s.v. Lud.

2. Gen. 10:6; 1 Chron. 1:8; Jer. 46:9; Ezek. 30:5; 38:5; Nah. 3:8; *Anchor Bible Dictionary* s.v. Put.

3. Gen. 10:18; 1 Macc. 15:23; *Anchor Bible Dictionary* s.v. Arvad.

4. See *Anchor Bible Dictionary*, s.v. Helech.

5. See ibid., s.v. Gamad.

6. E. K. Guhl and W. Koner, *Das Leben der Griechen und der Römer* (Berlin, 1872), p. 317; Pauly-Wissowa, Supplementband 5, col. 933.

7. Cf. Archibald Paterson, *Assyrian Sculptures: Palace of Sinacherib* (The Hague, 1912–1913).

8. August Köster, *Das antike Seewesen* (Berlin, 1923), p. 52, fig. 7.

9. On Kittim see also Isa. 23:1, 12; Jer. 2:10; Ezek. 27:6; Josephus, *Antiquities* 1:28; Targ. Onkelos ad Num. 24:24; Vulgate ad Ezek. 27:6 and Dan. 11:30; cf. *Anchor Bible Dict.*, s.v. Kittim.

10. Esther Rab. 2:1.

11. Cf. Samuel Klein, *Eretz Yehudah* (Tel Aviv, 1939), p. 59.

12. Cf. Joseph Klausner, *HaBayith haSheni biG'dulato* (Tel Aviv, 1930), p. 11.

13. Josephus, *Antiquities* 14:3:2.

14. M. A. Levy, *Geschichte der jüdischen Münzen* (Leipzig, 1862), pp. 58–73; Levi Herzfeld, *Handelsgeschichte der Juden des Altertums*, 2nd ed. (Braunschweig, 1984), p. 76.

15. Josephus, *Wars of the Jews* 2:21:8–9.

16. Ibid. 3:10:1.

17. Ibid. 2:10:2.

18. Ibid. 3:10:6.

19. Ibid. 3:10:9.

20. Ibid. 4:7:6.

21. Ibid. 3:9:2.

22. Cf. S. Tolkowsky, "Horban haTzi ha'Ivri . . . " in *HaAretz* (Tel Aviv, 27 Tishri, 1936).

23. Josephus, *Wars* 3:9:3.

24. Ibid. 7:5:5.

25. Cf. Emil Schürer, *Geschichte des jüdischen Volkes im Zeitalter Jesu Christi*, 4th ed., vol. 1 (Leipzig, 1901), p. 615, note 45, and literature, ibid.

26. Ibid. 1:688, and the sources listed there.

27. *Sefer ha Yashar*, edited by Lazarus Goldschmidt (Berlin, 1923), pp. 255–56.

28. Cf. Lionel Casson, *The Ancient Mariners* (Princeton, 1991), pp. 148, 151–155.

Chapter 10
Laws of the Sea and the River

1. A slightly different version of this chapter, under the title "Ancient Jewish Seafaring and River-Faring Laws," was published in John M. Lundquist and Stephen D. Ricks, eds., *By Study and Also by Faith: Essays in Honor of Hugh W. Nibley* (Salt Lake City and Provo, Utah, 1990), 1:389–416.

2. T. Qid. 1:7; cf. Y. Kethubboth 34b mid; B. Baba Bathra 76a.

3. M. Baba Bathra 5:1; T. Baba Bathra 4:1; Y. Baba Bathra 15a top.

4. M. Baba Bathra 5:1; T. Baba Bathra 4:1; Y. Baba Bathra 15a top; B. Baba Bathra 73a..

5. M. Baba Bathra 5:1.

6. B. Baba Bathra 34b, and Rashi's comment, ibid. [This was in accordance with the Talmudic legal principle according to which he who is stronger wins the right of possession in cases in which the judge is unable to decide because the two parties have an equal claim; for instance B. Gittin 60b —James Hornell]

7. B. Nedarim 38a.

8. M. Shebhi'ith 8:5.

9. Cf. B. Baba Bathra 97a.

10. B. 'Arakhin 18a; B. Baba Metzi'a 69b–70a, 79a.

11. B. Baba Qamma 97a.

12. Mid. Tehillim, Ps. 24:2.

13. B. Baba Metzi'a 79a–b.

14. Ibid. 79b. Cf. T. Baba Metzi'a 7:2.

15. T. Baba Metzi'a 9:14.

16. B. 'Abhodah Zarah 10b; Num. Rab. 2. Cf. also Matt. 9:9–10.

17. Tanhuma Buber, Terumah, 88. Cf. Chapter 6 above.

18. M. Baba Metzi'a 5:5; B. Baba Metzi'a 69b.

19. B. Baba Metzi'a 69b, and Rashi's comment, ibid. Cf. T. Baba Metzi'a 5:13; Y. Baba Metzi'a 10c top.

20. Cf. Georg F. Schoemann, *Griechische Altertümer*, 4th ed. (Berlin, 1897–1902), 1:474; William Smith, *Dictionary of Greek and Roman Antiquities*, 3rd ed. (London, 1872), s.v. *Fenus*, esp. p. 833; C. T. Lewis and C. Short, *Harper's Latin Dictionary* (Oxford, 1879 [1980]), s.v. *faenus*.

21. The printed text of the Y. has *risim*, which has been emended by Joseph Perles in his "Beiträge zur rabbinischen Sprach- und Altertumskunde," MGWJ 37/6 (1893):6–14, 64–68, 111–16, 174–79, 356–78, to *nesim*, i.e., the Greek *nesos*, islands; and by Immanuel Loew to *Qafrisim*, i.e. Cyprus, cf. Saul Lieberman, *Talmudah shel Qisrin* (Jerusalem, 1931), 14–15.

22. Y. Baba Metzi'a 10c bot.

23. Cf. B. Baba Metzi'a 65a, 68a; Y. Baba Metzi'a 10c bot.; Y. 'Abhodah Zarah 42a mid. On interest rates on ship loans in ancient Greece and Rome, see sources listed in n. 20 above.

24. B. Giṭṭin 73a; cf. B. Baba Metzi'a 106a.

25. B. Baba Metzi'a 69b–70a.

26. Cf. Theophile Meek, "The Code of Hammurabi," in ANET, p. 176.

27. B. Baba Metzi'a 80b.

28. Meek, "The Code of Hammurabi," p. 176.

29. T. Baba Metzi'a 11:26. These rulings should be compared with Codex Theodosius XIII:5:32 (*De naviculariis*), from the year 390, which provides that in case of shipwreck "if any measure of grain is said to have been lost in a storm at sea . . . the expense of such loss shall be allotted to the entire guild of shipmasters." See Clyde Pharr, *The Theodosian Code: A Translation with Commentary* (Princeton, 1952), p. 396a. The Theodosian Code (XIII:9:2–3) also provides that the sailors should be tortured in order to bring out "the full measure of truth" concerning a shipwreck.

30. B. Baba Qamma 116b.

31. Meek, "The Code of Hammurabi," p. 176.

32. B. Sanh. 32b.

33. T. Baba Qamma 2:10. Cf. Yer. Baba Qamma 3d mid.

34. B. Baba Metzi'a 107b.

35. Ibid. 107b–108a.

36. Ibid. 108a.

37. Ibid. 108b.

38. B. Mo'ed Qatan 4b.

39. Y. Baba Metzi'a 11a mid. Cf. also T. Baba Metzi'a 7:14; B. Baba Qamma 116b, where the text has to be emended according to the version of the Y.

40. T. Baba Metzi'a 7:14. Also the Theodosian Code (XIII:9:4) contains provisions for tossing cargo overboard to lighten the ship and thus save it from sinking in a storm.

41. M. Berakhoth 9:2.

42. Ibid. 4:6.

43. T. Berakhoth 3:9.

44. B. Berakhoth 54b.

45. Emil Schürer, *Geschichte des jüdischen Volkes im Zeitalter Jesu Christi*, 4th ed., vol. 3 (Leipzig, 1901), p. 50.

46. Cf. *Encyclopaedia Judaica* (Jerusalem, 1972), s.v. "Bet She'arim," and literature in the bibliography there.

47. B. Berakhoth 18a.

48. Gen. Rab. 6:5 and parallel sources there in the notes of the Theodor-Albeck edition, pp. 44–45. Cf. above, Chapter 8.

49. The Wisdom of Solomon 14:1–2.

50. T. Niddah 5:17; cf. also Y. Berakhoth 13b mid.

51. Sifrē Num. 76, fol. 29b.

52. M. 'Abhodah Zarah 1:3. Cf. also Philo, *Vita Mosis* 2:224.

53. T. Shabbath 13:10; B. Shabbath 19a.

54. B. Shabbath 19a.

55. M. 'Ērubhin 4:1; cf. B. 'Ērubhin 43a.

56. B. 'Ērubhin 42b.

57. M. 'Ērubhin 4:2.

58. Reading *la-limen* for *la-yam*.

59. T. Shabbath 13:11.

60. M. Shabbath 16:8; T. Shabbath 13:11.

61. T. Shabbath 10:16.

62. Ibid. 16:8. Cf. also Y. Shabbath 13c top.

63. Y. Shabbath 16a mid.

64. T. Shabbath 10:14; T. 'Ērubhin 10:2; B. Shabbath 100b–101a.

65. M. Shabbath 11:5; T. Shabbath 10:15.

66. Ibid.

67. B. Shabbath 100b; Y. Shabbath 13b top.

68. B. Shabbath 100b–101a.

69. M. Shabbath 15:1; B. Shabbath 111b.

70. B. Shabbath 111b.

71. Ibid.

72. T. 'Ērubhin 4:8.

73. M. Yoma 3:6; B. Yoma 85a, etc.

74. T. Pesaḥim 1:4.

75. In the identification of the town Mesha I am following Hirsch Hildes-
heimer, *Beiträge zur Geographie Palästinas* (Berlin, 1886), p. 38.

76. Y. Pesaḥim 30d mid.

77. T. Pesaḥim 1:24.

78. B. Pesaḥim 28a.

79. Cf. M. Rosh Hashanah 2:2; T. Rosh Hashanah 2 (1):2.

80. There were several Babylonian Amoraim by the name of Naḥman.

81. B. Rosh Hashanah 21a.

82. See above, Chapter 8.

83. T. Berakhoth 3:9.

84. M. Sukkah 2:3; B. Sukkah 23a; cf. Y. Sukkah 52d bot.; Y. 'Ērubhin 19b
mid.

85. M. Megillah 1:2; T. Berakhoth 3:91. Concerning the "closure of the sea"
during the stormy season, see the Theodosian Code XIII:9:3, which decrees that
"the month of November shall be exempt from navigation, but the month of
April, since it is nearest to the summer, shall be employed for the acceptance of
cargo. . . . Navigation shall be extended to the day of the *ides* of the aforementioned months." That is, navigation was suspended from November 15 to April
15.

86. M. Shabbath 9:2; B. Shabbath 83b; Y. Shabbath 11d bot. Cf. also
T. Kēlim Baba Qamma 2:3; M. Kēlim 2:3.

87. Y. Shabbath 7a mid.; B. Shabbath 83b, 84a.

88. M. Makhsh. 5:7.

89. M. Ohaloth 8:5.

90. Y. Sukkah 52d bot.

91. [This passage in Leviticus contains detailed ritual rules regarding the
"plague of leprosy" in a house. If the walls of a house should show greenish or

reddish stains (probably caused by some species of fungus), the house was regarded as unclean and ritual means had to be taken in order to clean it and
thereby render it habitable again. —James Hornell]

92. M. Nega'im 12:1.
93. M. Ohaloth 8:1.
94. M. Kēlim 15:1.
95. Ibid. 15:1.
96. M. Nega'im 11:11; T. Kēlin Baba Metz'ia 11:9.
97. M. Kēlim 20:1.
98. T. Kēlim Baba Metzi'a 1:1.
99. M. Makhsh. 5:7.
100. M. Kēlim 2:3.
101. M. Zabhim 3:3.
102. M. Taharoth 5:8; T. Zabhin 4:4.
103. M. 'Abhodah Zarah 5:4; T. 'Abhodah Zarah 7:13.
104. M. Miqwaoth 5:4, 6.
105. M. Ḥullin 2:9; T. Ḥullin 1:4; 2:29; 6:6; B. Ḥullin 13b, 88b.
106. M. Giṭṭin 3:4; B. Baba Bathra 153b.
107. M. Giṭṭin 6:5.
108. Cf. M. Yebhamoth 16:4; B. Yebhamoth 121a.
109. M. Ḥallah 1:2; T. 'Orlah 1:2, 3.

CHAPTER 11
SIMILES AND PARABLES

1. Cf. R. Patai, *HaMayim* (Tel Aviv, 1936), pp. 113ff.; Robert Graves and
Raphael Patai, *Hebrew Myths: The Book of Genesis* (Garden City, NY, ca. 1963),
index, s.v. Dragons.
2. B. Ḥullin 89a; cf. also B. Menaḥoth 44a.
3. Y. Sotah 22d mid.
4. B. Sanh. 68a.
5. B. Sukkah 51b.
6. Mid. Tehillim, p. 392; cf. W. Bacher, "Eine verschollene hebräische Vo-
cabel," MGWJ 41 (1975) 501.
7. Wisdom of Solomon 5:10, 13; R. H. Charles, *Apocrypha and Pseudepigrapha of the Old Testament in English*, 2 vols. (Oxford, 1913), 1:543.
8. Testament of Naphtali, Charles, *Apocrypha*, 2:338.
9. *Batte Midrashoth*, part 2, pp. 10ff.
10. Esther Rab. 5; cf. also Lev. Rab. 12:1.
11. Deut. Rab. 2:24.
12. B. 'Abhodah Zarah 10b.
13. Lev. Rab. 4:6..
14. Ibid. 21:5.
15. B. Berakhoth 28b; B. Baba Bathra 91b.
16. Tanḥuma Buber, Shelaḥ 31, p. 74.
17. Ex. Rab. 17:5, reading *liburnioth* for the corrupt *murnioth*.
18. Aggadath B'reshith, ch. 34.

19. Deut. Rab. 11:3.

20. Eccl. Rab. ad 6:5.

21. B. Megillah 16b; B. Baba Metzi'a 87a.

22. T. Menaḥoth 11:6, p. 529; B. Menaḥoth 87a.

23. B. 'Ērubhin 53b.

24. Esther Rab. 1:6.

25. Lev. Rab. 34:9; cf. Ex. Rab. 31:3.

26. Mid. Tehillim 19:5; cf. Yalqut Shim'oni ad Psalms 673.

27. Pirqē Rabbi Eliezer 5; Mid. Tehillim, Shoḥer Tobh 93.

28. Eccl. Rab. 1:15.

29. Gen. Rab. 22:6, Theodor-Albeck 210.

30. B. Mo'ed Qatan 28b–29a; Tanḥuma Buber, Miqetz 15, p. 200; Lev. Rab. 4:2, basing on Eccl. 6:7.

CHAPTER 12
SEA LEGENDS AND SAILORS' TALES

1. Cf. e.g. Targ. Yer. Gen. 1:7.

2. B. Ḥagigah 12a; cf. R. Patai, *HaMayim* (Tel Aviv, 1936), pp. 146f.

3. Eccl. Rab. 11:1; cf. variants in Y. Yebamoth 15d top; T. Yebamoth 14:5, p. 259; B. Yebamoth 121a.

4. Aboth diRabbi Nathan 3:9, Version A, p. 9a.

5. Eccl. 11:1, and Eccl. Rab. ad 11:1.

6. B. Bekhoroth 9a.

7. Mid. haGadol 1:9, p. 30; cf. Gen. Rab. 13, Theodor-Albeck 1:118; Eccl. Rab. ad 1:9 and 11:1.

8. Eccl. Rab. ad 11:1.

9. [The refusal on the part of the Jews to help a son of Esau, that is, an Edomite, must be viewed against the background of the bitter enmity felt by the two peoples against each other. In ancient times cruelty to shipwrecked persons was general among all peoples. In Rome, e.g., shipwrecked individuals were caught and sold as slaves, cf. Ludwig Friedländer, *Sittengeschichte Roms*, 10th ed. (Leipzig, 1922), 1:337. —James Hornell]

10. Eccl. Rab. 11:1.

11. Sifrē Deut., 354, p. 147a.

12. Ibid.

13. B. Nedarim 50a.

14. Eccl. Rab. 11:1.

15. Esther Rab. 2:1.

16. Pirqē Rabbi Eliezer, ch. 10. Cf. additional sources in Ginzberg 4:348ff., notes 26–40.

17. B. Ḥullin 95b, and Rashi there.

18. Eccl. Rab. 12:7.

19. On the Shetiyyah stone, see Ginzberg, *Legends of the Jews*, index, s.v. Foundation stone.

20. B. Yoma 38a; Y. Yoma 41a; T. Yoma 2:4, p. 183. According to Yoma 38a: the port of Acre.

21. B. Yoma 38a.

22. Ibid.

23. Josephus, *Wars of the Jews* 5:5:3; cf. Emil Schürer, *Geschichte des jüdischen Volkes im Zeitalter Jesu Christi*, 4th ed., vol. 2 (Leipzig, 1907), pp. 64f., note 165.

24. T. Niddah 5:17, p. 647.

25. Y. Berakhoth 13b mid.

26. Deut. Rab. 2:16.

27. Tanḥuma Buber, p. 89; cf. Yalqut Shim'oni, ad 363.

28. Y. Nedarim 36d mid.

29. B. Sukkah 51b.

30. B. Baba Metzi'a 59b.

31. B. Giṭṭin 56b.

32. Ibid. 57b.

33. B. Baba Bathra 74a.

34. Ibid. 73a.

35. Ibid. 73b. [The worm that caused the big fish to perish was probably some species of marine leech, or possibly some parasite crustacean. —James Hornell]

36. The reference to St. Brendan was supplied by James Hornell.

37. B. Baba Bathra 73b.

38. Ibid.

39. Lev. Rab. 22 end.

40. Mid. Shoḥer Tobh ad Ps. 93; cf. Yalqut Shim'oni, ad 93; Patai, *HaMayim*, p. 147.

41. B. Baba Bathra 74a–b.

42. B. Ta'anith 25a. Cf. Wilhelm Bacher, *Die Aggadah der Tannaiten* (Strasbourg, 1884), on Rabbi Yoḥanan.

43. On the purple-blue in rabbinic folklore, cf. R. Patai, "T'khelet (Purple-Blue)" in *Zikhron Yehudah: li-Khevod Profesor Yehudah Aryeh Bloi (621–696)*, edited by Tsadok Heveshi, Yeḥi'el Mikhl ha-Kohen Gutman, and David Shemu'el Lovinger (Budapest, 1938).

44. B. Baba Bathra 75a.

45. Ibid. 73a–75b.

46. Ibid. 74a. [This probably refers to the formidable Ox-ray (*dicerobatis sp.*) justly dreaded by pearl divers as an aggressive enemy, which is said to blanket the diver with its great "wings" and so drown him by preventing him from rising to the surface for breath. —James Hornell]

47. B. Baba Bathra 74b..

48. T. Sukkah 3:11–13, pp. 196–97. Cf. Ginzberg, *Legends* 6:21, note 129.

49. On Leviathan see Robert Graves and Raphael Patai, *Hebrew Myths: The Book of Genesis* (Garden City, NY, ca.1963), ch. 4.

50. B. Baba Bathra 74b.

51. Ibid.

52. Ibid.

53. Ibid. 75a.

54. Midrash Jonah, edited by Adolph Jellinek, *Beth haMidrash* (Leipzig, 1853; reprint, Jerusalem, 1938), 1:98.

55. Midrash Vayosha', ibid., 1:46–47.

CHAPTER 13
PORTS AND PORT CITIES

1. Cf. B. Maisler [Benjamin Mazar], *Untersuchungen zur alten Geschichte und Ethnographia Syriens und Palästinas*, vol. 1 (Giessen, 1930), p. 17; Nelson Glueck, "Explorations in Eastern Palestine," *Annual of the American School of Oriental Research* 14 (New Haven, 1933–1934); Franz M. T. Boehl, *Das Zeitalter Abrahams* (Leipzig, 1930), p. 13; *Anchor Bible Dictionary* (New York, 1992), s.v. Elath.

2. *Anchor Bible Dictionary*, s.v. Ophir.

3. Josephus, *Antiquities of the Jews* 8:6:4.

4. Targ. Y. ad Deut. 2:8 and elsewhere.

5. Josephus, *Antiquities* 8:6:4; Strabo, *Geography* 16:2:30; Pliny, *Naturalis historia* 5:12. Cf. *Encyclopaedia Judaica* (Jerusalem, 1971), s.vv. Elath, Ezion-Geber; *Anchor Bible Dictionary*, s.v. Elath, Ezion-Geber.

6. Cf. Jerome's translation of Eusebius's *Onomasticon*, edited by P. A. de Largarde, *Onomastica sacra* (Göttingen, 1870) 84, 25; 91, 21; 125, 7; 210, 75; 227, 44; 241, 33; Erich Klostermann's edition *Eusebius. Das Onomastikon . . .* (Leipzig, 1904; reprint Hildesheim, 1966), 63,10–13.

7. M. Yebhamoth 16:4; Y. Yebhamoth 15d mid.; cf. Samuel Klein, "Assia-Essia," in *Festschrift für Aron Freimann*, edited by A. Marx and H. Meyer (Berlin, 1935); Samuel Klein, *Eretz Yehuda* (Tel Aviv, 1939), pp. 122ff.

8. Qur'an 2:61; 7:161ff.

9. Istakhri, *Kitāb al-Masālik w'al-Mamālik* (Book of Routes and Kingdoms), edited by M. J. de Goeje, Bibliotheca Geographorum Arabicorum 1 (Leiden, 1870; reprint 1927), p. 33, lines 10–12; Muqaddasi, *Kitāb Aḥsan al-Taqāsīn*, edited by M. J. de Goeje, ibid., p. 178; cf. Yitzhak Ben-Zvi, *Sh'ar Yashuv* (Tel Aviv, 1936–1937), pp. 97–119.

10. Cf. *Encyclopedia of Islam*, new ed. (Leiden, 1960–), s.vv. Aḳaba, Ayla.

11. Josephus, *Antiquities* 13:15:4; idem, *Wars of the Jews* 4:11:5.

12. Josephus, *Antiquities* 13:15:4; 14:4:4; 14:5:3; and idem, *Wars* 1:7:7, 8.4; 4: 11:5; cf. *Anchor Bible Dictionary*, s.v. Raphia; ANET, pp. 285, 292; Yosef Braslawsky, *HaYada'ta et haAretz?* vol. 2 (Tel Aviv, 1946), p. 298; George A. Barton, *Archaeology and the Bible*, 7th ed. (Philadelphia, 1937), p. 467; A. Schalit, *HaMishtar haRomai bEretz Yisrael* (The Roman Administration in Palestine) (Jerusalem, 1937), pp. 4, 108; Emil Schürer, *Geschichte des jüdischen Volkes im Zeitalter Jesu Christi*, 4th ed., vol. 2 (Leipzig, 1907), p. 109.

13. See several works by Samuel Klein: "Derekh Hof haYam (Via Maris)" in Scripta Universitatis atque Bibliothecae Hierosolymitanarum, vol. 1 (Jerusalem, 1923), pp. 1–15; "Akko," and "Aschkalon," in *Encyclopedia Judaica* (Jerusalem, 1971); *Toldot haYishuv b'Eretz Yisrael* (History of the Jewish Settlement in Erez Israel) (Tel Aviv, 1935), p. 107.

14. Pliny, *Naturalis historia* 5:68:13; Ptolemy, *Geographia* 5:16:6; Schürer, *Geschichte* 2:108–9.

15. Braslawsky, *HaYada'ta* pp. 2:290–93.

16. Schürer, *Geschichte* 2:55; Braslawsky, *HaYada'ta*, pp. 255–98, 301; H. G. Liddell and R. Scott, *A Greek-English Lexicon*, new ed., 2 vols. (Oxford, 1925–1940), 1:689, s.v. eriphios.

17. Klein, *Toldot haYishuv*, pp. 101, 107.

18. Yitzhak Ben-Zvi, *Sh'ar Yashuv* (Tel Aviv, 1936–1937), p. 126.

19. ANET, p. 282.

20. Ibid., pp. 291, 294.

21. Herodotus, *History of the Persian Wars* 3:5.

22. Josephus, *Antiquities* 13:5:5; 1 Macc. 11:61–62.

23. Josephus, *Antiquities* 14:1:3 and *Wars* 1:4:2. Cf. *Anchor Bible Dictionary*, s.v. Gaza.

24. Josephus, *Wars* 1:20:3, 2:6:3, 2:18:1; Schürer, *Geschichte* 2:114.

25. Schürer, *Geschichte* 2:114.

26. Y. 'Abhodah Zarah 39d top; Klein, *Eretz Yehuda*, pp. 113ff.; Simḥa Asaf and L. A. Mayer, *Sēfer haYishuv*, vol. 2 (Jerusalem, 1944), pp. 48ff.

27. Josephus, *Antiquities* 13:13:3, 14:5:3; and *Wars* 1:4:2, 1:8:4.

28. Josephus, *Antiquities* 13:13:3, and *Wars* 1:8:4, 20:3, 2:18:1; *Encyclopaedia Judaica* (Jerusalem, 1971), s.v. Anthedon.

29. Schürer, *Geschichte* 2:120; Y. Press, ed., *Eretz Yisrael: Entziqlopedia Topografit-Historit*, vol. 1 (Jerusalem, 1946), p. 57; John Garstang, *The Foundation of Bible History: Joshua, Judges* (London, 1931), pp. 357–69.

30. T. Dothan, *The Philistines and Their Material Culture* (New Haven, 1982); A. Mazor, "The Emergence of Philistine Material Culture," *Israel Exploration Journal* 35 (1985), pp. 95–107.

31. Herodotus, *History* 1:105; Diodorus Siculus, *Bibliotheca historica*, 2:4:2.

32. Josephus, *Wars* 1:21:11.

33. Samuel Klein, in *Encyclopaedia Judaica* vol. 2 (Berlin, 1929) s.v. Askalon.

34. Schürer, *Geschichte* 2:119–24.

35. Ibid. 2:124–25.

36. Y. Shabbath 7a mid.; Schürer, *Geschichte* 2:120; S. Klein, in *Encyclopedia Judaica*, s.v. Askalon; Asaf and Mayer, *Sēfer haYishuv* 2:4–6; Press, *Eretz Yisrael*, 1:56.

37. Elias Auerbach, *Wüste und gelobtes Land*, vol. 2 (Berlin, 1936), p. 141; *Anchor Bible Dictionary*, s.v. Ashdod.

38. 1 Macc. 10:84; cf. 11:4; Josephus, *Antiquities* 13:15:4, 14:4:4, 17:8:1; and *Wars* 1:7:7, 8:4, 2:6:3.

39. Herodotus, *History* 2:157; Ptolemy *Geographia* 5:16:3; Josephus, *Antiquities* 13:15:4, 14:4:4; and *Wars* 1:7:7, Schürer, *Geschichte* 2:125; A. Schalit *Ha-Mishtar haRomai b'Eretz Yisrael* (Jerusalem, 1936), p. 47.

40. Klein, *Eretz Yehuda*, p. 8.

41. Cf. *Encyclopedia Judaica* (Jerusalem, 1971), s.v. Ashdod.

42. Pliny, *Naturalis historia* 5:13:68; Ptolemy, *Geographia* 5:16:2; cf. Pauly-Wissowa, vol. IX, 1, cols. 683–85; Josephus, *Antiquities* 13:15:4, 14:4:4; and *Wars* 1:7:7.

43. 2 Macc. 12:8ff., 40; cf. 1 Macc. 5:55ff., 10:69, 15:40; cf. Josephus, *Antiquities* 13:15:4, 14:4:4, 17:11:5, 18:2:2; and *Wars* 1:7:7, 1:8:4, 2:9:1, 4:3:2, 8:1; Philo, *Legatio ad Gaium*, par. 30.

44. Cf. *Encyclopaedia Judaica* (Jerusalem, 1971), s.vv. Jabneel, Jamnia.

45. Klein, *Eretz Yehuda*, p. 77.

46. Benjamin of Tudela, *Itinerary of Benjamin of Tudela*, edited by M. N. Adler et al. (Malibu, Calif., 1983), p. 88.

47. Pliny, *Naturalis historia* 5:13; Pomponius Mela, *Chorographia* 1:64.

48. See *The Tell Amarna Tablets*, translated by C. R. Conder (London, 1893) 214:32ff.; cf. 178:20; *ANET*, pp. 242, 475ff., esp. p. 478.

49. ANET, p. 287.

50. Ibid., p. 662.

51. Schürer, *Geschichte* 2:33.

52. Josephus, *Antiquities* 13:4:4; cf. 1 Macc. 10:69–76.

53. 1 Macc. 14:5, 34; Josephus, *Antiquities* 13:6:4.

54. Josephus, *Antiquities* 14:10:22.

55. Ibid. 14:10:6; *Wars* 2:18:10.

56. Josephus, *Wars* 3:9:3.

57. Klein, *Eretz Yehuda*, pp. 80–88.

58. Ibid., pp. 79–80; T. Demai 1:11, p. 45; B. Qid. 57b.

59. Samuel Tolkowsky, *The Gateway to Palestine: A History of Jaffa* (London, 1924), p. 74.

60. Binyamin Maisler, "The Expedition of Tiglath Pileser III to Palestine in 732 BCE" (in Hebrew), *Bulletin of the Jewish Palestine Exploration Society*, Jerusalem (April 1933).

61. Josephus, *Antiquities* 13:15:4; and *Wars* 1:8:4.

62. *Encyclopaedia Judaica* (Jerusalem, 1971), s.v. Apollonia; *Anchor Bible Dictionary*, s.v. Apollonia.

63. Y. Shebhi'ith 4, 36c top; Sifrē Deut. 51; Josephus, *Antiquities* 13:15:4, 15:7:3; and *Wars* 1:7:7, 20:3.

64. Y. Giṭṭin 43b bot.; Schürer, *Geschichte* 2:135.

65. Josephus, *Antiquities* 15:9:6; and *Wars* 1:21:5–8.

66. Josephus, *Antiquities* 17:11:4; and *Wars* 2:6:3, 18:1, 7:8:7.

67. B. Megillah 6a.

68. B. 'Ērubhin 76b; Y. Shabbath, passim; B. Ketubot 17a, etc.; Y. Sotah 7:1, 21b.

69. B. 'Abh. Zarah 39a; Y. Terumoth 47a bot.

70. Y. 'Abhodah Zarah 1:2, 39c; cf. *Encyclopaedia Judaica* (Jerusalem, 1971), s.v. Caesarea.

71. Cf. *Anchor Bible Dictionary*, s.v. Dor.

72. The expression "Dor and its towns" in Joshua 17:11 and Judges 1:27 indicates that Dor was the chief city of an area in which there were other towns as well.

73. ANET, p. 662

74. Josephus, *Antiquities* 13:12:2, 14:4:4, 19:6:3; and *Wars* 1:7:7; cf. Schürer, *Geschichte* 2:141, note 191.

75. Schürer, *Geschichte* 2:141.

76. Y. Demai 22c; Yitzḥak Ben-Zvi, "Athlit: Its Name and Its Ancient Remains" (in Hebrew), *Journal of the Jewish Palestine Exploration Society* 1 (Jerusalem, 1925).

77. Cf. *Encyclopedia Judaica* (Jerusalem, 1971), s.v. Athlit.

78. Josephus, *Antiquities* 13:12:3; Strabo, *Geography* 14:2:27; Pliny, *Naturalis historia* 5:19; Ptolemy, *Geographia* 5:14; Eusebius, *Onomasticon* 108:30; Klein, *Toldoth*, pp. 21–22; and idem, *Eretz Yehuda*, pp. 155–56.

79. T. Yebhamoth 6:8, p. 248; Y. Berakhoth 2:4; B. Shabbath 26a; Pesiqta diRabh Kahana 137a.

80. Mid. Tannaim ad Deut. 33:19–21, 219:5; cf. Sifrē Deut. 354.

81. Pesiqta diRabh Kahana 137a.

82. Lev. Rab. 23:5; Cant. Rab. 2:3, par. 5; Lam. Rab. 1:17; Mid. Shemuel, ch. 16.

83. Asaf and Mayer (eds.), *Sēfer haYishuv* 2:9.

84. *The Tell Amarna Tablets* 8:19; 88:46; etc.; cf. ANET, index, s.vv. Accho, Acre, Akko; Schürer, *Geschichte* 2:141–48.

85. 1 Macc. 10:39, 12:45ff.

86. Josephus, *Wars* 2:18:5; T. Ket. 5:10, p. 267.

87. Gen. Rab. 78, p. 923; Deut. Rab., as quoted by Klein, *Eretz Yehuda*, p. 119.

88. M. 'Abh. Zarah 3:4; T. Berakhoth 5:2; 11:23; Mid. Tannaim ad Deut. 68; 84:1; Y. Shebhi'ith 36c.

89. Y. 'Abhodah Zarah 39d; Gen. Rab. 47 end; cf. B. 'Abhodah Zarah 11b.

90. Gen. Rab. 78:5; B. 'Abhodah Zarah 34b; T. Shebhi'ith 5:2, p. 67; M. Nedarim 3:6.

91. Ex. Rab. 9:5 and elsewhere; B. Mo'ed Qatan 13b.

92. Gen. Rab. 5, p. 38; 13, p. 125; Deut. Rab. 7:6.

93. Josephus, *Wars* 2:10:2.

94. Cf. Raphael Patai, "Akhilat Adamah (Earth Eating)," in *Metsudah* (London) 5–6 (1948): 330–47, reprinted in Raphael Patai, *On Jewish Folklore* (Detroit, 1983), 174–94.

95. *Doctrina Jacobi nuper baptizati*, as quoted by Klein, *Eretz Yehuda*, pp. 120–21.

96. Cf. Samuel Klein, "Akko," in *Encyclopaedia Judaica* vol. 1 (Berlin, 1928).

97. ANET, index, s.v. Achshaph; M. Shebhi'ith 6:1; M. Ḥallah 4:8; T. Pesḥim 1:27, p. 157; T. Ma'aser Sheni 3:18, p. 92; T. Ohaloth 18:15, p. 617; B. 'Abhodah Zarah 25b.

98. T. Shebhi'ith 4:6, p. 65; T. Ḥallah 2:6, p. 99.

99. Ptolemy, *Geographia* 5:15; Pliny, *Naturalis historia* 5:17; Josephus, *Wars* 1:13:4; *Encyclopaedia Judaica* (Jerusalem, 1971), s.v. Achzib.

CHAPTER 14
LAKE KINNERET

1. Josephus, *Wars* 3:10:1.

2. T. Sukkah 3:9, etc.

3. Josephus, *Wars* 3:10:7.

4. B. Baba Qamma 81a–b.

5. Cf. e.g. M. Bētzah 3:1–2; Y. Pesaḥim 4:1; B. Shabbath 17b; B. Yoma 84b; B. Mo'ed Qatan 11a.

6. Cf. M. 'Arakhin 2:4; T. 'Ērubhin 1:2, p. 146; T. Megillah 4:3; Y. 'Erubhin 6 (5), 13; B. Megillah 2b.

7. Josephus, *Antiquities* 18:2:3.

8. Josephus, *Wars of the Jews*, 4:1:3.

9. Cf. Literature in *Encyclopaedia Judaica* (Jerusalem, 1971), s.v. Hamath.

10. Yer. Megillah 70a mid.; B. Megillah 6a.

11. Y. Megillah 70a mid.; B. Megillah 6a.

12. Cf. *Anchor Bible Dictionary* (New York, 1992), s.v. Rakkath.

13. s.v. Tiberias.

14. Y. Megillah 70a mid.; cf. B. Pesaḥim 8b.

15. Gen. Rab. 98:21, Theodor-Albeck 1,267.

16. Josephus, *Antiquities* 18:2:3; cf. *Wars* 2:21:6. Cf. above, under Hamath.

17. Josephus, *Antiquities* 18:2:3; cf. Y. Shebhi'ith 9:1; B. Shabbath 33b.

18. Y. Baba Qamma 6d; Eccl. Rab. 1:12; Gen. Rab. 2:1, Theodor-Albeck 1:79; Mid. Tehillim 1.

19. Josephus, *The Life of Flavius Josephus*, 12.

20. Y. Mo'ed Qaran 2 end, 81b; Yer. Pershim 3, 30d top.

21. Cf. Y. Megillah 1, 70a bot.

22. Josephus, *Antiquities* 18:2:1; *Wars* 2:9:1; *Life*, 72–73.

23. Cf. *Anchor Bible Dictionary*, s.vv. Beth-Saida and Herod Philip.

24. B. Pesaḥim 46b.

25. Josephus, *Life*, 32; Pliny, *Naturalis historia* 5:15; Strabo, *Geography* 16:2:45.

26. Cf. Emil Schürer, *Geschichte des jüdischen Volkes im Zeitalter Jesu Christi*, 4th ed., vol. 2 (Leipzig, 1907), p. 78.

27. Josephus, *Wars* 2:13:2; 2:21:3, 4, 8–9; 3:10:1; *Life* 27, 28, 59: cf. Matt. 15:39 (Magadan); Schürer, *Geschichte*, index, s.v. Tarichea.

28. Josephus, *Wars* 3:10:8; *Life* 72.

29. Cf. *Anchor Bible Dictionary*, s.v. Capernaum.

30. Josephus, *Wars* 3:10:8.

31. Josephus, *Life*, 65.

32. Josephus, *Antiquities* 14:4:4, 15:7:3, 17:11:4, *Wars* 1:7:7, 20:3, 2:6:3; Pliny, *Naturalis historia* 5:18, 74.

33. Y. Shebhi'ith 8:3, 38a; Lev. Rab. 23; T. Shebhi'ith 4:10.

34. Schürer, *Geschichte* 2:155–57.

35. B. Bekhoroth 51a; Y. Megillah 1:1, 70a.

36. Gen. Rab. 98:21, Theodor-Albeck 1267.

37. Cf. Schürer, *Geschichte*, vol. 1 (Leipzig, 1901), pp. 188, 1286; *Encyclopaedia Judaica* (Berlin, 1928), s.v. Bet Yerah; *Anchor Bible Dictionary*, s.v. Beth-Yerah.

38. I am indebted to my friend Issachar Ben-Ami of the Hebrew University of Jerusalem for making this material available to me.

APPENDIX
BIBLICAL SEAFARING AND THE BOOK OF MORMON

1. Hugh Nibley, *Lehi in the Desert. The World of the Jaredites. There Were Jaredites*, edited by John W. Welch, with Darrell L. Matthews and Stephen R. Callister (The Collected Works of Hugh Nibley, volume 5) (Salt Lake City and Provo, Utah, 1988), pp. 179–80.

2. John L. Sorenson, *An Ancient American Setting for the Book of Mormon* (Salt Lake City and Provo, Utah, 1996), pp. 110–19.

3. Hugh Nibley, *An Approach to the Book of Mormon*. 3rd ed., John W. Welch, general editor (The Collected Works of Hugh Nibley, volume 6) (Salt Lake City and Provo, Utah, 1988), pp. 340–48.

4. Ibid., pp. 348–58.

5. Warren P. Aston and Michaela Knoth Aston, *In the Footsteps of Lehi, New Evidence for Lehi's Journey across Arabia to Bountiful* (Salt Lake City, 1994), pp. 10–25.

6. Ibid., pp. 29–59.

7. Personal communication from Professor Noel B. Reynolds.

8. On the compass, called elsewhere in the Book of Mormon "liahona," see Hugh Nibley, *Since Cumorah*, 2nd ed., John W. Welch, general editor (The Collected Works of Hugh Nibley, volume 7) (Salt Lake City and Provo, Utah, 1988), pp. 251–63. On Jewish seafaring laws, see Raphael Patai, "Ancient Jewish Seafaring and River-faring Laws," in John M. Lundquist and Stephen D. Ricks, eds., *By Study and Also by Faith: Essays in Honor of Hugh W. Nibley*, 1:389–416, especially pp. 399–401. (Salt Lake City and Provo, Utah, 1990).

9. Sorenson, *Ancient American Setting*, p. 138.

10. John L. Sorenson, and Martin Raish, *Pre-Columbian Contact with the Americas: An Annotated Bibliography*. 2 vols. (Provo, Utah, 1990).

11. For all references to this literature, see ibid.

INDEX